"*Human in Death* offers a sustained and subtle inquiry into J. D. Robb's In Death books as novels of ideas. This is a groundbreaking contribution to the study of mass-market fiction, the ethics of reading, and the emerging field of popular romance studies."

—Eric Murphy Selinger, *President of the International Association for the Study of Popular Romance*

"Ali's fascinating forensic account of the sociological importance of the stories where we both escape and imagine ourselves into the future is a thought-provoking and accessible read for sociologists and laypeople alike."

—Tressie McMillan Cottom, *Assistant Professor of Sociology, Virginia Commonwealth University*

"A deeply engaging critical reflection, Ali deftly explores how fiction both shapes and reflects our complex lived realities, how fictional utopias can reiterate and justify the prejudices of the present. Under Ali's prescient analysis, J. D. Robb's popular novels become a venue for an exploration of American culture: what scares and what satisfies is revealed by Ali as saying so much more."

—Rafia Zakaria, *author of* The Upstairs Wife: An Intimate History of Pakistan

"Writing in an accessible idiom, Kecia Ali displays an expansive familiarity with the popular but understudied In Death series by Nora Roberts/J. D. Robb. *Human in Death* contains an evenhanded examination of the ethical stances visible in protagonist Eve Dallas' world, especially in relation to gender and sexuality, economic and bodily inequality, and personal and systemic violence. Ali's book is at heart a concordance replete with references to incidents, dialogue, and turns of phrase that bear out Ali's evaluation of what it means to recognize or repudiate someone's humanity in popular fiction."

—Jayashree Kamblé, *Assistant Professor of English, LaGuardia Community College*

Human in Death

Morality and Mortality in J. D. Robb's Novels

Kecia Ali

BAYLOR UNIVERSITY PRESS

Waco, Texas 76798

Cover Design by Andrew Brozyna, AJB Design, Inc.
Cover Art © iStockPhoto/ferrantraite, Alex_Schmidt, UroshPetrovic
Book Design by Diane Smith

Library of Congress Cataloging-in-Publication Data

Names: Ali, Kecia, author.
Title: Human in death : morality and mortality in J. D. Robb's novels / Kecia Ali.
Description: Waco, Texas : Baylor University Press, [2017] | Includes bibliographical references and index.
Identifiers: LCCN 2016027332 (print) | LCCN 2016053535 (ebook) | ISBN 9781481306270 (hardback) | ISBN 9781481306539 (web pdf) | ISBN 9781481306522 (mobi) | ISBN 9781481306294 (epub)
Subjects: LCSH: Robb, J. D., 1950– In death novel. | Mortality in literature | Ethics in literature.
Classification: LCC PS3568.O243 Z53 2017 (print) | LCC PS3568.O243 (ebook) | DDC 813/.54—dc23
LC record available at https://lccn.loc.gov/2016027332

Printed in the United States of America on acid-free paper with a minimum of 30 percent post-consumer waste recycled content.

For the unjustly bereaved and
those who struggle for justice

Contents

Preface

Writing a book is always murder.

I'm a scholar of religion and gender who first read the In Death series recreationally. Its characters, storylines, and ethics—often admirable, occasionally troubling—captivated me. I've written enough books to recognize the signs of an impending project. My copies of the novels began to bristle with color-coded tape flags. I proposed a conference paper, then sketched out a longer analysis. In November 2014, I met with an editor to discuss a relatively light-hearted little book focused on romance, friendship, and work in the series. The next day, a Missouri grand jury failed to indict Officer Darren Wilson for shooting and killing Michael Brown, an unarmed black teenager. I was ashamed to realize that although my outline and notes explored race and racism as well as gender and sexism, I hadn't written a single word about police violence. Before Ferguson, my inattention was deplorable. After Ferguson, it was inexcusable.

In its final form, this book grapples with brutality and inclusion in the In Death universe, alongside intimacy, friendship, and vocation. Critical engagement, not condemnation, is my task; I like the novels and think they're perceptive and thoughtful as well as entertaining. I've tried to make my reflections accessible to those who haven't read J. D. Robb's books. Although I unavoidably reveal plot points along the way, I don't think reading my book will spoil In Death for those who haven't yet read the series; instead I aim to prompt a different sort of reading (or rereading). Of necessity, *Human in Death* only scratches the surface of Robb's fictive world which, as of this writing, spans fifty-three installments and more than fifteen thousand pages. (Unless otherwise indicated in the text, all the quotations come from Robb's books.) I trust that Robb's devoted fans, used to backstory recap in each book, will forgive me for repeating things they already know in the service of exploring things they may not have considered. I hope that scholars and lay readers interested in pursuing my ethical arguments further will consult the extensive endnotes. Ideally, others will continue to analyze depictions of policing and punishment in the series, in tandem with urgent national conversations about state-sponsored violence, mass incarceration, and black lives. I also look forward to studies of aspects of Robb's writing about which I have said relatively little: mothers and fathers, both good and bad; the role of technology; the global political order; and the patriarchal conspiracy surrounding women's footwear.

I thank Carey Newman and his efficient staff at Baylor University Press; the mystery and detective fiction group at the Popular Culture Association, where I gave a paper on mentoring practices in In Death; the scholars in its popular romance studies group who talked with me about the genre; Eric Selinger, who commented incisively on a draft; and amina wadud, groundbreaking theologian and voracious reader, who several years ago gave me a copy of Toni Morrison's *Playing in the Dark*. It was an act of intellectual generosity and moral provocation, for which I remain deeply grateful.

Introduction
Reading in Death

In January 2058, Lieutenant Eve Dallas was a workaholic NYPSD homicide detective. She lived alone in a barely serviceable apartment, suffered regular nightmares, and kept aloof from would-be friends and lovers. In January 2061, she lives with an adoring husband and an affectionate, lazy cat in a home so magnificent that *mansion* seems too tame a term. Instead of borrowed suits and battered boots she wears cashmere and couture. She has friends and, after a fashion, family. She still has preternaturally vivid dreams, but the nightmares rarely come.

Despite being surrounded by wealth, her transformed life is anything but leisure and ease. She bears daily witness to brutality. Aided by her reformed rogue husband and trusted colleagues, she still investigates murders, gathers evidence, interrogates suspects, and apprehends killers. She endures violence and metes it out. She seeks justice for the dead and suffers for them. Her intimate partnership sustains her through physically and psychically exhausting cop work. She has no choice. She can do nothing else, be nothing else.

Eve Dallas is the heroine of J. D. Robb's best-selling In Death series, which comprises over fifty novels and novellas published between 1995 and 2016. Robb is the pseudonym of American romance legend Nora Roberts, one of the world's most popular and prolific authors.[1] In Death novels follow the recipe for police procedurals, leavened by romance and seasoned with science fiction.[2] The series is set in an imagined New York profoundly shaped by the devastating early twenty-first-century Urban Wars. Its central characters struggle with traumatic pasts as they navigate complicated personal and professional lives. Using intertwined stories of courtship and killing, friendship and betrayal, generosity and violence, In Death grapples with what it means to be vulnerable, mortal—in other words, human.

Like all literature, genre fiction explores the human condition. Crime novels wrestle with justice, law, and retribution. Speculative fiction prompts assessment of current social arrangements—class, race, technology—by showing strikingly changed ones. Notwithstanding the critical scorn and condescension heaped on them, popular romances interrogate social norms around masculinity, femininity, and relationships.[3] Yet even loyal readers of detective stories, romances, or science fiction may be reluctant to take such books too seriously. Perhaps they fear that analyzing pleasure reading will sap their enjoyment or that their favorite authors will wilt under scrutiny. But critical reflection need not oppose appreciation; it can enhance enjoyment. Though reading strategies may differ for escapist books and classic literature, all sorts of novels teach readers what matters.[4] They present situations and characters that do not really exist for readers to reflect on, sympathize with, detest, or admire.

By immersing readers in other worlds, fiction lets readers experience life differently. If this is the case for realistic fiction, it is even truer for speculative scenarios, where the utopian, dystopian, or merely markedly different aspects of the imagined setting come to the fore. It is certainly the case for New York in early 2058, where Eve Dallas, "murder cop and ass-kicker," stands for the dead.[5]

CHAPTER

1

Intimacy in Death

Lieutenant Eve Dallas is a loner. A New York City homicide detective with a troubled past and few close relationships, she disdains romantic entanglements and keeps her colleagues at arms length. She stands for the dead, bringing perpetrators to justice.

Roarke, a self-made billionaire with a shady past, rose from Dublin's alleys to dominate the global business world. Suave, sophisticated, and always in control, he has everything—except a woman he can love and trust. When their paths cross during a murder investigation, their connection threatens to topple her carefully constructed barriers and throw his ordered world into chaos. Will the potent chemistry between steely-eyed cop and reformed criminal suffice for the much more difficult work of making a life together?

A slow motion one-two punch

Shortly after the reader meets her, Dallas stands over a prostitute's corpse. Sharon DeBlass, a twenty-four-year-old woman from a wealthy, prominent family, has been shot three times. Dallas, "barely thirty," has been working for the New York Police and Security Department since her graduation from the academy a decade earlier.[1] Her single-minded devotion to the job took her rapidly from uniformed officer to detective to lieutenant. Like many of her hard-boiled predecessors, her professional success does not betoken a vibrant, well-rounded personal life. She works hard. She does little else. Despite her years as a murder cop, Dallas had never seen a gunshot victim. This victim's manner of death is shocking because, unlike in early twenty-first-century America where guns are legal and prostitution proscribed, in 2058 sex work has been legalized while, in the wake of the vicious Urban Wars that roiled cities worldwide beginning in the second decade of the twenty-first century, firearms have been outlawed.[2]

From the first pages of the series, as Dallas tracks a murderer who kills licensed companions (LCs), sex and violence intertwine. In addition to the focus on loving sexual partnership between the main characters, and brutal sexual violence as a trauma, sex work is a recurring thread in the novels. Sex clubs and strippers appear regularly, and the government regulates male and female licensed companions—serving men, women, or both—running the gamut from street level to pricey and exclusive. Licensure screens out the unsuitable and allows prosecution of the unlicensed. Sexual violence, sex work, and sexual connection appear often in the background, and sometimes in the foreground, of the novels' plots.

The commingling of sex and violence echoes the series' genre blending. In addition to setting the stage for this brave new world, the first novels in the series interweave a courtship plot with the procedural. Both have their own logics and narrative conventions.[3] Plot points do double duty. The romantic hero comes to the heroine's notice as a murder suspect: Roarke had gone on a date with the victim shortly before her death. Dallas researches him. She learns of the suspicions of criminal activity that have dogged him as well as the global corporate empire he has built. His legendary physical attractiveness is matched only by his phenomenal wealth; one character, admittedly prone to exaggeration, estimates that he owns "approximately twenty-eight percent of the world, and its satellites."[4] While learning about his business activities and dodgy past, Dallas is, to her chagrin, immediately attracted, later recalling "that she'd started falling for him the moment she'd seen that face."[5]

The meeting—a requirement of any romance—fits into her homicide investigation. Roarke attends DeBlass' funeral as a family friend. Dallas seeks him out to interrogate him about his connection to the victim: he is a suspect, not a potential romantic interest. The meeting is all clichéd attraction. They are palpably drawn together. She looks at him. He reacts: "her gaze, as physical as a blow . . . had coiled his muscles, tightened his gut." When their eyes meet, "another blow. A slow motion one-two punch he hadn't been able to evade."[6] When he learns that she is a detective, Roarke, who has not lived a precisely law-abiding life, finds his attraction to a cop disconcerting.[7]

The procedural plot creates the barriers to union that the romance structure requires. Although their early interactions are charged with distrust, Dallas quickly rules him out as the killer. Their mutual attraction steadily increases. As long as he remains under formal suspicion, personal involvement breaks the rules. The regulations preventing Dallas from dating a person of interest in an open investigation are less of a hindrance than their divergent perspectives on the merits of strict adherence to the law. They have other differences: she is brash, he is smooth. Still, like recognizes like. Both had difficult childhoods, are passionate about their work, and ruthlessly pursue their objectives. They have chemistry. Ultimately, they cannot withstand their attraction for each other: though Roarke takes the initiative, Dallas participates enthusiastically in their physical encounters. She does not, however, wish to take it any further than sex.

Dallas' unromantic, utilitarian approach to sex had been foreshadowed at an early murder scene. The officer standing guard is clearly shaken up by seeing a gunshot victim. Dallas asks if he's involved with someone; when he says he's engaged, she remarks on cops who have had a difficult experience "losing it in a warm body." It is, she says, better than drinking. Her crude remark portrays an unhealthy ethic of sex: using another as a means to an end.[8] She thinks of sex as either violence or a simple release of tension.

Dallas' reluctance to involve herself emotionally with Roarke stems from wariness of his reputation and wealth as well as of intimacy more generally. She is emotionally closed off, in part because of childhood trauma revealed over the course of the series. As she much later confides to her detective partner, "He's the only man I've ever had a real relationship with."[9] Where Dallas is skittish, Roarke is intrigued. He is emotionally more self-aware than she. He must confront his own uncertainties, but the barriers to intimacy that she erects are the first and main obstacles to be demolished for them to become a couple and begin to build a life together.[10] She resists; he pursues.

A woman wants glitter

Roarke's pursuit of Dallas illustrates retrograde gender dynamics. He is persistent, even pushy. He wields power effectively, sometimes in worrisome ways. Using the skill in reading people that has made him professionally successful, he tailors his overtures. He entices her with real coffee, an expensive luxury in a world of soy substitutes, first in his car leaving the funeral, then when he sends her a gift. Mavis Freestone—Dallas' only close girlfriend at the start of the series—assumes he has sent diamonds. Learning otherwise, she rants, "The man's got more money than God, and he sends you a bag of coffee? . . . I don't care what the damn stuff costs a pound, Dallas. A woman wants glitter." She replies, "Not this woman. The son of a bitch knew just how to get to me."[11] His gift illustrates that he knows her. She is no anonymous cipher of femininity but a person with tastes and preferences.[12] Yet even as the coffee thoughtfully reflects her individuality, Roarke makes a power play: he owns her building and has the package delivered to her apartment though she has never told him where she lives. Thoughtful shades into creepy.[13]

If the early stages of Eve and Roarke's relationship reflect a pursuit dynamic premised on (ambivalent) male dominance and male agency, the relationship quickly arcs toward egalitarianism with a feminist bent. Robb inverts expected nurturing patterns and centers the wife's rather than the husband's career. Partly, this focus reflects the importance of the detective stories in the series: solving crimes is Dallas' bailiwick. Mutuality comes to the fore for two additional intertwined reasons. One is external to the story: from the 1990s onward, romance heroes moved further away from the model of controlling males prominent in the 1970s and into the 1980s. What is considered romantic shifts quickly, and gender norms become dated fast.[14] The second factor is internal to the series: courtship is one thing; marriage, another. After they have been married for some months, she reminisces about his "exciting" actions during their courtship: "wanted," "pursued," "demanded," "taken." Shifting registers, she ends with "cherished."[15] Social norms surrounding dating (who asks, who pays, who tags whom via link) shift but still presume men's power in a way that is increasingly outdated for marriage.[16] Thus, both because marriage means the end of pursuit and because of changed notions of what is romantic, this imbalance fades in later novels.

Popular romances convey ideas about love and sex as well as gender and marriage.[17] Male dominance is a major theme of romance novels, both longed for and contested. Authors and heroines alike express deep ambivalence about certain elements of normative masculinity. Emotionally inscrutable, implacable, and capricious heroes have fallen out of fashion, but novelists still write taller, older, stronger, wealthier, virile heroes who can provide for and protect the women they love. Yet heroines' independence and ability to hold their own in all realms of life is a precondition for their worthiness to receive love from these reformed but still capable and masculine heroes.

Though Dallas and Roarke have an egalitarian relationship, he dominates elsewhere. He lives by his own code of honor rather than strictly by law. He has the "killer instinct," and "though he'd never taken a life without cause, he'd killed."[18] At the same time, his attempts to control Dallas involve not attaining his own interests but fulfilling hers, at least as he perceives them. He wants her to accept gifts, nurturing, and eventually his love. She does not fall neatly into line.

Their road from attraction to involvement to marriage is bumpy. Emotional involvement follows physical intimacy, as does the increased intertwining of Roarke with Dallas' professional life. During their courtship, he is tangentially connected to a series of crimes, not only because of his suspicious connections, which he has been slowly shedding, but also because with "his clever fingers in too many pies to count . . . it was inevitable that his name would pop up in connection with so many of her cases."[19] As the series proceeds, he becomes an occasional and then a frequent civilian consultant, routinely helping Dallas and her colleagues solve crimes. Personal and professional merge, if not seamlessly then inextricably.

The romance element, at the fore in early volumes, alternately surfaces and recedes. Even when no real drama happens in their marriage, Roarke and Dallas' relationship occupies the emotional center of the series. In an online fan poll of favorite couples in Roberts' books, Dallas and Roarke received more than half the votes. Roarke handily won a similar poll for favorite Roberts hero, scoring

35% of the votes shared over ten candidates; Dallas did similarly in a poll about heroines. One fan's list of the top ten reasons she loves Roberts includes three references to Roarke. Asked why In Death novels are shelved with Roberts' romance fiction, a bookstore clerk explained, "At heart, they're romances. After all, without Eve and Roarke, you wouldn't have a series."[20]

Still, the courtship proceeds over the course of only three novels, mere months in the compressed series timeline.[21] After Eve and Roarke meet and become involved in *Naked in Death*, they date off-page for several months. (This is the only substantial gap between novels, which otherwise begin within weeks or days of the previous installment's ending.) When *Glory in Death* opens in late May of 2058, they are involved but struggling over commitment and love. Declarations, recriminations, and reconciliation occur mid-book; at book's end, Roarke proposes and she accepts. They are engaged and planning a wedding during *Immortal in Death*, in which she half-heartedly pulls away but does not get far. The July wedding takes place before *Rapture in Death*, which opens on their honeymoon. After the arc from meeting to marriage, that they will remain together is never seriously in doubt. In this sense, their relationship conforms to the single most important requisite of the romance genre: the Happily Ever After or, as the Romance Writers Association guidelines put it, an "emotionally satisfying and uplifting conclusion."

Some disdain romances for such pat endings. As feminist cultural critic bell hooks points out, "True love does not always lead to happily ever after, and even when it does, sustaining love still takes work."[22] Yet focusing only on the ending obscures the complex storylines and meaningful character developments along the way.[23] In any case, in a series where the end is indefinitely deferred, tidy closure is rejected.[24] Things happen happily, but not once and for all; there is a commitment to ongoing adjustments. Occasional crises test the strength, though not the endurance, of their bond. Marriage is only an early step in their intimate relationship. Complex negotiations and balancing acts persist long after courtship and commitment.

A wifely duty dispensed

The ethics of intimacy and companionship constitute a fruitful, sometimes fraught, basis for thinking about what Dallas calls marriage rules: unspoken as well as explicitly negotiated habits to accommodate a partner. One central rule is to communicate, both about important events and feelings and about things as minor as arriving home late.[25] Some routine communication involves avoiding unnecessary friction. Both Dallas and Roarke err in this regard; both also improve over time, endeavoring not to make the same mistakes repeatedly.

Other communication is more fraught, since each has sensitive professional and personal loyalties.[26] Becoming privy to confidential information—which happens in couples, in loving relationships, and among people who share households—is especially difficult when that information involves police investigations, corporate secrets, or dramatic and traumatic personal histories. Even after a few years of marriage, the revelation of information can threaten their equilibrium: a past girlfriend intent on rekindling an affair, revenge murders one has committed, a past as a smuggler, a long-repressed trauma, the truth about one's mother, or the involvement of a secret government agency in covering up a killing. Dallas works in a profession in which confidentiality is paramount; with Roarke's shadowy past, competing loyalties emerge. Both, however, come to put each other first and confront challenges together.

Mundane factors also complicate their shared life. Both have demanding careers. Dallas has an unpredictable and intense schedule. Dispatch summons her to murder scenes in the wee hours. She comes home late only to hole up in her home office.[27] In the midst of a case, she works herself to exhaustion. Not only does Roarke tolerate the demands police work makes on Dallas' time, he respects and understands the work and her.[28] He calls her "Lieutenant" far more often than he uses any other endearment.[29] Although she tries for some time to keep him separate from her work, he becomes increasingly drawn into her cases. Dallas' work structures the life they build together.[30]

Roarke too works many hours, by choice. He alters his schedule to be available to Dallas. He travels with her when she has an emotionally challenging trip: "What's the point of being master of all you survey if you can't ditch meetings when it suits you?"[31] She recognizes how fortunate she is, when, instead of heading home after a dinner out that served double duty as a chance to question a potential witness ("Meaning," Roarke notes, "you can put a check in the column that reads: Went out to dinner with Roarke, and consider that a wifely duty dispensed"), he assumes they'll go follow up another lead.[32] When she apologizes for missing a dinner she had not relished attending, he reassures her, "You don't let me down. . . . It adds considerably to my cachet when I apologize for my wife, who's been called to duty on a case."[33] She reflects that "he made a much better cop's husband than she made corporate wife."[34]

In addition to Roarke's control of his own schedule, his near-imperviousness to fatigue allows him to do his own work and collaborate with Dallas on hers.[35] Just as late capitalism functions round the clock, so (nearly) does he.[36] Dallas is astonished by how little sleep he requires, noting that "he seemed to get by on less sleep than a normal human."[37] She wonders whether he is "man or machine"—a question that takes on a new resonance in a universe where droids fill numerous roles, mostly in household service but also as clerks, bartenders, and even beat cops.[38]

Roarke, though, is a flesh and blood man. His ability to survive on minimal sleep echoes other romance heroes' personae, signaling competence, protection, and vigor. Yet heroines may worry about men who rest insufficiently. Inverting these expectations, Roarke is frequently concerned with Dallas' level of work-related exhaustion and repeatedly coaxes her to rest.[39] The contrast between Dallas' entirely human susceptibility to exhaustion and Roarke's superhuman ability to get by on little rest could be read as affirming male strength and female weakness. But her dedication is admired by her colleagues and friends; she struggles valiantly to overcome fatigue. She alone perceives her natural physical limits as flaws. It is not that Roarke is exemplary and she is less so; he, exceptional, sets a standard of work and wakefulness that ordinary people, regardless of gender, cannot possibly be expected to meet. She works to, and sometimes beyond, her limits. She consistently ignores her body's cues of fatigue, pain, and hunger and pushes through as best she can. Because she will not simply comply, Roarke adapts. As she is prone to nightmares, Roarke alters his resting schedule and minimizes his travel to suit her needs; she sleeps better when he is with her.[40] The rest he accomplishes with a mixture of cajolery, browbeating, and sneakiness.

Why don't we try a little role reversal?

Contrary to stereotypes that associate women and femininity with care work, Roarke is the main caregiver in their relationship, even as he fulfills the masculine norm of providing. He offers tempting luxuries, but also basic nurture: food, medicine, rest.[41] When she complains about his frequent reminders, he responds, "If I didn't nag you about eating and sleeping, you'd do precious little of either."[42] Early in their courtship, his overtures—except coffee—meet resistance or outright rejection. As their relationship progresses, Dallas gets better at accepting most forms of caretaking from Roarke, and she occasionally reciprocates.

She still resists medical treatment for illness and, more often, injuries. Roarke has "dragged, strong-armed, or carried her into their emergency treatment centers a number of times. When, she thought now, she'd have been perfectly fine with a first aid kit and a nap."[43] Except under extreme, rare circumstances, as when a race against the clock tests the strength and endurance of abducted victims as well as the police officers searching for them and their would-be killer, Dallas is unwilling to take authorized stimulants to keep herself awake.[44] Habitually choosing the more difficult path, she avoids even legal chemical management of energy and pain; Roarke occasionally forces her to take blockers.[45] The series presents positively accepting others' care and nurture, even when it goes against one's habits and temperament.

Her resistance to sleep arises out of the conviction that there is too much work to be done; her objections to medical treatment stem both from a resistance to anything that smacks of coddling and from a childhood hospitalization after escaping years of trauma and brutality.[46] She has no objection to food, but often forgets to eat in the face of pressing duties. When she insists that she can take care of herself, he scoffs: she can, "when she remembers."[47]

Food is a central way Roarke expresses his caring. He coaxes her to eat, and, when she eats, to eat more healthfully.[48] He feeds her steak and other foods designed to entice. Once they are married, he alternately accedes to her preferences for pizza and waffles and pushes healthier, though still tasty, food at her. He sneaks green vegetables into her pasta and tempers the disappointment of oatmeal for breakfast with berries and bacon on the side.[49]

Occasionally the tables turn, but rarely enough that it occasions comment: she suggests dinner; he says, "Now you're stepping on my lines."[50] When he thanks her for "tending to" him, she highlights reciprocity: "I've had a lot of practice on the other side of it."[51] Sometimes she takes a direct approach. One night she says, "Why don't we try a little role reversal? I'll make you eat, sneak a soother into your food, then tuck you into bed."[52] On another occasion, she uses subterfuge. He's "a little frazzled" and "a little weary" because a killer is targeting his employees, so Dallas ensures that he rests by asking him to stay with her while she sleeps.[53] After she brings him coffee the next morning, he observes, recognizing her manipulation, "You're very wifely these days. Are you taking care of me, Eve?" She asks, "And so what if I am? *And* don't call me wifely. It pisses me off." Roarke responds that "pissing you off by calling you wifely is one of my small pleasures."[54] Even where her behavior is stereotypically nurturing, their interactions carry an edge.

Their mutual caretaking is cemented by rituals centered on meals, including breakfast together in their bedroom sitting area and dinner in her home office looking at her murder board. Both reject a neat separation of work and life.[55] When they take temporary custody of a girl who witnessed her family's murder, Roarke insists that they all eat together in the dining room since "that child needs as much normalcy as we can manage. Dinner, at the table, is normal."[56] It is not typical for them, though, and neither cares to make the change permanent. Although the gender equality of their physical relationship and the flipped dynamics of their habitual patterns of nurturing pass mostly without comment, they do reflect on the fact that talking death over dinner and working in their connecting home offices suits them.[57]

Though they provide a temporary respite for that young survivor, and stay in touch with her once she finds a more permanent home with another family, they do not try to adopt her. Their consuming careers would be impossible if they had children. (Stepping away from the internal logic of the novels to the genre choices of their author: given the work-centrism of the novels, the central protagonist must remain child-free if the novels are to retain their focus.[58]) Even megawealthy Roarke cannot buy more hours in a day. Managing two demanding careers and a relationship involves time clashes and conflicts as well as a struggle for leisure.[59] Moreover, both have hesitations around becoming parents, though Dallas' are more pronounced.[60] Around their second anniversary, they have a theoretical conversation about naming any future progeny. Roarke begins, "When we have children," and Eve responds, "If we have a kid." They are out of sync as to how likely it is they will have children or how many.[61] This mismatch reflects both the widespread mainstream assumptions that married couples will procreate and resistance to this conventional wisdom.

New York circa 2060 resembles the present-day United States in many ways. Many people live in committed couples or aim to do so. Although some biological families fail—Dallas and Roarke reaped different consequences of spectacular parental failures—the series typically presumes couples who reproduce biologically and parent their children in nuclear families. Most women, including mothers, seem to work outside the home. Some mothers who work outside the home employ nannies; a few are married to men who stay home.[62] The immensely popular Professional Parent Act allows parents to draw a stipend while they withdraw from the paid workforce to raise children.[63] Although some old-fashioned figures believe that the compensation should be eliminated, arguing that motherhood is a duty, an honor, and its own reward, they are a small minority.

Dallas and Roarke's egalitarian relationship, too, may owe in part to their childlessness: Dallas does not dwindle into wifehood and motherhood. The series obliquely addresses the relationship between wifehood, motherhood, and habitual patterns of responsibility for the emotional and logistical labor of running a household and sustaining a marriage. In twentieth- and early twenty-first-century America, even as new patterns of sharing household labor have been worked out among heterosexual married couples, wives often absorb household duties, including the mental managing of other people's schedules and activities, regardless of whether they performed such duties before marriage. When cohabiting partners become spouses, they often slide away from egalitarian assumptions about household work. It is widely assumed in contemporary America that wives more than husbands are responsible for ensuring the success of marriages by adapting to the husband's needs; that is less the case in Dallas and Roarke's marriage.[64]

Luckily for their domestic happiness, Roarke has no desire to have her be other than she is. "And to think some men come home after a day of work and are greeted by their woman," he says one day when he arrives to find her mid-workout, about to spar with a droid. She invites him to practice hand-to-hand combat with her instead. "A smile, a kiss, perhaps a cold drink. . . . How tedious for them."[65] For some time after they are married, Dallas remains insecure about whether he really does not mind how consumed she is with work. She harbors unspoken assumptions that a woman will be more available to her husband than the reverse.[66] Listening over the wire when Roarke, working with her, lies to trap a suspect ("I want my wife, not a bloody cop. I prefer having my woman available at my convenience, not running around all hours of the day and night investigating cases. . . . A man's entitled to that, isn't he?"[67]), she asks, "All that business about a man having this right and that right, and wanting your woman when you want her. That was just show, right?" Roarke reassures her that they'd both be "bored brainless" with that sort of life.[68]

That Dallas escapes the fate of arranging her life around his owes both to Roarke's love and respect for her and also to his temperament, competence, and inexhaustible financial resources. Since, unlike her, he enjoys socializing, he typically orchestrates gatherings, including Dallas without demanding her attendance. And though she had "married Roarke in spite of his money," his wealth enables him to pay for a vast array of services, including household help, both human and droid.[69] However, if money frees women from drudge work it can sometimes bring new expectations. When an investigation shows Dallas the range of semisocial, semiprofessional tasks one society wife assumes for her husband's career, she wonders who does these sorts of tasks for Roarke. Whether it is Roarke himself, his frighteningly efficient admin Caro, or perhaps Lawrence Summerset, a fixture in their lives, it is clear that this role will not fall to Dallas.[70]

Our happy little family

Dallas and Roarke's romantic relationship and much of its caring work take place in dyadic relationship, but though they have no children, their household—and thus their imbrication in caregiving—includes others. When Dallas moves into Roarke's home, she brings her newly acquired fat cat Galahad, who becomes part of "our happy little family."[71] She and Galahad join Summerset, majordomo and more to Roarke. The four of them, counting the furry one, illustrate forms of family and household formation that surpass or replace marital ties or nuclear families.

Though Roarke considers Eve and Summerset "the two people he believed knew and understood him best," his love and his longtime friend and mentor have a fractious relationship.[72] Summerset, "Roarke's man of everything and resident pain in her ass," at first harps on Dallas' unfitness to be wife to a man of Roarke's stature.[73] He is rude to her, and vice versa.[74] Mavis observes that it as if "Roarke is his first and only born or something instead of his boss."[75] In fact, she is not far off the mark.

Like Dallas, Roarke survived an abusive childhood. His father, Patrick Roarke, was a handsome, brutal charmer who expected Roarke to steal. He beat him if the take was low and also sometimes out of sheer temper. Then, "after one particularly enthusiastic beating" left Roarke, not yet twelve, "unconscious in an alley" and "half-beaten to death," Summerset rescued him.[76] Widowed in the Urban Wars, Summerset was raising his daughter Marlena alone. He took Roarke into his home and helped him hone his skills at theft and deception.[77] Roarke sometimes describes their relationship as an alliance or partnership rather than a filial bond; at other times he acknowledges the paternal role the older man played.[78] This variability points to the inadequacy of existing categories. Their connection merges commerce and caring, family and friendship.

One obstacle Eve and Summerset must overcome is distrust. He initially fears that Dallas will use what she learns against Roarke.[79] Eventually, he realizes that she will always put Roarke's well-being foremost.[80] She comes to appreciate his role in overseeing the home's management, though she remains uneasy with, for instance, his handling of her clothing. Despite their détente, their mutual antagonism does not fade entirely; they continue "exchanging swipes."[81] Dallas typically lobs crude insults that express annoyance. Summerset utters snide, judgmental comments that often foster, in a roundabout way, her well-being. Once, for instance, she comes in late without having notified him. He tells her she's missed dinner and suggests she have her aide "notify me of your plans so the household could maintain some order." She refuses, and heads off to grab dinner—though she "would have been mortified if she'd known Summerset had planted the thought of dinner in her mind, knowing she would remember to eat out of spite if nothing else. Otherwise, she most likely would have forgotten."[82] Actions matter more than affect.

Portrait in Death takes place when Dallas and Roarke have been married just over a year. Its intertwined plots focus on relationships, familial and otherwise. Family, care, and love stand at the center. Early in the novel, Roarke learns distressing news about his family history. Even as he reels from this disclosure, Summerset takes a bad fall. Usually able to thrive on minimal sleep, Roarke becomes fatigued and overwrought.[83] Even more uncharacteristic, since he is typically the one pushing for greater spousal communication, he clams up, shutting Dallas out.[84] Roarke is thrown off his game, disrupting the couple's—and the household's—typical patterns of nurture and caregiving. Instead of Roarke (and, obliquely, Summerset) caring for Dallas, Dallas must serve as primary agent in rebalancing the relationships and providing caregiving. Giving and receiving care, emotional and physical, is central to the storyline. She conspires with "her personal nemesis" to care for Roarke, even as both she and Roarke care for Summerset.[85]

Summerset resists, as Dallas usually does, having someone care for him. He refuses hospitalization. He does not want a nurse at home. Roarke strains to arrange his care; though money is no object, Summerset's physical vulnerability is difficult for both men. A few months earlier, Summerset had been attacked as part of a plot to distract Roarke, and they sparred over whether Summerset would leave town.[86] Roarke later admits to Dallas, "He's been the only constant in my life, until you. Scared me brainless to see him hurt that way."[87]

The idea of family, and questions about what makes a family, stand at the core of this novel. Summerset is among those who came to stand in for parents who, by choice or not, did not fulfill their roles. Dallas helps manage Summerset's care and also shoulders part of Roarke's emotional burden. Her interventions largely concern affect: Dallas tells Summerset's chipper caregiver that he will respond better to clear directives than coddling. She also suggests to Summerset, conspiratorially, that he might want to "stash a bottle" of booze in easy reach. Even without stereotypical nurturing, Dallas is effective; she empathizes with Summerset's temperament and knows people in pain lash out.[88]

Roarke is in pain too. With Summerset laid up and cranky, Roarke discovers that his mother was not the callous woman he had thought abandoned him to his abusive father, but a younger, loving woman his father killed. Keeping that information secret, he pushes both Dallas and Summerset away. Summerset, despite his ongoing hostilities with Dallas, calls on her to intervene.[89]

Though the source of Roarke's distress is emotional, his symptoms manifest physically as his inner turmoil saps his vitality. He avoids Dallas, but she eventually pins him down, prepares a meal for him, and slips a tranquilizer into his soup. He realizes it as he begins to go under, and she cheerfully announces that she understands why he sometimes doses her: it's gratifying.[90] Despite having finally confided in her about his worries, Roarke leaves the next day while Dallas is on the job, heading for Ireland to track down both information about his mother and to find his newly discovered maternal relatives. Unsure of his welcome, he believes he must go alone; he is unwilling to drag Dallas away from her case. "She's not only my wife," he explains to Summerset. "Not even always my wife first . . . People's lives depend on her."[91] His stubborn refusal to ask for her help results partly from a laudable respect for her work, but also from shame and guilt. He eventually realizes that he wants nothing more than to have her with him, just as she arrives. She in turn has overcome her own fear of depending on others, asking Summerset to help arrange transport and arranging for her colleagues to cover for her at work. She reasons, "She wasn't the only cop on the NYPSD. But she was Roarke's only wife."[92]

Roarke may have only one wife, but both Dallas and Roarke have others who care about them individually and as a couple. *Portrait* shows the value of interdependence, the crucial importance of caring work, and the inevitability of vulnerability.[93] Intimacy extends beyond the romantic pair and does not depend on the emotions relationships evoke but rather on the closely held, if not secret, knowledge and personal attention they involve.[94] Intimacy can tolerate asymmetry and even a degree of hostility but not the complete absence of mutuality.[95] People depend on each other at different times.

Although unhappy marriages and relationships generate a good deal of her cop work, most of those around Dallas are happily, if sometimes tumultuously, coupled; Dallas and Roarke's marriage does not take place in a vacuum.[96] Dallas and Roarke, who acknowledge that they have "become a unit" (or, as a character who previously held a torch for Dallas puts it, "so married I see little lovebirds circling over your head"), are surrounded by secondary and tertiary characters who are married or who couple up in the course of the series.[97] Dallas and Roarke consider how others perceive their relationship, and at times they use others' relationships to provide a new perspective on their own. (One junior colleague appreciates their connection as "an education in the tug-of-war of relationships."[98]) In the midst of a conflict with Roarke, Dallas asks a long-married colleague for advice, saying, "I feel stupid." Psychiatrist and police profiler Dr. Charlotte Mira replies, "No, sweetheart. You feel married."[99] Mira affirms that marriage is not "for the weak or the lazy. It's work and it should be."[100] On another occasion, Dallas complains to Mira that "a lot of marriage is a pain in the ass." Mira concurs.[101]

Marriage is a pain in the ass in part because Dallas and Roarke are "two strong-headed, strong-willed people, both not only used to giving orders but to having them obeyed." Instead of tranquility, they have "an interesting and stimulating life."[102] Rightly or wrongly, they anger each other frequently.[103] Dallas "wondered why two people who loved each other to the point of stupid managed to aggravate each other as often as they seemed to."[104] Yet even if they "just weren't peaceful people," their love remains unshakable.[105] They do not have a straightforward happily ever after. They are committed but also complicated. Their life together is not easy. But it is rewarding precisely in proportion to how complicated it is. Neither would be satisfied with something simpler.

There was never anybody before you

Robb adheres to the romance convention that the love story between the hero and heroine must be truer—and the sex must be better—than in any previous relationship. Dallas' prior experiences with consensual sex were casual, neither especially meaningful nor emotionally or physically powerful.[106] With Roarke, not only is her physical satisfaction greater, so is the emotional involvement.[107] She tells him, "There was never anybody before you."[108] Though it is not literally true of lovers, it is true of love and lovemaking. Roarke has had "a lot more" lovers than she has had; she crosses paths with several in the course of the series.[109] Unlike her, he has cared deeply for some of them, "but they were never more than momentary pleasure."[110] The attraction between Eve and Roarke, which they hope will never fade, is strengthened by their emotional connection.[111]

Sex functions as an emotional and ethical barometer of their relationship. Eve's greater satisfaction with Roarke symbolizes the truth of their relationship. Conventional wisdom associates orgasm, especially simultaneous orgasm, with emotional connection: strong orgasm equals strong emotion.[112] Before Roarke, "she'd always equated [orgasms] with the subtle pop of a cork from a bottle of stress, not the violent explosion that destroyed a lifetime of restraint."[113] Sex plays this role not just in the courtship arc but throughout the series. In *Brotherhood in Death,* set three years after they became involved, she offers a disquisition on the emotional truth of sex: "She knew what this physical act could mean when driven by violence, by a quest for power, when it was driven by need, by passion and lust. And she knew, from him, what it meant when driven by love." Love plus sex becomes salvation; it "had saved her."[114]

In addition to being an arena for ethical and unethical behavior, sex can both reiterate and subvert gender norms. Dominant ideas about active masculinity and receptive femininity affect their courtship. Roarke initiates both physical and emotional intimacy. After they spend the night together at her apartment, their second sexual encounter, he waits for her to take the next physical step. Yet he controls the pacing. As their relationship solidifies, Dallas is a willing, active, initiating participant in their sexual encounters.[115] Sex here, as in romance novels generally, centers on women's physical as well as emotional satisfactions; it affirms women's desires as legitimate. It also serves, ideally, to epitomize equal partnerships. It does so here: for Dallas and Roarke, lovemaking is "a dance either could lead, both could follow."[116] Their encounters range from tender to frenzied, from playful to passionate.

As they are finding their footing, Robb emphasizes Roarke's physical power. He picks Dallas up and carries her as a prelude to sex. They wrestle in bed. Though Eve gains the upper hand, Roarke subdues her: no force, but power. On another occasion, in his office, she pins him, but their early couplings mostly emphasize male power. Robb uses terms evoking violence (pummeled, assaulted, invaded) in Dallas' reflection after their first encounter, but his attack on "the parts of her she'd thought impregnable" was a physical assault on emotional barriers.[117] The novels categorically affirm that Roarke never hurts women. He says as much directly when she later punches him.[118]

Other encounters emphasize their physical parity. In earlier novels, she has to taunt him to spar with her: "You know, some men are still stuck in the mindset that a woman can't go toe to toe on a physical level. Since I know you're above that, I can only assume you're afraid I'll whip your ass."[119] They come to spar routinely, both restraining their power.[120] They simulate a sword fight to understand how a murder occurred; she appreciates "the thrill of battle against a perfectly matched opponent."[121]

The irrelevance of physical superiority to masculine desirability manifests in mundane ways too. Roarke sits on a hallway floor, working and waiting, while she surveys a murder scene. "Eve straightened, then held out a hand. Roarke grasped her forearm, and she his, to help him to his feet."[122] Companionable female strength coexists with a more pointed denial of male dominance as necessary for hot sex: "uncontrolled" lovemaking in the kitchen leaves both exhausted, "lying on their backs on the floor in a sweaty heap." She says, "I don't suppose you could pull one of your macho routines and carry me." He responds, "I don't suppose. I was hoping you'd carry me."[123]

I'm good at saving myself

Dallas and Roarke's equality extends beyond the sparring mat and the bedroom (or kitchen) into their life together. Early in their relationship, she reflects, "I guess we do a lot of juggling of the controls, end up heading in the same direction anyway."[124] Their power struggles continue but are smoothed by the commitment they've made. An ethic of mutuality permeates their work together and never slides into a representation of a woman in jeopardy needing to be saved by a macho male. Rarely if ever does Roarke unambiguously rescue her. Even in situations of extreme danger, she extricates herself without assistance or is on the brink of doing so when the cavalry arrives.[125] One instance in which Roarke clearly comes to the rescue is when he defuses a bomb that would have destroyed the Statue of Liberty and killed all of the police on scene, including Dallas. This happens directly after she establishes her capability by hauling him to safety when he ends up dangling by one hand over the water.[126] Not only can she save herself, when necessary she can also save him.

If caring is most often explored as an inversion of expected gendered roles, physical and emotional protection is mutual. Though each acknowledges that the other is capable of looking out for him or herself, Roarke wants to protect her from both physical and emotional harms—past as well as present and future.[127] She says to him that it's okay that he didn't save her: "I'm good at saving myself."[128] After they have been married nearly two years, a vicious former foster mother of Dallas' visits, attempting blackmail. Roarke takes measures to protect her. Dallas rants, "Male of the fricking species. Do I look like some wilting, helpless *female*?"[129] When the threat is more directly physical, she calls out his gendered double standards. On one occasion when she wants to ensure his safety, he resists, saying it would be different if he were protecting her. She retorts, "Because you have a penis?" Ruefully, he concedes her point.[130]

His protective instincts merge with nurturing instincts around her role. He does not try to thwart or hinder her professional life; to the contrary, he facilitates it in large and small ways. The first time she spends the night at his house, he has the heater in her decrepit police-issue car fixed.[131] Eventually, he commissions a nondescript car with a wide array of special features; as regulations permit the use of private vehicles, she uses her custom DLE Urban instead of a standard cop car. Similar anecdotes illustrate her ongoing struggle with Maintenance, like her running feud with the vending machines at Cop Central; they also expose a more sinister reality: the privatization of social functions. To get functional equipment, public servants must draw on private wealth.[132]

Nurture, gendered indulgence, worry, and protection manifest also in Roarke's provision of her clothing. He regularly provides her with gloves and sunglasses, which she continually forgets or loses.[133] He gives her a custom-made leather jacket with stun-proof protective lining, illustrating the inadequacy of her standard-issue gear but also reflecting her priorities: function over fashion. Like the gift of coffee rather than diamonds, the coat illustrates that Roarke knows her and appreciates who she is, including her job.

Friends, lovers, partners

Roarke and Dallas emerge from courtship into a complicated, loving, intense marriage. Moments of high drama, such as life-or-death fights or emotional confrontations with past trauma, thread through activities of daily living, including sharing meals, getting dressed, giving gifts, and socializing. Perhaps the most surprising outcome of Dallas and Roarke's meeting is that they have become friends. At the end of a case involving both envy turned murderous and friendship turned romantic, Roarke says, "I know love, and what it does to you, for you, I know that it can bloom out of friendship, or that friendship can open out of love. Both are precious. And when you have both, there's little that can't be done." Dallas reflects that "she and Roarke had taken [the] route" of love to friendship rather than the other way around. "It seemed to be working out just fine." Earlier, she had told him, "Friends, lovers, partners. You get a check in the all-of-the-above column."[134]

The relationship between self and other is a fundamental ground for ethical inquiry. When two selves come together in intimate partnership, both are transformed. The relationship between Dallas and Roarke, forged across difference, is exemplary in part because of their dogged commitment to its well-being. Neither changes radically to fit what the other requires nor merely makes a series of grudging compromises in order to live peaceably. They move closer to each other on some issues, but the similarity is not the point. Rather, in finding their way together they are able to grow into better versions of themselves.[135] In Roarke's case, being "utterly besotted" is motivation for fully divesting himself of "criminal associations and activities."[136] They maintain their independence even as they develop interdependence. They forge a working partnership.[137] Their relationship, in turn, serves as the practical and emotional foundation for a more expansive life in which Dallas develops friendships with an array of others, mostly women.[138] Instead of losing herself in an all-encompassing romantic partnership that leads her to neglect existing friendships, the stability of her intimate partnership with Roarke enables her to preserve and deepen her few existing friendships and to begin to build new ones.

CHAPTER

2

Friendship in Death

Fantasy in Death, set in mid-2060, centers on a quartet of longtime friends who run a successful game business start-up. When one is mysteriously beheaded in a locked holosuite, suspicion falls on his three partners. To solve the murder, Dallas must explore how friendship can twist into violence and how loyalty may presage betrayal. The mystery and complexity of human connection beyond romantic partnership involves sameness and difference, self and other. Trust, closeness, and their opposites must be negotiated; healthy friendships are shown to be vital, even as they require conscious nurturing and create vulnerability. These friends were, or seemed to be, like family, their closeness and interdependence apparent. The violent rupture of their seemingly unified group calls into question whether any relationship is ever viable.[1]

During a brief break from the investigation, Dallas reflects on her own friendships. Over dinner with Roarke at a pizza place where she had eaten shortly after arriving in New York, she reminisces about realizing the city was where she was meant to be. It suited her because one was "rarely alone, but never intimate."[2] The city was full of people, but she had no friends, no lovers. Though satisfied in her work, she was not yet a homicide cop.

Before Roarke, she had "only been close to two people in my entire life."[3] One was Mavis—the friend who complained when Roarke hadn't given Dallas diamonds. The other was Dallas' colleague Ryan Feeney. As with Roarke, who she met during a murder investigation, Dallas' relationships with Mavis and Feeney began on the job. She arrested Mavis for small-time theft, and, mostly through Mavis' persistence, they became friends. After a lucky bust brought Dallas to then-homicide detective Feeney's attention, she worked as his trainee, then partner.[4] When he was promoted to captain and transferred to head another division at Cop Central, they remained friendly, collaborating on cases when she required his e-skills and sometimes meeting for a beer after work.

When she met Roarke, she was back to working alone. Shortly thereafter, she met beat cop Delia Peabody at a crime scene. Peabody eventually became her aide, then partner, then closest friend other than Mavis.[5] Mira, source of marital advice, has been Dallas' colleague and, as her relationship with Roarke allows her to open up more about her childhood abuse, comes to be a semimaternal confidant. Heiress and do-gooder physician Louise DiMatto, met during the course of an investigation, likewise becomes a friend, as does intrepid reporter Nadine Furst.[6] Not quite a friend, beauty consultant Trina cuts Dallas' hair and preps her for special events.[7] Eventually, feminine but "fierce" Assistant Prosecuting Attorney Cher Reo becomes part of the circle.[8]

Girl territory

These women and others met along the way excel in their chosen fields. As one says, "We're women of position and authority."[9] Some, like Mira, are in high-ranking roles when readers meet them; Louise has established herself medically, though her free clinic is struggling. Like others, she finds increased success as the series proceeds, due in no small part to a major infusion of Roarke's funds. Others advance professionally from their own merits in conjunction with their association with Dallas and Roarke. Mavis, who "had come a long way from the street grifter Eve had once busted, to performance artist in third-rate clubs, and now to bona fide musical star," has a dramatic and singular style; Roarke, who listens to her at Dallas' request, recognizes as much and connects her with a producer.[10] Nadine, crime reporter for Channel 75, gains her own news show and publishes a best-selling account of one of Dallas' cases, which is eventually made into a vid. Even Trina benefits professionally from her association with Dallas.[11]

These women share other key characteristics. All are partnered or involved with men; there is no indication that any has ever been involved with a woman. (Although laws permit marriage and legal cohabitation no matter the gender of the parties, no significant characters have same-sex partners.[12]) Mira has been married for decades. Mavis becomes involved with fashion designer Leonardo and marries swiftly, despite an earlier distaste for marriage.[13] Louise meets and dates licensed companion Charles Monroe, whom she meets through Dallas; he becomes a sex therapist before they marry. "The sturdy Peabody . . . a cop from the brown of her dark bowl-cut hair to her shiny regulation shoes," hooks up, dates, and cohabits with e-detective Ian McNab.[14] Heterosexuality is normalized and unmarked; coupledom seems to occur naturally, although Dallas periodically speaks up for women who choose not to pursue relationships and Nadine dates men but dithers about whether to pursue a relationship or just continue to have flings. Marriage still seems the logical end point for relationships. Only Peabody and McNab, still in their twenties, opt for legal cohabitation, and they too eventually imagine marriage.

Despite sharing a sexual orientation and achieving success in their chosen fields, these women "didn't really have that much in common." Dallas thinks of them as "a strange mix."[15] Apart from her, though, all embrace certain cultural norms of femininity.[16] Across their varied styles and temperaments, all are far more interested than she in fashion and babies.[17] While Mavis insists that "being a girl is the frostiest," Dallas likens observing women at a baby shower to "watching aliens."[18] "Never fully at ease in girl territory," Dallas expresses her discomfort with "girl stuff" like jewelry and cosmetics.[19] When she grudgingly agrees to a haircut from "terrifying Trina with her bottomless case of glops and goos," Mavis encourages her to "enjoy being a girl." Dallas replies, "I don't think that means the same thing to you as it does to me."[20] She cannot comprehend why any woman would voluntarily wear high heels. Instead, she speculates on their utility as potential weapons.[21] Purses flummox her.[22] If she carries a purse to a gala, it is only to hold her badge and police-issue stunner.[23] Her evening wear is tailored for weapon access.[24]

Mira serves as a counterpoint to Dallas. At the top of her profession, "soft and pretty" Mira manages to be "the perfect example of gracious femininity" without detracting from her professional competence: "One of the top profilers in the country, and she wore pearls to work, Eve thought."[25] Dallas frequently reflects on how different Mira is from her and on her own inability to comprehend how "some women" can always look so put together and can match and coordinate outfits with aplomb.

A telling encounter illustrates diverse approaches to clothing, accessories, and recreational shopping. On her way to meet Mira for a case consultation over lunch, Dallas breaks up a "hair-pulling, scratching, teeth-snapping tangle" on the sidewalk outside a store. The delay makes her late, and she explains, "There was a fight over a Laroche triple roll bag. In peony." Mira reacts with astonishment that Dallas, "a woman who'd prefer a blow with a blunt instrument to shopping for an afternoon," would fight over a purse.[26] Dallas explains that she had broken up a scuffle between two women who both wanted the purse on sale. She was incredulous that anyone would want such a thing, let alone fight for it, and heaps scorn on the women involved: "I don't get it. Scratch, bite, squeal, slap. Why do women fight like that? They've got fists. It's an embarrassment to our entire gender." Mira, who has taken a moment to call the store to reserve the bag for herself, replies dryly that "a fistfight over the triple roll would have been much less embarrassing for all involved."[27] Later, when Detective Darcia Angelo, chief of police at Roarke's off-planet Olympus resort, visits New York and asks for shopping advice, Dallas directs her to the store with "stupidly expensive handbags and shoes."[28]

Though Dallas finds purses inexplicable, she recognizes that her colleagues and friends feel differently. Having a circle of friends enmeshes her in webs of reciprocal obligations. Some are semiprofessional. ("Stupid damn friendships," Dallas complains, when reminded that she will appear on Nadine's show that week. "They always cost you."[29]) The scariest involve socially prescribed female bonding rituals. When Mavis is expecting, Dallas grouses, "Coaching classes, baby showers, now shopping. Is there no end to the price of friendship?"[30] Dallas is "more comfortable in the morgue than in a baby boutique." Having agreed to serve as matron of honor for Louise, she is less at ease throwing the requisite bridal shower than asking her help—or being relied upon by her—to solve a murder, catch a criminal, or deal with recent or impending death.[31] "The fuss, the frills, the frenzy" of wedding preparations, even her own, perplex Dallas.[32] Already wary of marriage, she had panicked at the "horrifying" thought of "a wedding—clothes, flowers, music, people."[33]

As she explains to Mira, "I feel different from most of the women I know. Never can figure out how I end up pals with them, when half the time they're like another species."[34] Fortunately, the skills that stand her in good stead for police work help with one of friendship's obligations: gift giving. The ability to observe closely and follow a trail of clues, even ones that are not obvious, and to rely on previously cultivated contacts to garner inside information, make her a good gift giver, even if an impatient and temperamental shopper. In *Festive in Death,* set over Christmas 2060, she buys purses and matching accessories for her friends; Peabody, befitting her status as partner, receives a coat like her own—long, leather, and lined with Kevlar-like protection—but in pink rather than black, acknowledging both the professional need for such protection and Peabody's predilection for pink. Dallas' bafflement at why anyone would want such things is tempered by the realization that gifts are about what will please the recipient. By giving purses—or a pink coat—she accepts her friends as they are rather than as she is or thinks they should be. Gifts signal acceptance, if not celebration, of difference.

Not exactly a friend

Though the series dwells on differences among Dallas' friends that range from the superficial to the fundamental, one form of sameness passes entirely without comment: these women's whiteness. Despite the racial heterogeneity of New York, most of In Death's key characters, and all of Dallas' female friends, are white. In white-authored genre fiction, including private eye or police procedurals as well as some chick lit, racial and sexual others often appear as sidekicks: a gay best friend or a sassy black woman pal or assistant.[35] By making Dallas' subordinate partner white, Robb avoids this trap; instead, various modes of femininity coexist within whiteness. But in striking contrast to the way the novels explicitly juxtapose and reflect on varying gender norms as well as concerns about class, there is little acknowledgment let alone interrogation of whiteness or racism.[36]

In Death mentions race or skin color frequently. Many witnesses, victims, and suspects, and occasionally colleagues, are mixed race. A few are Asian, Latinx, or black. White ethnicity appears in matter-of-fact forensic descriptions of victims or suspects. Otherwise whiteness goes mostly unspoken. Characters with white skin are typically described by hair and eye color alone.[37] Whiteness or paleness more often describes sickly pallor due to injury, illness, or distress.[38] Otherwise, skin tones are likened to warm beverages (café au lait, dark coffee, cocoa) or gooey deserts (caramel, chocolate).[39] Dallas frequently encounters mixed marriages during the course of her investigations.[40] Though racial mixing is common, as attested by ubiquitous mixed-race characters and occasional interracial marriages, readers learn nothing about how racial categories are different in the future, if they are. Race and racism get little attention or discussion, even as at least one structural feature of racism persists: social segregation. Dallas' world includes many people of color, but her circle of friends includes strikingly few, none of them female.

Over the course of the series, Dallas accumulates a slew of female friends. Some of these relationships begin with initial wariness if not outright hostility. When Dallas first encounters Louise in the course of investigating a murder near the doctor's Canal Street clinic, it is unclear whether they will take to each other. She signs Louise on as a consultant. Louise tells Roarke, "I believe we'll either be fast friends or hate each other before we're done."[41] At a crunch time in the case, Dallas bribes Louise with a massive donation to the clinic, which Louise supports as much as her own family trust fund will allow.[42] Case solved, their friendship endures.[43] Dallas' friendship with Nadine, too, though it begins with prickly territorial wrangling, is followed by mutually beneficial collaboration. Another potential friendship is thwarted by circumstance. Dallas is wary of Amaryllis Coltraine, a white detective who moved to New York becoming involved with Chief Medical Examiner Li Morris before getting murdered. Dallas considers her "an interloper" but assumes that had she not died, they would have become friends; at a minimum, Coltraine would have been included in their social circle: "I think if [Louise's bridal] shower deal had been another six months or so down the road, she'd have been there."[44]

In contrast, non-white women fail to gain admittance to Dallas' inner circle even when they recur as characters. Colombian Chief Angelo's exclusion can perhaps be attributed to her off-planet residence; when she visits New York, she and Dallas meet up. But Garnet DeWinter, a mixed-race forensic anthropologist introduced late in 2060's *Concealed in Death*, remains apart despite the fact that she is local.[45] DeWinter, who identifies her own heritage as partly black and Asian, collaborates with Dallas on a few cases. They generate significant friction.[46] She is "not exactly a friend."[47] Dallas grudgingly accepts owing her a drink when DeWinter is helpful; both agree that they should really learn to communicate. It remains unclear whether they will do so in future novels.

One might explain the unrelieved whiteness of Dallas' circle of women friends as Robb's conscious recreation of, and commentary on, contemporary patterns of racial-social segregation. If so, it is at odds with her dispensing with equally common segregation on the basis of class, education, profession, or age. Dallas' friends differ from her and from each other in striking ways, as she repeatedly observes. Moreover, the racial homogeneity of Dallas' female friends is notably greater than that of the men around her. Although Roarke, Summerset, McNab, Feeney, and Charles are white—described as such or presumptively—male secondary and tertiary characters are somewhat more diverse. Morris is part Asian.[48] Dallas' squad detective Santiago is presumably Latino.[49] Mavis' "copper-skinned" husband Leonardo is likely part Native American.[50] Dallas' immediate police superiors, Commander Whitney and Chief Tibble, are dark skinned. The sole recurring black-identified character is a club owner named Crack. A tertiary figure, Crack provides an important foil for considering how difference and sameness play out.

Hey, big black guy

Dallas meets dive bar bouncer/owner Crack in *Glory in Death* while she is investigating a murder that took place near his club, the Down and Dirty. From their first encounter, he insistently names her whiteness in racially charged, gendered, and sexualized encounters. He hails her with "Hey, white girl."

> Brows knit, Eve turned at the interruption. The man was tall as a house and from the deepness of his complexion, a full black. He sported, as many did in this part of town, feathers in his hair. His cheek tattoo was vivid green and in the shape of a grinning human skull. He wore an open red vest and matching pants snug enough to show the bulge of his cock.
>
> "Hey, black boy," she said in the same casually insulting tone.
>
> He flashed a wide, dazzling grin at her from an unbelievably ugly face. "You looking for action?" He jerked his head toward the garish sign of the all-nude club across the street. "You a little skinny, but they be hiring. Don't get many white as you. Mostly mixed." He chucked her under the chin with fingers the width of soy wieners. "I be the bouncer, put in a word for you."
>
> "Now why would you do that?"
>
> "Out of the goodness of my heart, and five percent of your tips, honeypot. A long white girl like you make plenty jiggling her stuff."
>
> "I appreciate the thought, but I've got a job." Almost with regret, she pulled out her badge.
>
> He whistled through his teeth. "Now how come I don't be seeing that? White girl, you just don't smell like cop."
>
> "Must be the new soap I'm using. Got a name?"
>
> "They just call me Crack. That's the sound it makes when I bust heads." He grinned again, and illustrated by bringing his two huge hands together. "Crack. Got it?"[51]

Dallas questions him about his whereabouts concerning the time she's interested in, pays him for information, and gives him her card so he can get in touch. He agrees to "keep it in mind" and adds, "You decide you want to earn a little extra shaking those little white tits, you let Crack know." Leaving, "he loped across the street with the surprising grace of an enormous black gazelle."[52]

This encounter foregrounds race, gender, sex, and embodiment. Crack addresses Dallas in terms of her sex and race: "Hey, white girl." *Girl* applied to a thirty-year-old woman is disrespectfully infantilizing, as Dallas points out in another context, but not racially laden.[53] She responds to his casual sexism with casual racism. "Hey, black boy" echoes a long history of denying black males adult status.[54] In later meetings, Crack continues to initiate these exchanges. He offers, "Hey there, white girl"; she responds symmetrically, "Hey back, black boy."[55] To "Hey, skinny white girl," she responds, "Hey, big black guy."[56] Occasionally, he calls her "white girl" and she replies with "black man."[57]

These greetings rely on paired opposites: skinny/big, female/male, and above all, white/black. White and black oppose each other. They also contrast with the mixed shades in between. Phenotype equals racial identity: Crack's "complexion" tells Dallas he is "a full black." Her whiteness distinguishes her from the "mostly mixed" women who work in the "all-nude" club and also makes her like the "big, important, fancy" as well as "dead" lawyer. Crack observes, "White girl, wasn't she? Just like you, honeypot."[58] Dallas' whiteness is both unusual ("Don't get many as white as you") and desirable. It increases her sexual appeal: "A long white girl like you make plenty jiggling her stuff." Even after Crack learns she is a cop, he repeats his suggestion that she work in the club "shaking [her] little white tits."[59]

Crack, too, is relentlessly embodied. Dallas notes his skin color, his size, and, along with his flamboyant clothing, the visible outline of his genitalia.[60] Crack combines grotesque appearance ("unbelievably ugly," "enormous") and animality ("gazelle," "loped") with physical prowess ("surprising grace").[61]

Other regular characters have dark skin, but only Crack is black. Dallas' immediate supervisor, Commander Whitney, is "an imposing man with a hard face and tired eyes." He's routinely described as having a wide face and dark skin, occasionally likened to coffee, cocoa, or, once, "glossy oak."[62] Also "enormous," the "formal and distinguished" Chief Tibble is likewise "dark," with skin like "polished onyx."[63] Crack's skin is also "polished onyx," but if Tibble and Crack share skin tone, they do not seem to share a race.[64] Blackness is social. It involves a host of stereotypical allusions and connections to an urban underclass environment.[65] Though Robb repeatedly explains his nickname as resulting from his skull-cracking work as a bouncer, the allusion to crack cocaine, scourge of the inner cities, is unmistakable.[66]

Just as he is the only recurring character whose blackness gets attention, Crack is the only character who names whiteness.[67] Not only does he continually refer to Dallas' race, he points out the whiteness of FBI agents who Dallas arranges to meet in his club. "More white meat. Whiter than white. They ever hire color in the effing-bee of eye?"[68] Prior to that moment, no racial descriptors were used for the men, only Dallas' not entirely complimentary "clean-cut."

Coded terms such as *clean-cut* name whiteness obliquely. Such language clusters around innocent, "fresh," "undeniably adorable" Officer Troy Trueheart.[69] He first appears in *Conspiracy in Death* as a young rookie poorly treated by his trainer. When he impresses Dallas with his insight, she draws him into her investigation. She explains to Commander Whitney that he has "excellent potential" and pairs him with one of her detectives, the slick, fashionable, and reliable David Baxter.[70] Trueheart, with his "hero's face," is seldom described with any color other than "green"—a term used elsewhere for inexperience and Midwestern identity.[71] "Hardly more than a boy," "Officer Baby Face" is "the kid with the peach fuzz on his face that looks like a screen ad for toothpaste."[72] When Trueheart, then age twenty-two, gets badly injured shortly after he joins her squad, Dallas says to Roarke, "I've got a man down. A boy . . . He's a goddamn boy."[73] Even when he later earns his detective shield, he looks "young, a little pale, and daisy fresh," both "handsome and homespun."[74] He has "a good brain and an idealism that was bright and shiny as polished silver," but for the most part he is described in terms of looks and general demeanor.[75] Though "tall" and "soldiery," "Trueheart's a nonthreatening presence" with "a kind of Officer Friendly way about him."[76] "Everybody likes Trueheart."[77] He's buff and built, but any potential sexual charge gets blunted through references to his "sweet" disposition or retiring manner: he's "young, studly, and shy," blushes when embarrassed, and moves with glacial slowness when interested in a girl.[78]

He and Crack anchor opposite ends of the spectrum: the former "remarkably ugly" with "a face even a besotted mother would have a hard time loving," and the latter a "cutie-pie."[79] "Earnest" and "All-American" Trueheart is "as wholesome and harmless as apple pie."[80]

With these sorts of oblique connections, the identity "American" simultaneously depends on and conceals its racial implications.[81] For all of the series' references to mixed-race people, race is still consistently iterated through the dichotomous opposition between and hierarchical positioning of black and white.[82] Yet white racial identity masquerades as no identity. Trueheart's whiteness, like that of Dallas' female friends, goes unspoken, while Crack's blackness is visible, obvious, and frequently mentioned. It is only in contrast to blackness that whiteness becomes noticeable. Nearly two years after their first encounter in the harsh streets outside his club, Crack attends Thanksgiving dinner at Dallas and Roarke's home. The whiteness of Roarke's relatives shows up only when juxtaposed to Crack's blackness: "The Irish white skin of the little girl [Crack] had on his hip glowed against his ebony."[83]

Such interesting friends

The path from reluctant informant to friend of a sort involves twists and turns. From an unpromising start, Crack and Dallas develop a working collaboration. She periodically meets informants or colleagues at his club, where "the drinks were next to lethal, the music was hot, and many of the patrons had spent as much time in a cage as out of one."[84] Though she refers to him as "a friend" in late 2058—and Nadine remarks, at one meeting, "You have such interesting friends, Dallas"—Crack and Dallas do not socialize; she continues to pay him when he provides information.[85] After all, "Friendly only went so far."[86]

Tragedy bridges this gap. In *Portrait in Death*, set in August 2059, a serial killer murders NYU medical student Alicia Dilbert, a "pretty black girl" aged twenty. A search for next of kin turns up a brother named Wilson Buckley, which the reader learns is Crack's legal name. Neither Dallas nor Peabody knew he had family. Peabody remonstrates with herself: "I didn't even know he had a sister. It feels like I should've." Yet Crack had chosen to keep his club persona and his personal life separate. As a protective big brother, he lived close but not too close to his "baby sister" while keeping her "distant from his business." He didn't want her sullied by "the dregs that frequented the club."[87]

When Dallas and Roarke visit his home to notify him that his sister has died, careful separations collapse. His appearance as a "huge black man naked but for a purple loincloth and many tattoos" contrasts with refined but exotic surroundings: a "spacious and tidy" apartment "tastefully decorated in what she supposed was African art, the masks, the bright colors, the lush fabrics."[88] Primitive blackness meets cosmopolitan African heritage. His language shifts too. Crack greets them with dialect: "Shit. Gonna need coffee if I gonna be talking to some skinny-assed cop this time of day. Roarke, can't you keep this white girl busy enough so she leave me be?"[89] When Dallas tells him the awful news, "the jive vanished from his speech."[90]

Grief, like any shared ordeal, can bring people closer. Given a family (albeit one he must immediately mourn) and a home, a distraught Crack moves from stereotype to individual, from informant to friend. After they view his sister's body at the morgue, Dallas comforts him, kneeling beside him after he collapses "into a weeping puddle on the floor." Incongruously, "the huge man curled into her like a baby wanting comfort. And she rocked him while he wept." She convinces him that she will find Alicia's killer, bringing justice. He wouldn't have accepted such assurances from anyone else: "you're not any other cop, white girl. You take care of my baby sister."[91] In this encounter, only whiteness is named; Crack's size remains salient, but his infantilization ("like a baby wanting comfort") removes any potential sexual charge to their sustained embrace.[92]

Dallas eventually apprehends the deranged photographer who, intent on capturing the innocent energy of his victims, had killed Crack's sister and nearly killed Trueheart as well. Whatever Crack's own grey areas, his sister and Trueheart share an essential purity of spirit. Although many characters have awful family members, the inclusion of a respectable, high-achieving sibling helps humanize Crack. So, too, does his vulnerability in grief. The case creates a bridge between Crack and Dallas. From friendly but professional acquaintanceship they move to reciprocal connection and mutual obligation. Dallas and Roarke plant a tree to memorialize his sister, as Dallas had earlier done for Roarke's mother. Crack subsequently refuses payment for information, favors, or use of a room at his club.[93] Dallas passes along greetings from Roarke when they encounter each other—something one could not imagine her doing with other informants—and invites him for a cookout with colleagues and others, a large holiday party, and even the more intimate Thanksgiving dinner, where his blackness brings whiteness into relief.[94]

A personal friend

All of Dallas' relationships sooner or later involve the intersection of personal and professional interactions. An interaction with Chief Tibble's formidable wife at a memorial service for a murder victim whose death Dallas is investigating highlights both the potential conflicts that Dallas seems to pooh-pooh but also the impossibility, at least within the In Death narrative universe, of separate work and personal spheres. Mrs. Tibble, a friend of the widow, tells Dallas it's inappropriate for her "to speak with a reporter at the victim's memorial." Dallas responds that Nadine "is also a personal friend." Pressed further, she suggests that it is equally inappropriate for the police chief's wife to "attend the memorial of the victim of an open homicide case" and talk with potential suspects. Mrs. Tibble concedes the point: no clear divisions are possible.[95]

Work is central to Dallas' life. She meets her friends through the exercise of her profession, their profession, or more often, both; she neither believes in nor practices segregation of work life and personal life. It makes sense that with a reporter, a profiler, and a prosecutor, professional interactions continue alongside, interwoven with, and occasionally in conflict with social and personal engagements. But this is also true for Dallas' friends whose professions do not directly intersect with police work. Dallas asks Trina for advice about cosmetics and enhancements as they intersect with her cases.[96] She seeks Mavis' advice on how one might conduct a psychic con, asks her for information to understand the troubled girls killed by a serial murderer, and has her impersonate a clerk for a sting operation.[97] Dallas hosts Louise's sleepover bridal shower; the next morning, when Louise, Nadine, Mira, Reo, and Mavis gather in Dallas' office, Mavis has the breakthrough insight that helps crack the case.[98]

Apart from such collaborations on Dallas' assigned cases, an improbable number of Dallas' personal connections become embroiled in murder. Mavis is accused of murder, and Dallas "professionally and personally" must deal with it.[99] Although she convinces her commander to keep her on the case despite the conflict of interest, she recognizes the problem with having Mavis and Leonardo, whose ex-girlfriend was the victim of the murder of which Mavis is suspected, stay at her home: "The primary, the defendant, and the tenant of the murder scene, who also happens to be the victim's former lover and the defendant's current. Are you all insane?"[100] Peabody's brother is (falsely) suspected of murder when he visits New York, Mira's husband is attacked by his cousin's killers, the daughter of Roarke's admin Caro is thought to have killed her cheating husband, and Summerset briefly becomes a suspect in a string of murders.[101] Trina calls Dallas when, sozzled, she and a friend discover a dead body during a prank.[102] Largely through Dallas' efforts, all are ultimately vindicated.

The fraught boundaries between friendship and professional obligations are nowhere clearer than with Nadine. What began as a wary professional acquaintance deepened out of "a sense of debt": after Dallas saved Nadine's life from a murderous fellow reporter in *Glory in Death*, she could trust that Nadine would be fair in her reporting and would not betray her personal secrets.[103] There is occasional friction, something to be expected with "two hardheaded, strong-willed women who believed absolutely in their duty to their profession."[104] Their relationship is built on respect, like, and mutually beneficial exchanges, not including the low-level bribery—cookies and brownies—that Nadine relies on to smooth her way through the bull pen into Dallas' office. They explicitly negotiate the lines between friendship and professional relationship and acknowledge how tricky it is to maintain them.[105] (Nadine: "Nice doing business with you, Dallas."[106]) Dallas uses Nadine to spin stories for desired effects; Nadine, in return, gets a scoop or an exclusive interview. Dallas must tread carefully when giving Nadine access lest "other members of the Fourth Estate" grumble.[107] She trusts that Nadine will not use information improperly.[108] That such close collaboration, or Nadine's other friendships with cops, might lead to collusion between media and police to cover up police misconduct is never explored.[109]

Since profiler Mira works for the police department, no such worry exists; Mira knows as much about Eve as anyone does—perhaps, Dallas speculates, even more than she herself knows.[110] Some of that sharing was involuntary, as Dallas was stripped bare both literally and metaphorically in required evaluations. Mira also urges her to confide voluntarily; as the series progresses, she does so, disclosing memories and fears. They have a deep and asymmetrical relationship.[111] Dallas is not Mira's subordinate, but neither is she quite an equal. Though Dallas wants to protect Mira and steps in on occasion to do so, more often Mira is the one who provides additional, personal help to Dallas beyond her work as profiler.

Mira at times acts as surrogate mother as well as friend and colleague; she has "strong and deeply maternal" feelings for Eve.[112] Dallas says, once, "We're friends," but thinks, "or something more complicated . . . that was tangled in friendship."[113] After Dallas recovers a memory she has been suppressing for years, Mira tries to dissuade her undertaking physically and psychologically grueling Level 3 Testing.[114] Mira says, "I have children I love. . . . I have friends who are vital to me and acquaintances and colleagues I admire and respect. . . . I have all those feelings for you." "If you were my daughter . . . I'm asking you, as a friend, to reconsider."[115] In Mira's arsenal of reasons are reassurances about Eve as a competent adult woman capable of deep and reciprocal connections to people.

If Mira is in some respects the senior partner in relationship with Dallas, with Peabody the reverse is true. Dallas and Peabody's mentor/mentee relationship combines partnership with hierarchy. Dallas has, and uses, the upper hand. Yet as Peabody becomes more experienced, their friendship grows steadily. Partners on the job have a certain sort of intimacy. Dallas frequently pulls rank; their friendship is unequal though reciprocal.[116] At the same time, especially after Peabody earns her detective shield, Dallas comes to confide in her about her past.

Showing up, even if one would prefer to be somewhere else, doing something else, is part of the job of friendship; Dallas does it.[117] Listening to discomfiting confidences—from pregnancy news to oversharing about a relationship—is part of the deal.[118] When Peabody and McNab hit a rocky patch, Dallas fulfills the dictates of friendship, which she likens to "her job."[119] She listens, inquires, and eats copious quantities of ice cream.[120] Peabody is a foil for Dallas. Since the latter grew up without girlfriends, Peabody advises her about the passionate and changeable nature of loyalties during the teen years while they are dissecting and analyzing communications from a serial killer who has fixated on Dallas and considers herself Eve's sole "true friend."[121]

Your true and loyal friend

Friendship can be a force for good. It can also be a force for evil. *Obsession in Death*, set at the very end of 2060, tracks a deranged fan of Dallas' who believes that by killing, she's revenging slights to the Lieutenant. She begins by murdering those who might reasonably be construed as Dallas' antagonists if not enemies, leaving a note to Dallas at the scene identifying herself as "your true and loyal friend."[122] She murders a lawyer who had opposed Dallas in court and a criminal who had injured her in a minor scuffle. Then she turns her attention to those she decides are not Dallas' real friends, making attempts on Nadine as well as young computer prodigy Jamie Lingstrom. Ultimately, she turns on Dallas herself when Dallas does not recognize or reward her overtures.[123]

The books devote relatively less attention to male friendships, either casual or deeply intimate, than to female friendships. Roarke and McNab connect over beers occasionally; Roarke socializes with Feeney and occasionally with Dallas' ranking officers. He throws a bachelor party for Charles before his marriage to Louise. Roarke's true friends, however, are those from childhood. They play significant, if intermittent, roles in filling in his backstory. One shows up and intends to swindle Roarke.[124] Eventually, this man/old friend puts himself in harm's way to enable Dallas to catch the crook who went beyond theft to murder. In the end, he ends up taking a blade meant for Roarke and dying to save his life.[125] This is a brotherhood truer than that of those who claim the mantle to justify their bad deeds.

The male friendships that do come under close scrutiny, however, are far from healthy. Twisted partnerships among privileged elites figure in two books centering on pairs of murderers (*Indulgence in Death* and *Seduction in Death*) and another on a gang of serial rapists (*Brotherhood in Death*).[126] The "arrogant, smug, wealthy, privileged" perpetrators in each case believe themselves legally untouchable.[127] They have gotten away with things their whole lives. In *Seduction*, the predators are in their twenties; in *Indulgence*, in their forties; in *Brotherhood*, in their late sixties. In *Brotherhood*, the friends affirm their fraternal bond by jointly raping young women. The predators in *Seduction* start off intending only rape, but graduate quickly to rape-murder. *Indulgence*'s killers target high-end service providers, mostly female, befitting the pair's sense of being above the ordinary run of humanity.

Brotherhood plays with the categories of villain and victim as it weaves a narrative around sexual violence, masculine and class privilege, and loyalty. The story begins with the sexualized torture-murder of a former US senator and conservative politician. Another victim soon follows: a judge and close friend of the senator. Dallas and Peabody discover that these men were part of a self-proclaimed brotherhood formed nearly half a century earlier at Yale, cemented with the yearly abduction, drugging, and gang-rape of a young woman, typically a student. The murderers are several of their victims who banded together to enact what they perceive—though Dallas disagrees—as justice. These men profaned the notion of friendship while believing that their brotherhood justified their actions.

In *Seduction* and *Indulgence*, too, pairs of men, born to wealth, consider their friendship a law unto itself. One young man refers to the other as "his friend, his oldest and most constant companion" and believes "he deserved some sympathy and support" when he inadvertently kills the woman he intended merely to seduce, using date-rape drugs, as part of a competition for points.[128] The friend ups the stakes to include deliberate killing in his own turn. Considering that, despite similarities in the methods used, there may be two killers, Roarke points out, if so, "they know each other intimately. Brothers of a sort. . . . Partners." Their friendship proves more powerful than family ties. Yet after they are caught and the less dominant partner has confessed, the other poisons him in an attempt to save his own skin.[129] The older pair of killers has a more reciprocal connection. Their relationship with each other is more intimate than with the women they have dated and married: Dallas calls them "freaking soul mates."[130]

These cases involved a kind of game, competition, or ritual: a deeply dysfunctional partnership or brotherhood. These twisted refractions of healthy relationships serve as a foil for the true friendships that Dallas maintains: with Roarke, with Peabody, with Mavis and others. Though her partnership with Roarke is sexually exclusive—both insist on monogamy—their emotional connection is enhanced, not imperiled, by friendships with others.[131] Unlike these rapists and murderers, however, they do not cement their friendships by joining together to victimize outsiders.

Privileged villains in these three novels as well as others commit bad acts to keep or extend their power. Their wealth facilitates impunity. It does not, however, guarantee it. Eventually, rich wrongdoers get their just desserts. Ultrawealthy sport murderers are brought to justice. Two privileged young white men do not get away with rape and murder. A serial-killer diplomat gets stripped of immunity; a socialite is charged with two homicides; a sociopath from a wealthy family ends up in custody.[132] The guilty parties in the murders Dallas investigates are disproportionately wealthy and powerful, like the woman who relies on a relationship of patronage to pressure a poorer woman into an exchange of murders.[133] Seldom did the butler do it.[134] Robb allows readers to notice pervasive inequality and the different standards that apply to rich and poor before bringing wealthy malefactors to justice.

Yet as "the richest man in the known world," Roarke circumvents the law regularly.[135] Roarke is an exception to the rule that rich men are not above the law, though it is mostly his skills rather than his billions that make him untouchable. Given the series' ambivalent critique of capitalism and of elite privilege, his fantastical wealth poses a problem; it is both appreciated and subverted. The "difference between multigenerational wealth and wealth more recently and personally acquired" partly accounts for his different moral status.[136] His experiences of deprivation and his empathy and charitable activity make a difference. He does not believe that his wealth makes him better than others; he can relate as an equal to those in wildly different circumstances. Perhaps most importantly, his experience of true friendship protects him from the deforming effects of great wealth. If a perverted form of friendship nurtures murderous impulses, true friendship benefits individuals and society.

In critiquing inherited wealth and snobbery, In Death implicitly critiques white privilege as it intersects male and class privilege.[137] Robb mentions racism directly only a handful of times in over fifteen thousand pages. Yet unlike in *Obsession in Death*, where the female killer is motivated by individual psychopathology, in the series' first and most recent installments, wealthy, educated, privileged white men, rich and politically connected, commit sexual crimes, persistently harm women, and expect their privilege to protect them. It doesn't.

CHAPTER

3

Vocation in Death

Lieutenant Renee Oberman is a dirty cop. She uses subordinates, accomplices, and criminals to collect bribes and skim drugs and money from evidence. The daughter of a retired, decorated officer, Oberman wields sex, influence, and violence to protect her enterprise. Her activities come to light by accident. At the outset of *Treachery in Death*, set in the sweltering summer of 2060, Dallas assigns newly promoted Detective Peabody as primary on a convenience-store robbery–homicide. A scuffle ensues when they confront the neighborhood toughs responsible. Dallas criticizes Peabody's fighting technique. Taking her superior's criticism to heart, Peabody works out in an underused gym at headquarters. There she overhears Oberman and a crooked colleague discuss a murder committed to cover up their corruption.

As it chronicles Dallas and Peabody's investigation and apprehension of these crooked cops, *Treachery* brings together themes that weave through the series. It contrasts good and bad uses of a superior officer's power, addresses the importance of mentoring and training, and attends to the variety of ways women wield power. It explores the centrality of work to individual identity, raises questions about the relationship between work and wealth, and foregrounds the ethical dilemmas that arise in the course of work life, for police officers as well as for others. It connects the rule of law to personal and professional ethics, while acknowledging that the system does not always guarantee justice and that other worthwhile moral codes exist.[1]

Doing what they were meant to do

The novels reflect both in various characters' affirmations and in structure, which centers on one woman's work, the conviction that success and satisfaction in one's work are vital, especially for women.[2] A working heroine is nothing new. From the 1980s onward, the vast majority of popular romance heroines work, whether in low-status occupations offering little beyond a paycheck and some hassles, or in dynamic and successful careers.[3] An array of female professionals figure among Dallas' friends and those she encounters in her job: lawyers, surgeons, police officers, politicians, entrepreneurs, performers, and artists.

The place of work in Dallas' life goes far beyond employment, though, to serve as the backbone of the novels, her relationships, and her character. For her, being a cop is a calling. A priest compares Dallas' vocation to his own.[4] Others are called to different work. Someone says about a murder victim who knew (of) Dallas: "She admired you. She believed, strongly, in women leaving a deep mark doing what they were meant to do."[5] Similarly, after Dallas broke up a global cloning ring, Nadine wrote a book, *The Icove Agenda,* about it: "We're damn good at what we do, Dallas, you and me." They're "damn good" in part because the work "matters."[6] Nadine's book becomes a best seller and is made into a vid. The actor playing Dallas respects Dallas' "important" work while emphasizing her own suitability for her acting career: "I'm good at my work. I'm damn good at it and I feel strongly what I do is important. It's not uncovering-a-global-cloning-ring important, but without art, stories, and the people who bring those stories to life, the world would be a sadder, smaller place."[7]

As the actor insists, a variety of kinds of work are important for a richer world. Moreover, some people are suited to certain kinds of work and are both good at it and fulfilled by it. (Killers too may understand their activity as work; being good at a certain type of work does not mean the work is good.[8]) People are drawn to particular careers out of a mix of talent, personal history, and simple pull.[9] Louise explains, "I became a doctor because I have a need, and a talent, to heal." Medicine is her family-approved "passion," but, she says, "I practice it my way." Licensed companion Charles

Monroe, whom Dallas had met in the course of an investigation and introduced to Louise, explains his own professional history similarly: "I have a need, and a talent, for giving pleasure."[10] Talent is a necessary but not sufficient ingredient for success. Personal satisfaction in one's profession matters. Peabody declares, "If you're not excited about your work, life's crap."[11]

Suitable work brings together affinity and tenacity to get results. That work is not always paid. Roarke's Aunt Sinead, whom he and Dallas visit at the family farm in Ireland, remarks that she likes to care for people and has "a talent for it," just as Dallas has a talent for her work. Sinead's cooking and caretaking are no less a vocation for being unpaid. Indeed, they might be more so. Although Dallas dismisses the few backward figures, including a retired police officer and a politician, who want to eliminate stipends for professional mothers, thinking money makes the work less sacred, nonparents who perform waged caring work in the home need not have a calling to do it. The work performed by nannies, house managers, home care nurses, and housekeepers is never disparaged, but few if any celebrate it as their calling as Sinead does.[12]

Dallas' work, for which she earns a "slightly less pathetic" salary than her subordinates, involves little obvious nurturing and arises less out of pleasure than need. In the aftermath of a case involving a vicious gang rape and ritual murder, Roarke says to Dallas, "It's a hard life you've chosen, Lieutenant. A brutal road that brings you to that so often." "It chose me," she answers.[13] Her personal experience of violence led to her job: "I wanted to be a cop. Because cops have control. They stop the bad guys."[14] Sexual homicides affect her particularly strongly.[15] Her past—and how she processes it—enables her to do what she does and, sometimes, to have special "insight" that allows her to outthink her quarry.[16] Her job helps her "overcome" or integrate or work through or live with her past: "Once she'd been a victim—helpless, used, and broken. Now, she was a warrior."[17]

Peabody's stable family and loving upbringing in a pacifist, rural hippie-like community could not be more different than Dallas'. Yet Dallas, recognizing "a spark," takes her on as a trainee.[18] Explaining to Dallas why she is "not growing alfalfa, weaving mats, and raising a brood," Peabody declares, "I like to kick ass, Sir."[19] Peabody's Free-Ager parents accept her unconventional choice. When they visit her in New York, her mother Phoebe tells Dallas, "We understood that this was her calling, and trusted that she would do good work." Later, having watched her daughter draw a confession from a suspect, Phoebe tells her that police work is "a very difficult job. And one you were meant to do."[20]

You've got potential

If Dallas was impressed by Peabody's competence on scene and by her spark, Peabody already knew about Dallas, who had been her "hero" and a "mythical figure" while she was at the academy.[21] Peabody is not the only one in awe of Dallas. A uniform at crime scene awaits her arrival with trepidation: "She had a rep. You didn't want to screw up with Dallas. . . . He'd heard it said she chewed up lazy cops for breakfast and spit them out at lunch. He wanted to make it through the day."[22] He mixes wariness with respect. Dallas' impressive record of solved cases and arrests generates envy from underperforming colleagues and admiration from others. For instance, Officer Ellen Bowers, introduced in *Conspiracy in Death,* was senior to Dallas at the police academy and has harbored resentment since that time, though Dallas does not remember her. Their careers provide striking contrasts: Bowers remains in uniform and on "homicide-lite" duty, while Dallas has earned a shield and rank.

Her reputation extends beyond other officers to members of the public, owing to her involvement in several high-profile cases and her marriage to Roarke. Her profile is burnished by occasional public feats of impressive athleticism and bravery. She catches a toddler hurled at her by a fleeing suspect.[23] She falls two stories from a terrace, then leaps from a moving walkway in pursuit of another killer.[24] Yet she shuns media attention, deflecting it unless it serves her purposes. She stresses the routine aspects of cop work. Even where a particular lead seems unlikely to generate results, it must be pursued. When Roarke remarks on the "unholy tedium" of an investigation, she responds, "It's not all land to air chases and busting in doors."[25] Elsewhere she notes, "Homicide, like most cop work, was walking, waiting, asking questions, and paperwork."[26]

Still, the media (and hence the public) largely ignore the boring elements in favor of drama.[27] The relative of a victim says, "When people talk about Roarke's cop over their cocktails and canapés, they say she's a little scary, a little mean, and very relentless."[28] To her, that is a good thing; Dallas' tenacity will lead to justice. Some civilians, though, are disdainful, often in gendered ways. One man describes Dallas as a "female storm trooper bitch," and a suspect calls her a "two-bit dyke bitch cop."[29] She plays to this stereotype when it suits, intimidating suspects in a rough neighborhood as a "bad bitch cop" who will retaliate if her car is damaged or stolen while she is about her business.[30]

Persistent sexist attitudes infiltrate the workplace. In addition to occasional politicos who spout backwards notions about women's place in the home, and several killers who are hostile to powerful women, a few police officers display explicitly chauvinist attitudes toward women, especially those who hold rank.[31] Other sexist elements are subtle but pervasive. Dallas' professional life involves solving homicides and managing her "men"—a squad of male and female detectives.[32] Her working style and mentoring activity show an ambivalent relationship to ideals of femininity. The presence of other female cops, both subordinates and superiors, illustrates a variety of ways of being female and professional.

Drawing on her own training by Captain Feeney, who now runs the Electronic Detection Division, Dallas keeps an eye out for promising junior officers, female and male. Mirroring the way Feeney "had plucked her out of the pack when she'd still been in uniform, and made her his," she recruits Peabody to help with a case after being impressed by her competence at a crime scene.[33] Peabody does well; Dallas asks if she wants to be her aide. Dallas tells her, "You've got potential—brains and guts. That's what Feeney told me when he brought me in under him."[34]

When Dallas brings rookie Trueheart into an investigation, she rescues him from the bitter and incompetent Officer Bowers, who had been assigned to train him. She pairs him temporarily with Detective Baxter, who subsequently agrees to train him. Later, she reflects that both are "good cops" and that "tucking the earnest Trueheart in as the smart-ass Baxter's aide had been one of her better ideas."[35] The training relationship shapes both trainer and trainee. It also affects Dallas, as Baxter's superior: she oversees Baxter's oversight of Trueheart, just as her commander oversees her supervision of her detectives and their aides.[36] She consistently and dependably attends to her subordinates' professional development.[37]

Training occurs via professional apprenticeship. Dallas trains Peabody to use her own judgment and instincts, slowly leading her toward independence.[38] In addition to grunt work and fetching coffee, Dallas assigns her incrementally more responsibility. She tasks her with getting warrants from the prosecuting attorney's office, has her figure time of death and identification at a crime scene, orders her to update their Commander, conduct a briefing, put teams together for a raid, and take the lead in an interview.[39] She lets her handle an interview and booking for a suspect who turns himself in and sends her to interview someone independently and to follow up on a lead arising from her hunch.[40] She assigns her responsibility for a cold case, requiring Peabody to do the interrogation but nudging her toward the right tactics when she flounders.[41] At Dallas' instigation, Peabody prepares for, takes, and passes the detective exam.[42] After Peabody earns her shield, Dallas assigns her to serve as primary on a straightforward case—in the aftermath of which she learns of Oberman's treachery.[43] Dallas drags Peabody to the podium at a press conference and sends her to appear on Nadine's news show, NOW, explaining to her superiors that Peabody "needs a shove into the deep end of the pool."[44]

Along the way, Dallas repeatedly tests Peabody's mettle, offers (gruff) encouragement when deserved and measured correction when necessary. Peabody is typically uneasy with expanded responsibilities, enough so that Dallas periodically warns her "don't say *Me?* in that stupid tone" before reminding her that she knows how to perform the task in question.[45] Still, being ordered to update their Commander leaves Peabody "pale and speechless."[46] When Peabody is nervous about receiving a medal for extraordinary service, McNab tries to cajole her out of the mood.[47] Dallas' brusque manner reassures more than her cohab's solicitousness.[48] In another instance, when Peabody frets that she is not living up to expectations, Dallas forgoes soothing for directness. She acknowledges Peabody's anxiety but asks, "Has there been any time since you came under my command that I've hesitated to tell you when I felt you didn't do the job to my requirements, or that I was dissatisfied with your performance or that you'd screwed up in any way, shape, or form?" Peabody acknowledges that she hasn't: "Ah, well, no, sir."[49]

As Dallas mentors Peabody through the Oberman case and others, her mentoring style plays to her own strengths at the same time it undoes gendered stereotypes. Her peevish manner masks concern for her underlings' welfare.[50] When Peabody vomits at a particularly gruesome crime scene, Dallas asks Mira to check on her later, since Peabody is "brooding about it. Like she's the first cop to puke on her shoes." Dallas recounts the stress Peabody is under, including apartment hunting with McNab, and suggests that Mira "could find a minute to pat her on the head about it or something. Whatever. Shit." Mira replies, "It's very sweet for you to be worried about her." Dallas recoils. She neither "want[s] to be very sweet" nor "to worry about her." As she puts it, "This isn't the time for her head to be up her ass."[51]

Do I look like a lady?

As such exchanges make clear, Dallas is neither refined nor ladylike. She prefers that her underlings call her *Sir. Ma'am,* she says, is "somebody's tight-assed aunt."[52] She insists that people respect her rank. When she intervenes in a street fight, one combatant says, "This is none of your business lady, so just move before you get hurt." She corrects him: "That's Lieutenant Lady."[53] Investigating a suspicious death while on vacation at Roarke's off-planet resort, she tussles with the resort doctor over what he will call her. (He proposes Lieutenant Roarke as a compromise.[54]) She corrects a store owner who calls her Mrs. Roarke; he offers instead the deferential Mrs. Lieutenant Dallas Roarke.[55] Believing herself disrespected, one crotchety witness persists in calling her "Miss Dallas." They reach an accommodation after Dallas informs her that "respect's a two way street."[56]

Dallas' preference for *Sir* also reflects her ambivalent relationship to femininity. Dallas makes crass jokes and talks about tits. Yet she tolerates neither misogyny nor harassment. She allows Baxter's lewd comments to her about the women he observes during an operation but quickly rebukes Detective Santiago when he tells his partner to "move [her] hot buns." Detective Carmichael quickly assures Dallas that she asked him to say it as motivation to avoid holiday weight gain. Dallas relents, but orders Santiago not to "give any motivation in public."[57] She occasionally encounters prejudiced men who think women should not be cops, who resent female authority, or who hold overly restrictive notions of appropriate female behavior. When she curses during an interrogation, a suspect insists that "ladies don't use bad words like that." She asks, "Do I look like a lady?" He replies, "You're a girl." She retorts, "I'm a cop. I'm a murder cop, and I eat assholes like you for breakfast."[58] When a visiting deputy from Arkansas uses the word "bullshit," then apologizes for using "hard language," Dallas scoffs, "The day 'bullshit' is hard language in a cop shop, that's the day I turn in my badge."[59]

Dallas accepts at some level stereotypical notions of feminine weakness, but such weakness crosses gender lines. She calls the male suspect most likely to break in interrogation "a weak sister."[60] When Roarke suggests that there is something spooky about a house rumored to be haunted, Dallas taunts, "Want to wait in the car, Sally?"[61] Later, she insults a female killer, saying, "Jesus, you fight like a girl." Girly fighting, however, is not inherently gendered: the killer's male victim also fought "like a girl," while Dallas does not.[62] When a man working out at an all-male gym she's investigating insists, "Guy can't bench his weight, he's a girl," Dallas does "ten slow, steady reps" at her own weight and tells him, "I ain't no girl."[63]

Dallas rejects things she views as "uncoplike," many of which are coded female.[64] Indeed, when she assumes an e-cop they are discussing is male, McNab corrects her: "She. DS Melodie Reedway." Dallas grumbles, "A cop named Melodie. It's just not right."[65] When Trina gives Dallas a French manicure, she is horrified: "Do you understand that I'm a cop? Do you understand that should I have to restrain a suspect and he gets a load of my shiny yet neutral French job, he's going to break his neck laughing?" She continues hyperbolically, imagining an internal affairs "investigation for the death of a suspect at my hands."[66] When Peabody gushes about the engagement of mutual friends, Dallas forbids her from saying "the words 'sweet' [or] 'romantic' . . . in my bullpen unless they are coated and dripping with sarcasm."[67] When, in the course of a confrontation between Peabody and Dallas, Peabody tears up, Dallas tells her, "No crying. We're on duty. There is no crying on duty."[68] On other occasions, she extends her edict to hugging, squealing, giggling, and "hair obsessing."[69]

Rejecting dominant ideas of femininity does not mean rejecting being female.[70] Even as her idea of how cops dress and behave is male-normed, Dallas insists that police work is ungendered. She bristles when a young woman at a party declares, "I don't see why a girl would want to be a cop. . . . It's not very feminine."[71] Being female has nothing to do with capacity for police work.[72] When (unlikable) characters suggest otherwise, she proves them wrong. Both civilians and fellow cops who underestimate her because of her sex learn their error. Her disdain for feminine fripperies is surpassed by her intolerance for misogynist assholery.

While Dallas' tone and manner are effective for her, she recognizes that her way is not the only way. She allows for a variety of professional approaches and accepts that skills can be complementary. As Peabody and Dallas work together, Peabody quickly learns that Dallas is not a "mythical figure," but she continues to consider Dallas "the best damn cop [she] had ever known."[73] Still, even as Peabody "looks at Dallas like the lieutenant has the answers to the mysteries of the universe" (as McNab observes), she does not want to mimic her.[74] Instead, Dallas has taught Peabody to play to her own strengths: "I learned I didn't want to be like you. You taught me to want to be me."[75]

Fancying up for cop work

Since the second wave of feminism in the 1960s and 1970s, clothing and fashion, and their links to femininity, have been hotly contested. Historian of gender and clothing Jo Paoletti frames the debate: "Was fashion a form of oppression created and perpetuated by a patriarchy or a pastime enjoyed by many women as a means of self-actualization?"[76] Although some of her colleagues and friends lean toward the latter—including Mavis and Mira, who have radically different styles—Dallas takes the first position.[77] She waxes contemptuous on the discomforts of high heels, though she grudgingly dons them for certain events.[78] Her critique involves the male preference for such shoes, but, as Roarke notes, women are complicit in this process.[79] Dallas complains about the "stylish but impractical heels" that make Nadine reluctant to walk with her, but Nadine likens her heels to Dallas' sidearm: "Tools of our respective trades."[80]

The same clothes on different people can mean different things. While towering shoes worn by Nadine, Mira, and Mavis merely confuse Dallas, they render Oberman a "high-heel-wearing, smug-ass bitch."[81] If uniforms define officers, plainclothes define detectives. Dallas mostly cares that her clothes do not interfere with her ability to do her work.[82] In contrast, Oberman suits up fancy, feminine, and sexy. Baxter, a "fashion-plate" who is a "solid cop" despite his "slick wardrobe," worries over damaging his fancy duds.[83] (Informed that they'll be going to a club in a seedy part of town, he laments, "Underground . . . I just bought these shoes."[84]) The younger detectives in Feeney's Electronic Detection Division wear flashy items in wild colors, including McNab, who "dress[es] like a psychotic clown."[85] His "pretty face" and "silly clothes" prove helpful occasionally when he needs to go undercover; he looks nothing like a cop.[86]

Peabody sometimes uses fashion as part of her professional duties. She transforms to undercover honeypot, geek skank, and earth mother Free-Ager for surveillance and investigation.[87] After she receives her detective's shield, she experiments to find a look that suits her. Her first outfit combines several shades of purple. Her high-heeled shoes click—a sound to which Dallas objects strenuously. By the end of the day, Peabody's feet hurt and she vows to destroy the shoes when she gets home.[88] Dallas does not attempt to squelch Peabody's style, before or after her promotion, but warns repeatedly that heels will slow her down in a chase.[89] Whereas Roarke compliments Peabody on a "chunky" carnelian necklace, Dallas' "only thought on seeing it around her partner's neck was that in a chase it would probably swing up and put Peabody's eye out."[90] Although Dallas often expresses her (usually negative) opinions of particular outfits, she keeps this observation to herself. She recognizes, as good mentors must, that her job is not to turn her protégé into a copy of herself, but to help her develop her own strengths as well as the confidence to use them. Although Peabody ultimately settles on a relatively straightforward approach to dressing herself ("simple lines, interesting colors, and matching airsneaks or skids"), she maintains an inexplicable preference for pink.[91] Still, for Dallas, "pink shoes or not, Peabody was a cop right to the bone."[92] Behind her ridiculous rainbow sunshades, Peabody has cop eyes.[93]

Unlike Peabody, Dallas is mostly indifferent to clothing. "In her view, cops shouldn't wear anything they had to worry about getting yucked up."[94] (She praises the laundry service she used before she married Roarke: it did a good job removing bloodstains.[95]) Though she does appreciate some fine things, she resists "fancying up for cop work," focusing instead on clothing that allows her to perform the physical aspects of her job. She evaluates a pair of new boots as to how well they'll enable her to chase suspects and "kick some teeth in."[96] She also rejects anything that would interfere with her safety. When Roarke suggests that she add a scarf to an outfit for "polish," Dallas replies, "Oh sure, I'll hang something around my neck some bad guy can grab onto and strangle me with."[97] She is like consistently rumpled Feeney, who dresses badly but not outrageously; his wife, to whom "he's been married since the dawn of time," intervenes frequently to advocate for "less disreputable" clothing.[98]

Eve's spouse, too, prevents fashion faux pas and, when possible, enhances her appearance.[99] When she does manage to look "stylishly professional" on her own, it is "a happy accident" rather than a deliberate undertaking.[100] Roarke believes that dressing appropriately is part of her job. Befitting his business focus, he addresses her need to look authoritative while presenting her case to higher-ups.[101] She accepts his interventions, either because it is easier to acquiesce or because a power outfit lets her do her job more effectively, no different than boots that allow her to run fast or kick hard.

She defers to Roarke's expertise. Though she once insists, "I don't need you to pick out my clothes" (Roarke replies that she "so absolutely" does), she asks for help sometimes.[102] For a meeting with Oberman, she wants to look "seriously in charge." He finds something easily, since "he'd selected every one of [her jackets] himself as wardrobe—much less shopping for wardrobe—was dead low on her list of priorities." She likes his choices, especially since the jacket's burgundy color means "if she got blood on it, it might not show. Much." Her attire matters because Oberman notices and cares about clothing. "She's going to know, on every level I can manage, she's dealing with power.'"[103] Though the clothing exudes symbolic power in a confrontation between women, it is a man who speaks its language.[104]

Homicide bitches

Oberman's activities came to light only because of Peabody's accidental eavesdropping. When Dallas learns what Peabody has overheard, she initially blames herself for having criticized Peabody's fighting style, setting in motion the events that put Peabody in danger. Perhaps she should have simply let it go. Roarke reassures her, "You're not just her partner, Eve, you're still training her."[105] Although Dallas recognizes that she couldn't have foreseen what happened, her self-questioning reveals her blend of responsibility and protectiveness toward her junior partner. This dynamic plays out on numerous other occasions as well: spread the credit but claim the blame. She stands between her subordinates and punishment where possible.[106]

The contrast between Dallas and Oberman could not be clearer.[107] Dallas mostly fulfills the ideal of good cop and ethical person that Robb weaves throughout the novels; Oberman emphatically does not. There are similarities. Both work in a profession where sexism, though it does not reign unchecked, remains a concern. As another ambitious female officer, Captain Roth, tells Dallas, "Women are still more closely scrutinized in the department and more strictly judged."[108] One of Roth's corrupt subordinates exemplifies this sexism: "Wants to make commander. Plays a good game of politics, but she's got this problem. She don't have a dick and wishes she did."[109] Another hot-headed officer refers to Dallas and Peabody as "homicide bitches" and makes other derogatory, sexist remarks about Dallas.[110] In contrast to Dallas, Oberman uses her sexual appeal to get ahead in the department and tends to despise other women, particularly those whom she perceives as threatening.

On the surface, Oberman is consummately professional. She requires spit-and-polish formality from her detectives and uniformed officers and insists on a near-sterile squad room; the door to her well-appointed office is usually closed. Dallas' command style is less rigid, her bull pen at times raucous. The door to her miniscule office, with its single, narrow window and uncomfortable visitor's chair, usually stays open. She gives her detectives significant leeway, as "pulling rank had never been her style."[111] She lets one juggle; she knows that when another has his feet on the desk and eyes closed, he's thinking through a problem.[112] She expects excellence and also initiative: subordinates must be capable of more than mechanically following orders; they must adapt plans to prevailing conditions.[113] Unlike Oberman, Dallas rewards independent judgment. Her people are able to give more of themselves to their work. Superiors are responsible for the behavior of their subordinates. In return for dedication, Dallas gives credit and a measure of protection. Dallas deflects blame from her subordinates; Oberman proves willing to sacrifice not just good cops who stand in her way but also her partners in crime to save her own skin.

Both Dallas and Oberman are ambitious. Yet while Dallas zealously secures recognition and advancement for her subordinates, she's less concerned with her own promotion to captain. She cares more about collars than credit.[114] Despite her rank, she works cases, actively investigating rather than managing from her office. She wants neither to move off the streets and behind a desk nor to maintain a sufficiently diplomatic demeanor for politics.[115] Yet "command," Mira observes, "fits her like skin."[116] Her superior officers all assume that Dallas will eventually advance to captain and that she could do so more quickly if she made slightly different choices. When her commander observes that political concerns, stemming in part from her marriage to Roarke, have hindered her promotion, he offers to call in favors to secure her captaincy; she refuses, to the relief of both. He declares, "Frankly, Dallas, I'm not ready to have one of my best street cops riding a desk. And you're not ready to comfortably ride one."[117]

In contrast, Oberman commands from her flashy office. Whitney, who believes Oberman is angling for his commander's chair "and very likely has a timeline for when she'd drop her ass into it," was not supportive of her even before learning of her corruption. Though suited for "the politics, for the grips and grins, for the paperwork and public relations . . . she lacks compassion, and she sees her men as tools, and the job as a means to an end."[118]

The connections and disjunctions between Dallas and Oberman have a shadow history. Feeney considered training Oberman when she graduated from the police academy.[119] He later opted to train Dallas, which he might well not have done had he supervised Oberman.

Mentoring seems to depend on chance encounters that transform careers: senior officers recognize the potential of their juniors and may arrange for their transfer and reassignment. The NYPSD of the mid-twenty-first century is in many respects a meritocracy; women are, despite lingering prejudice, well integrated.[120] But those at the top have a great deal of discretion in choosing whether and how to support the career of a junior colleague. In this as in many other ways, the series asks how history, genetics, chance, personal character, and choice combine to shape lives. Despite the parallels between Dallas and Oberman, the differences are more significant: Oberman's supportive father is a respected police veteran—"Saint Oberman" previously held Whitney's job—while Dallas' abusive father was a brutal criminal.[121] In distinct ways, both women's chosen profession owes to their family history.

Not all cops are heroes

Divergent childhoods led the two lieutenants to the same profession but disparate ethical systems. Throughout the series, other codes of conduct emerge, some admirable and some despicable. These alternate codes of conduct are held by Dallas herself and those who, like her, appear as good cops; by the Internal Affairs Bureau (IAB) that investigates police misconduct; by other, corrupt detectives and officers—some who merely skim, others who are murderously violent; and by businesspeople of all sorts, from embezzlers to the earnestly honest. The codes governing police work are first and foremost in Dallas' consideration, though. The series assumes loyalty and solidarity among police officers but also insists that corrupt officers, of whom it offers numerous examples, must be stopped.

This conflict between the duty to protect fellow officers and the need to root out misconduct leads to clashes. Cops mostly resist complaining about or pursuing police misconduct, even though "not all cops are heroes just because they're supposed to be."[122] Many cops perceive the IAB—or, less flatteringly, the "rat squad"—as somehow disloyal.[123] All agree that "wrong cops" are a problem, but many are reluctant to break the blue line.[124] Yet Dallas insists repeatedly that dirty cops do not deserve other cops' loyalty; in fact, they "smear us all."[125]

Opinions differ on what behavior constitutes misconduct and when serious consequences are warranted. Setting aside, for the moment, corruption and brutality, the series presents a range of perspectives on how closely one must hew to regulations and at what point cutting corners or violating rules becomes a problem. Dallas prefers to adhere strictly to rules, apart from her semiregular violation of the profanity ban, yet on-page reference to her rule-bound nature nearly always signals a breach of procedure. She and Roarke disagree as to how precisely methods must be followed. In *Conspiracy in Death,* Dallas, framed for killing Bowers, who had filed repeated meritless complaints against her, must surrender her badge. Without the accoutrements of authority, she operates further outside the parameters of the law than she normally would. Even after the suspension is revoked and "expunged from [her] record," she faces ongoing temptation to sidestep official constraints on her investigative powers.[126]

Sometimes these restrictions come into question when the investigation targets the powerful and connected. Dallas first acquiesces to using Roarke's unregistered equipment to investigate the corrupt chief of police.[127] In *Treachery,* ordinary investigative channels must be avoided because it is unclear how far Oberman's tentacles reach.[128]

Such questions are even more prominent when the organization is not the NYPSD but other government agencies. "Spec Ops" soldiers from the military receive dangerous training and then wreak havoc once off their leash.[129] More prominent in the series' plots, the Homeland Security Organization (HSO), "formed at the Dawn of the Urban Wars," raises crucial questions about government surveillance and impunity.[130] Although both Dallas and Peabody accept that the organization was initially needed "to protect the country, to police the streets and gather intel covertly from radical factions," it has become a problem. Dallas agrees with those who believe that "it had morphed into something closer to a legalized terrorist group than a protection and intel operation." Considering how to interact with it, she says, "This is the HSO. The antiterrorist organization that employs methods every bit as dirty as the terrorists they were initially formed to seek out and destroy." She feels justified in violating protocol: "Since we're playing with spooks screw the rules." Peabody considers them "just another kind of organized crime."

Attributing her dislike to her Free-Ager roots, she accepts that "governments need covert organizations to gather intelligence, to help predict terrorist attacks, to help dismantle terrorists and politically fanatic groups" but laments that "the fact that they don't always have to play by the rules . . . can corrupt the individuals that make up the whole."[131] With these unanswered and perhaps unanswerable questions, the novel stages a debate about the purpose, limits, and dangers of government surveillance.

Yet when it comes to the moral dimensions of HSO practice, the series focuses on individual accountability and individual action. *Divided in Death* reveals that some HSO operatives knew about Dallas' father's abuse of her. Because they discovered it as part of a larger weapons-smuggling operation, they opted not to intervene. Dallas sums up: they chose to focus on the "big picture, and fuck the people in it." Roarke wants to mete out justice, according to his own "moral ground," to the individuals who left her to suffer.[132] Dallas admits that she wants "payback" badly, but worries about being able to live with him having taken such action.[133] Playing by the key rules of her job is vital to her sense of self, to her moral compass. As she says to Roarke, "You can't stand there and talk about doing murder to a murder cop and expect me to ignore it and pretend it's nothing."[134] Ultimately, Roarke comes to accept that she would not be able to live with his mode of meting out justice.[135] Neither considers taking aim at the larger organization or structure.

In later cases Dallas cooperates with HSO operatives where unavoidable, as with a series of chemical weapon attacks—personally rather than ideologically motivated—in *Delusion in Death,* set in late 2060. She is reassured somewhat to learn that the people responsible for leaving her with her abuser decades earlier are long gone. Still, she harbors significant doubts about the organization as a whole. Thus, although she cooperates with the agents assigned to her in that and other cases, in "Missing in Death" she lets a killer who created a dangerous device escape, recognizing not just that his killing of the paid assassin who murdered his family might have been its own sort of justice but also that, were he taken into custody by the shadowy Homeland Security agency, his knowledge would be used in unacceptable ways. After the events of *Delusion,* she is skeptical that the agency will keep its word to keep the chemical formula entirely secure. She takes measures available to her because of her private resources: "She'd have Roarke keep an eye on things on his unregistered equipment." She also considers other options, including her "ace reporter in the back pocket" should she need to mobilize public outcry.[136]

It's all just ends and means

Some of Dallas and Roarke's disagreements about acceptable conduct concern weighty matters such as taking bloody revenge against others for past crimes against vulnerable children. Still, they draw lines differently about what means are acceptable in the pursuit of justice even in mundane circumstances. As Dallas increasingly relies on Roarke's help in her investigations, she confronts questions about acceptable investigative shortcuts. She disregards procedure in exceptional circumstances, typically resulting in less respect for civilians' legal protections. She uses unregistered equipment, obtains information without warrants, and—even when she goes back and obtains the same information through legal channels—dithers about upholding certain protections.[137] When she admits that an unauthorized search is "a gray area," Roarke responds, "Your gray is broader and darker than mine."[138] Her criterion for bypassing procedure is often whether lives are in immediate jeopardy.[139] When she insists on following regulations, he reminds her that he's "not a cop . . . and it's annoying to be asked to perform minor miracles while toeing the line you set." She replies, "I've moved it plenty, and you know it." To his request that she "move it again," she offers, "Every time I do, I worry I won't remember where I left it." Ultimately, she agrees when he says, "I know where you put it, and how far you can nudge it and feel you've done the right thing. You ought to know the same of me."[140] Roarke is comfortable saying, "Ends and means, darling. It's all just ends and means." Yet Dallas continues to worry. After she has (temporarily) lost her badge during the investigation into Bowers' death, she tells him, "I must have lost my mind. I keep crossing lines." He replies, "The lines keep moving. You're just keeping up." She retorts, "I continue keeping up this way, I'll end up wearing security bracelets. I used to go by the book. Now I just rewrite the pages."[141]

Roarke changes too. "Most of his life had been spent avoiding, evading, or out-thinking cops . . . but [now] he spent a great deal of his time in a consultant capacity for the NYPSD."[142] He has "a knack" for the sort of work required, maybe because "he'd lived on the other side of the law most of his life."[143] By the time Dallas meets him, Roarke had already sloughed off most of his shadier activities. He extricated himself from the remainder because they might cause trouble for her, not because they caused him qualms.[144] He lives by his own code of acceptable conduct: yes to smuggling, no to human trafficking ("even I had my standards"); yes to hacking, no to intellectual property theft ("it's low and common"); yes to killing for vengeance, no to murder for hire and cons that involve posing as a priest ("well, it's rude, isn't it?").[145]

Though Roarke will not hesitate to break certain rules, he mostly respects Dallas' need to obey them. She and Roarke begin on opposite sides of the line. Roarke comes closer to her way of thinking about the potential worth of the police.[146] ("I'm more inclined to believe in the face of the law, since I look at it every day, than I ever did before I saw it."[147]) As he notes, "He'd actually worked with the cops, the very element that had once been the enemy."[148] He sometimes even works in cop shops, not just at Cop Central in New York but even, in one instance, in Texas.[149] Dallas does not gain the same level of respect for civilian lawbreakers that Roarke does for police, though she knows that the system does not always deliver justice.[150] She occasionally stacks the deck in its favor.

Apart from large questions of policy and procedure, Dallas draws on Roarke's resources but tries to avoid relying too heavily on them.[151] He wants to put all of his resources at her disposal all of the time, but he respects her limits even if he finds some of her choices puzzling, as she does his, telling him, "Your moral compass continues to baffle me."[152] Dallas draws on his wealth to bribe coworkers with expensive liquor or tickets to sports events. She never bribes exotically sexy, always fashionable medical examiner Morris, with whom she has a friendship of sorts.[153] She routinely mixes threats with bribery to get quick results from creepy but capable lab chief Dick "Dickhead" Berenski.[154] She jokes with Peabody that she should "beg, bribe, threaten, offer sexual favors of any kind" to Requisitions to get a functioning car.[155] Peabody, too, learns the system. She offers

VIP access to one of Mavis' concerts to induce a police sketch artist to work rapidly. Dallas praises: "Good bribe. I'm so proud." Peabody demurs: "I had an excellent trainer."[156]

Bribes to grease the wheels with otherwise upright colleagues stand distinct from the intolerable corruption that is a sustained concern of the series. Dallas acknowledges persistent misconduct but conceives of it as a matter of individual vice, not structural power. She admits but does not accept "cops on the take."[157] Indeed, rather than excessive force, it is stealing or skimming that puts a cop outside the pale.[158] One detective has a few reprimands for being overly physical; another has gotten a slap for harassing a licensed companion.[159] But ultimately, these men are taken down for engaging in long-term fraud and bribery. Their routine brutality draws half-hearted condemnation as compared to the other troubling behaviors with which it goes hand in hand. Corrupt police officers repeatedly get their comeuppance. The greedy police chief she exposes in *Naked in Death* loses his job to the sturdier Tibble. Dallas and her comrades oust Lieutenant Oberman and her badged miscreants. Another corrupt squad run by the ineffectual Captain Roth gets cleaned up in *Judgment in Death,* which begins with the vigilante murder of a black detective mistakenly suspected of corruption by a cop who takes it on himself to root out offenders—revealing many layers of misconduct, attributable in part to disregard for proper procedure and channels. Dallas perceives recurrent abuses of power but does not consider police power itself abusive: wrong cops are always outliers no matter how frequently they appear.

In contrast, Roarke recalls endemic police corruption from his childhood. In the aftermath of the disruptive Urban Wars, some cops tried to keep order but most were unethical. Roarke recalls "many cops in the pocket of the cartel whose territory I trespassed on." Not only did they hassle those who threatened their bosses' interests, they ignored widespread violence perpetrated by those paying them. A particularly infuriating example of police inaction involves Summerset. He had brought Roarke to live with him and his delightful daughter, who was a few years younger than Roarke. As a blossoming adolescent, Marlena developed a crush on then-teenaged Roarke, who rejected her overtures. She left the house, upset; some local criminals' angry at Roarke's refusal to join them, abducted, tortured, and murdered her, then returned her mutilated body to the house the three of them shared.[160] The corrupt cop assigned to investigate Marlena's death chalked her obvious torture-murder up to "death by misadventure."[161] Likewise, when Roarke's father murdered Roarke's mother, the police failed to investigate, even when prompted by his mother's family.[162] In *Treachery,* the main theme of which is good cops versus bad cops, Summerset says that Dallas is "the first cop he'd had contact with who worked so tirelessly or cared so much about real justice."[163]

If the system will not provide justice, then one must pursue justice outside the system. Roarke, who hunted down and killed the men responsible for Marlena's death, describes that result as justice. Dallas demurs, while acknowledging that sometimes the system fails.[164] "She felt the weight of her badge, tangibly. Not in her pocket but on her heart." When she tells Roarke it "wasn't for you to decide," he refuses to "apologize for what [he] did" because "the law doesn't always stand for the innocent and the used. The law doesn't always care enough." However, given that the past has come back in the form of murders in New York seeking revenge for those revenge killings, Roarke does regret putting Dallas "in the position of choosing between me and your duty."[165] In order to investigate properly, Dallas must inform Peabody about Roarke's past actions. Even though he broke laws, Dallas is confident that Peabody will "stand with" her and remain silent. Roarke affirms, "She's a good cop. You've taught me the phrase isn't a contradiction in terms."[166] Being a good cop here requires seeing the moral dimensions as separate from the legal dimensions and being willing to overlook private vengeance taken in the name of justice.

Dallas is capable of stepping outside the legal, but only temporarily. Having viewed a holograph of Marlena's beaten and broken body, what Roarke terms "the ruin of innocence," she declares, "I'll only say this once, I may only mean it once, now, while I've still got her image in my head. You were right. What you did was justice."[167]

Absolving Roarke of past sins differs from allowing a current killing in retaliation, hence his restraint in *Divided in Death* when he learns of the HSO's inaction during Dallas' childhood and when he pursues the truth about his mother's murder. But if Dallas can forgive the man she loves, she is less flexible with herself. She insists on following procedure when, early in her relationship with Roarke, she realizes, in a nightmare flashback, that she killed her own father to defend herself during a violent assault in which she feared for her life. Once she recovers that memory, despite the fact that there are no files on record (she learns later of an HSO cover-up), she feels honor bound to tell her superiors about the killing—perhaps making her unfit for police work.[168] Although police work is all she knows how to do and a major component—*the* major component—of her identity, she is prepared to give it up if she is unfit for the job. She honestly feels compelled to explain.

However, it is clear to everyone but her, and eventually even to her, that she is not guilty of anything, that she knows what it is to take life, but that what she did was not murder, but rather self-defense. Roarke strenuously objects both to her attempt to resign and her attempt to end their relationship: "Goddamn the law. What good did it do either one of us when we needed it most? You want to chuck your badge because the law's too fucking weak to care for its innocents, its children, be my guest. Throw your career away. But you're not getting rid of me."[169]

This confrontation highlights both Dallas and Roarke's commonalities and their key differences. Each was subject to arbitrary, abusive power. Dallas joined "the system that had failed her when she was a child"; Roarke accumulated sufficient wealth to counter any possibility of deprivation.[170] "His buffer against yesterday was money, power, control. Hers was a badge."[171] Dallas eschews a rose-colored view of government or the NYPSD but she is essentially committed to following its rules. Her commitment wanes the longer she is married to Roarke, who has less respect for rules qua rules even as he values integrity not precisely coextensive with laws.[172] The law's failure to protect the weak and the innocent, to provide substantive justice, is not the same as conceiving of the law and law enforcement as the source of violence or oppression, but it suggests a fundamental divergence of perspectives that never fully resolves.

Capitalist opportunist

One morning a year or so into their marriage, Eve asks Roarke whether he's "already started today's quest for global economic domination." In turn, he comments on her timetable for "today's quest for truth, justice, and ass-kicking."[173] Though these ways of describing their respective work emphasize money and power in his case and doing good in hers, Roarke enjoys and finds meaning in his work, not just the wealth it brings. Although the foundation of the series is Dallas' work rather than Roarke's, his character—as well as the skills at lock-picking, hacking, and ferreting out financial shenanigans he brings to collaboration with her—are inescapably formed by his personal history and ongoing occupation. It is not merely his wealth that matters but how he obtains it; were he the scion of an obscenely wealthy family rather than a "clever man who'd built an empire out of guts and guile and a wily kind of genius," he would be much less compelling.[174] Instead, his work and his relationship with Dallas are impossible to disentangle.[175]

In *Loyalty in Death*, set in winter 2059, a terrorist organization called Cassandra plants a bomb in an unoccupied warehouse. The building belongs to Roarke, who, as Dallas periodically points out with varying levels of frustration, resignation, and amusement, owns "every damn thing."[176] The organization releases a manifesto full of what he terms "tedious political jargon. . . . the redistribution of wealth, the exploitation of the poor by the rich." It calls him a "capitalist opportunist," which, he agrees, "is absolutely true."[177] Cassandra's rhetoric turns out to be a sham. Its prediction of "the uprising of the masses, the toppling of corrupt governments . . . and the overthrow of the greedy upper class" masks personal greed and pathological delusion. Still, its critique of capitalism is far from the only one in the series.[178] As literary scholar Jayashree Kamblé notes, "the novels legitimize free-market capitalism" and, at the same time, "continually interrogate it."[179]

Dallas serves as a primary voice against pervasive consumerism: she objects to ubiquitous ad blimps and compulsory acquisition. Although she luxuriates in her endless mugs of real coffee and her home's inexhaustible hot-water supply, she wears her T-shirts to rags.[180] She wonders, "Why does there have to be a gift for every damn thing?"[181] She refuses to buy unneeded things when she discovers that her credit card entitles her to obtain anything produced by Roarke Industries at no cost.[182] (Also frustrating is the memo Roarke sent to all employees of his properties and companies, directing them to provide her with their full cooperation; she would have preferred to command, browbeat, or force their assent herself, although his way, she admits, saves time.[183]) When Peabody wants to "gaze longingly" at expensive shoes, Dallas suggests dryly that "people who longingly imagine having things they can't afford" end up with "a life of crime."[184] At the same time, wealth is seductive. As with power, it is difficult to resist its blandishments.

Capitalism appears primarily as a mode of consumption and ownership rather than a system of alienated production. Roarke Industries brings new products to market, with emphasis on the brain-work of design rather than the physical labor of manufacturing or the consumption of resources in their production. In depicting Roarke's work, the series plays up his savvy deal making and downplays—indeed, deflects attention from—the extraction of wealth from workers' toil.[185] Roarke unabashedly claims the title "capitalist opportunist" but with emphasis on *opportunity* rather than capitalism. Put slightly differently, master of the corporate world = sexy; living the high life on the backs of factory drones = decidedly unsexy.

Roarke purchases and accumulates. He buys more than he sells, and likes it that way. Dallas jokes about his buying islands, countries, planets, and solar systems.[186] His acquisitions lead to repair and betterment. He turns around companies in distress. He restores or improves residential and commercial real estate. He builds from scratch too, everything from off-planet luxury resorts to computer games, vitamin drinks, medical devices, and military technology. He attends holo-conferences with counterparts in Tokyo and Prague and occasionally intimidates underperforming employees in person.[187]

Roarke is a good boss. Though he does not get chummy with his employees, they like and respect him—not only Summerset, who is a special case, and Roarke's assistant Caro, but the maids at his flagship hotel and the waitstaff in restaurants he owns.[188] When a serial killer targets women who work for Roarke, he feels responsible for them.[189] He understands when an employee goes through a "rough patch" and gives second chances to those who, from fear or softheartedness, fail in their duties.[190] Even outside these extraordinary circumstances, "He paid well, and the working conditions that were found in all his companies, factories, subsidiaries, and offices throughout the world and its satellites were unquestionably high." Such policies arise at least as much from pragmatism as from idealism. Though his own desperate circumstances had prompted the desire "to achieve more" through fair means or foul, "for most, a stingy wage and an airless box in which to earn it [foster] hopelessness, resentment. And pilfering."[191] Still, the series devotes little attention to these arrangements and never suggests workers' labor generates a surplus for him; instead, his acquisitions of underperforming companies provide opportunities for their employees while generating profits for him.[192] His money seems to come from the pockets of other, undeserving, rich people.

Still, occasional glimpses of Roarke's ordinary employees—doormen, clerks, maids—show commonalities with many of the witnesses, suspects, and victims Dallas encounters. Delivery people, dishwashers, strippers, and clerks have jobs, not careers. They cannot restructure their work calendars to accommodate a trip to the police station let alone a visit to Italy to pursue a suspect.[193] Dallas must sometimes intervene with bosses to excuse a witness' lateness or absence; people worry about losing jobs they do not even like.[194] Even as the series' main characters pursue vocations that challenge, delight, and reward them—emotionally as well as financially—a counternarrative winds through the background: work as a grind, pursued for the sake of making a living, not making a life.

Political theorist Kathi Weeks suggests that the way work has become central to individual identity and deeply interwoven with notions about human fulfillment "is one of the most stubbornly naturalized and apparently self-evident elements of modern and late, or postmodern, capitalist societies." The Protestant origins of the "ethic of work—the willingness to dedicate oneself to work as an end in itself, living to work instead of working to live" are largely submerged by the twentieth century, overshadowed by new emphasis on "work as a path to individual self-expression, self-development, and creativity." Dallas' continual battles against fatigue and exhaustion reflect the way " 'Life' with its wealth of possibilities is subordinated to the disciplinary demands of work. This injunction to delay other gratifications and focus instead on methodical effort for productive ends remains at the core of later formulations of the work ethic." The ethic, Weeks observes, is effective precisely because it is not enforced by external authority but rather "internalized by the individual."[195]

Work is central not only to the plotlines and structure of the In Death novels, but also to their imagined good life. Dallas' integration of work into her life, and life into her work, puts to rest tired saws about work-life balance and calls into question notions of bounded identity.[196] A romantic partner becomes a professional collaborator; a work partner becomes a close friend; colleagues become a kind of family.[197] Intimacy, friendship, and work are interwoven in complex ways. On the other hand, work and its rewards mean different things for people of various classes, who do work of various types. For Dallas, her friends, and her mate, work is a vocation, not merely a way to earn a wage—a seductive, compelling, and seemingly natural state of affairs that merits critical scrutiny. Within this fictive world, it's fortunate that the "slick talking, sticky-fingered civilian" and his beloved "mean-tempered, single-minded cop" both have work for which they are suited, and which suits them—just as they suit each other.[198]

CHAPTER

4

Violence in Death

Violence pervades the In Death novels, stretching far beyond the murder(s) at the core of each plot. Robb explores violent acts and their traumatic aftermaths: the vicious parental abuse meted out to Dallas and Roarke as children; the Urban Wars which laid the groundwork for this fictive future; individual and group terrorism; government uses of force—through secretive agencies, federal authorities, and the NYPSD—in the prevention and punishment of crime. Violence in policing and incarceration appears, sometimes criticized and sometimes capriciously exercised by her sympathetic protagonist. Structural violence permeates the novels, too, with grinding poverty appearing then quickly lapsing into the background as murder takes precedence, fading from many plots just as real-world suffering too quickly fades from privileged readers' attention. Questions about state, organizational, and individual violence simmer through the series.

Murder may be, as detective novelist P. D. James writes, "the contaminating and unique crime," but In Death reveals it to be contiguous with other forms of mundane and extraordinary lawbreaking, including petty thefts, burglaries, muggings, rapes, and assaults.[1] Urban violence is omnipresent but, like municipal services, unequally distributed.[2] The broader social world, even the architecture of the city, has passed the immediate aftermath of the cataclysmic Urban Wars, which began in the second decade of the twenty-first century. A massive bombing at the Pentagon killed 8,000 people, civilian as well as military, children as well as adults. Rather than cave to terrorist demands, the U.S. government responded by putting a $5 million bounty on the head of the leader, "no questions asked."[3] New York and other American cities as well as London, Dublin, and Paris had large-scale physical destruction—still noticeable in dilapidated slap-dash post-war construction in poor areas—as well as high death tolls.[4] Summerset, who lived through it, recalls, "To say the world was in disarray is the least of it. Looting, burning, bombing, indiscriminate killings, rapes. At first it seemed the police and the military would quell it, all would right again. . . . But they didn't quell it, and it didn't right again, not for a very long time. It became a tidal wave of rage and violence that wouldn't be stopped."[5] Gun bans attempt to prevent a repeat of those explosive years of violence. While, as Dallas notes, "Taking such impulsive killing devices off the street saved lives," she thinks, "there were always new ways to kill. The human mind never tired of dreaming them up."[6]

Through violence and tragedy

Human nature makes violence inevitable. Being a victim or a perpetrator of violence shapes one's perspective. Dallas' job regularly presents her with potentially devastating, incapacitating sights and scenes; violence is her quotidian: "Seeing death, violent death, was nothing new."[7] She encounters abuse, loss, and trauma in her job—and in her relationships. Many regular characters have experienced loss and trauma. People witness unspeakable things, suffer unbearable losses, and continue with their lives. Summerset loses a child. Readers eventually learn both that Mira was raped by her stepfather and Mavis was abused by her mentally ill mother. Childhood abuse plays a major role in the backstories of both Dallas and Roarke, and its effects, particularly for Dallas, continue to resonate.

Violent backgrounds are part of what join Dallas and Roarke.[8] "They had both come from misery, she thought, and survived it. They had been drawn together through violence and tragedy, and had overcome it. They walked different paths and had found a mutual route."[9] On another occasion, she asks him, "Would you kill for me?" and he responds immediately, "I would, yes, of course." He elaborates: no need to think about it as he'd do it "to protect you, to save your life, to save you from harm," without any second guessing. He need not speculate about what he would do if she made a frivolous request because she'd never ask.[10]

Violence weaves Dallas' story into the larger narrative arc of the series. At the outset of the series, she sleeps poorly. The immediate cause is a trauma: she was unable to intervene in time to stop a father from killing his young daughter; immediately thereafter she had to kill him before he killed her. This becomes mixed up in her head with her own scanty memories of childhood. When she undergoes Testing, a psychologically invasive procedure to examine her memories of and feelings about the event in which she discharged her weapon fatally, Mira offers to help her recover her other memories. Dallas rejects the offer but begins to remember bits and pieces.[11]

Readers learn at the outset of the series that she was found wandering outside at about eight years of age, bloody and confused, arm broken, raped, with evidence of substantial prior ongoing abuse. No one came to claim her. A social worker eventually gave her the name Eve Dallas, the surname for the city where she was found. She grew up in foster care and state schools. When she reached majority, she moved to New York to study at the Police Academy. She has occasional flashbacks. As she feels increasingly safe in her relationship with Roarke, she recalls more and more of her childhood. She remembers that it was her father who abused her, and, ultimately, she recalls killing him in self-defense during one attack. (To Mira, she recounts, " 'My father raped me, abused me, beat me,' Eve said flatly. 'I killed him. I was eight years old. I survived.' "[12]) When she visits the city Dallas as part of another investigation, she goes back to the hotel room where she killed her father decades earlier. Roarke accompanies her.

In their hotel later, Roarke damages his hands in beating up a speed bag. Dallas mentions he could have worn gloves. Roarke points out that his way was more "cathartic." She agrees, "There's nothing quite like beating something into pulp with your bare hands for relaxation. . . . We come from violent people. We've got that in us. The difference is we don't let it loose whenever we feel like on whoever's handy."[13] In the aftermath of that outburst, they make love tenderly. Violence is a connective thread between her old life and her new life, but it is the disjunctions that matter: a luxurious suite replaces the seedy room; consensual, tender lovemaking replaces brutal rape; loving husband replaces abusive father.

Still, rhetorical violence underscores their mutual attraction and their equally mutual insistence on fidelity. Roarke says, when Dallas (accidentally) engages in what she worries is "virtual adultery," " 'You can indulge in fantasy professionally or personally. I'm not your keeper. . . . Try it in the flesh, even once, and I'll have to kill you.' Her pupils widened, and foolishly her heart gave a pleased little leap. 'Oh, well, that's fair.' "[14] In a similar vein, were he unfaithful, she'd kill him and/or his partner and "do the rumba on [his] corpse."[15] Possessiveness and threatened violence toward the cheating partner or the cheating partner's lover appear as signs of love. Male violence toward women suffuses the series, but surprisingly few of its homicide cases have jealousy as a motive; where they do, the woman tends to be the perpetrator.[16] Perhaps these simply do not make for very difficult or intriguing mysteries. In the cases Robb presents to her readers, women are more often killed by serial murderers with a penchant for elaborate torture than by current or estranged male partners.

Since jealousy-triggered partner violence plays a relatively limited role in the series, and since readers understand that neither Eve nor Roarke would ever cheat, hyperbolic threats become acceptable. Despite these jokes between Eve and Roarke about physical retaliation for infidelity, there is a clear distinction between temper and violence.[17] It is ludicrous to imagine Roarke beating or raping a woman; the question is to be scoffed at.[18] Eve occasionally shoves or punches him; he never retaliates.[19] Even when he is furious at her, he restrains himself physically.[20] Roarke's tightly leashed potential for violence emerges clearly when Eve investigates his former underworld associate Max Ricker. Roarke is very angry after he discovers she has lied about having been to see Ricker, who had grabbed her roughly, leaving marks. As they argue, Roarke takes hold of her arms. But "even when he was furious, he didn't hurt her, and was careful to keep his grip away from the bruise." This does not mean, however, that Roarke forswears violence. Instead, he threatens to kill Ricker if he hurts Eve again.[21]

Nothing like punching your fist into a face

Violent and traumatic backgrounds do not necessarily explain character. The series asks, repeatedly, what effect nature and nurture have on people's development. Characters prove, over and over, that one's parents or even one's upbringing and experiences do not determine outcomes, even if they can lead in certain directions. Individuals make choices, moral and immoral; those choices, in turn, make them. Dallas' potential for violence is neither only innate nor merely a result of circumstance. She takes her experience and carefully tempers it. For cops, violence is sometimes a duty: precision in its exercise can be admired.[22] But at some level, Dallas, whose aura has a "dark shimmer of violence," simply "like[s] a good fight."[23] As she says after a holographic brawl, "Nothing like punching your fist into a face to brighten up the day."[24] In her propensity for violence, she is not alone of all her sex. Women are plentiful among the series' villains, and some revel in brutality.[25] Serial killer Julianne Dunne in *Reunion in Death* respects women, despises men, and enjoys watching her victims die; Oberman, who "intimidates or eliminates" women, uses violence instrumentally and impersonally but does not shy away from it.[26] Both Dunne and Oberman have father issues: The former despises the weak stepfather she manipulated into a sexual relationship; the latter resents her father's professional ethics.

All characters agree that violence, including killing, is sometimes justifiable; they disagree over when it is legitimate or illegitimate. Summerset, who Mira describes as "one of the most nonviolent personalities I've ever encountered," and who finds "true violence . . . abhorrent," presumably killed Roarke's father.[27] When Dallas asks Summerset directly, he evades the question, since "there is no statute of limitations on murder." When she persists ("It's not the cop who's asking you"), he offers only, "I had children to protect."[28] His use of violence is always in the context of other violence, actual or possible. Though not precisely self-defense in the way her killing her own father was—immediate protection in the face of overwhelming force—Summerset's justification appeases her. It also makes clear that, under the right circumstances, anyone can kill. The teenaged Jamie Lingstrom—who had threatened to avenge his sister's death at the hands of those who also killed his grandfather, a police officer—ends up killing in the heat of an encounter. Dallas covers it up, making it seem as though the death occurred in the course of her struggle with the suspect.[29]

Killing in the course of an apprehension is not routine. Some officers go their entire careers without killing or even firing their weapons.[30] Yet when the suspect is threatening to kill the officer or someone else, the suspect's death is not a moral problem. It requires Testing to ascertain whether it was necessary. It need not occasion angst.

Testing is Robb's imperfect answer to the imperfect mechanisms available to assess an officer's use of deadly force.[31] The least invasive level of Testing does not differ too much from intense questioning; other routine check-ins, or instances in which an officer's fitness is questioned, might necessitate deeper Testing. When an officer kills in the line of duty, Testing becomes harsh and nearly impossible to fool.[32] As Dallas notes, "Testing after a termination's pretty intense. More intense than the screening, the evals, to get a badge."[33] She undergoes it in the first novel, after she has killed a man who just slaughtered his young daughter and then attempted to kill Dallas.

Shortly after he joins the squad, Officer Trueheart discharges his stunner in self-defense and the man dies. Trueheart's account of events does not jibe with expectations. Had his stunner been at the setting he described, used from the distance he described, only once as he asserts, it should not have led to death. Unbeknownst to investigators, the individual he stunned was under the influence of a computer virus, distributed by a vigilante group, which made him vulnerable to this reaction. Shortly thereafter, a police officer similarly infected in the course of an investigation also becomes uncontrollable and eventually dies. In due course it becomes clear that Trueheart was telling the truth. The investigation exonerates him for the killing of a low-level junkie, and the police pursue and apprehend the vigilantes who caused the man's death. The police are the good guys, in contrast to those who operate outside the law, with its checks and balances.

Before the investigation is complete, other uniformed officers bristle at the inquiry into Trueheart's actions. Rather than accept that Testing will provide a clear answer as to what transpired, they resent the oversight.[34] Trueheart, conscience clear, passes Testing. Indeed, though the possibility of failing Testing is ever present, in the cases described, all pass. However, such results are sometimes questionable, even in cases of termination; the benefit of the doubt goes to the officer in such cases. Among the many examples of misconduct turned up by the investigation into Oberman's squad was a case where Testing exonerated an officer in a termination that appeared suspicious. Misconduct could not be proven, though the subsequent deaths of witnesses made it seem even more likely. With the officer under investigation for other forms of corruption, that case may be reopened.[35] Corrupt or disturbed cops use various strategies—substances, a complicit psychiatrist—to bypass the routine screenings that are substantially less invasive than those that follow a termination.[36]

In addition to formal Testing, there are tests of moral fortitude associated with the exercise of lethal force. On at least two occasions, Dallas engages in life-or-death struggles with killers and, after she has subdued them, must wrestle with the temptation to end their lives. In *Survivor in Death*, she and Roarke temporarily take in young Nixie Swisher, the sole survivor of a home-invasion massacre. The same killers who killed her parents, brother, housekeeper, and young friend (mistaking her for Nixie) later kill police officers they think are guarding Nixie. When Nixie asks Dallas if she'll kill them "because they killed your friends," Dallas replies, "I'll want to. Part of me will want to, but that's not the job. Unless my life or someone else's life is in danger, if I kill them because I'm just pissed off and sad and sorry, it puts me in the same place as them."[37] The actual takedown, though, tests her resolve. In the struggle, one of the attackers breaks her neck falling down the stairs as she and Dallas grapple. This death occasions no moral searching. On the other hand, when Dallas finally subdues the ringleader behind the Swisher murders, she barely stops herself from stabbing him to death with his knife.

She faces a similar test when she finally (re)apprehends the serial rapist, abductor, and killer Isaac McQueen. A frighteningly intelligent, vicious pedophile, McQueen plays a central role in Dallas' professional story. She had arrested him as a rookie, in the process freeing twenty-two girls he had been holding captive. This apprehension, which occurred in the course of performing other duties, brought her to Feeney's attention, leading to the offer to be his aide, setting her eventually on the path to homicide detective. When McQueen escapes from prison a decade later, Dallas tracks him down only to discover that he has become entangled in her personal history too: unknown to either of them, the woman he has taken as a new partner in crime is Dallas' biological mother, who turns out herself to be abusive and vicious. Before he comes after Dallas, McQueen has killed her mother, who has outlived her usefulness as a partner.[38] In the course of fighting off McQueen, who threatens to rape her before killing her, Dallas has a flashback to her father's final rape of her, when she killed him. She nearly kills McQueen as well.

Both with the Swishers' killer and with McQueen, the weapon she holds and (barely) prevents herself from using is a knife. Though her primary police weapon is a stunner, these knives evoke the one she used to kill her father.[39] She is morally tested in both cases, wanting to kill the men but ultimately not carrying it through.[40] Roarke, present both times, does not intervene on the first occasion, confident that she will not kill the subdued suspect. On the second occasion, he calls her back to herself and coaxes the knife from her.[41] Ultimately, her conscience prevents her from stabbing the men to death: she is capable of killing where necessary, but not killing cold-bloodedly.[42]

Killing is unacceptable, the books declare, except in defense of self or others. Although Dallas keeps the secret of Roarke having killed the men who murdered Summerset's daughter Marlena, she has difficulty countenancing it. She can accept it as part of his past, but cannot accept that he will continue to do such things. Roarke, too, has changed. When he discovers that his father murdered his real mother, he goes to Ireland to investigate the cover-up. In a marked departure from how he would have behaved years earlier, he neither kills nor seriously injures the conspirator from whom he seeks information. Vengeance is no longer necessary.[43] Still, when the crime is against Dallas, restraint proves more difficult. Roarke longs to retaliate against the Homeland Security operatives who, they learn, had left Dallas with her father despite their awareness that he was abusing her. Dallas cannot accept Roarke's need to retaliate. This divergence occasions a rift between them. He ultimately decides not to pursue revenge, not because he couldn't live with it, but because she could not.[44]

The sweet scent of first blood

Most tests of Dallas' forbearance have less potentially lethal outcomes. Often, she must rein in her temper and curb violent impulses. Her restraint gets a workout when a surly and unprofessional cop files a groundless complaint against her. Bowers, for whose murder Dallas will later be framed, is not merely incompetent but actively mean and petty in her treatment of civilians: she harasses sidewalk sleepers in addition to the nuisance suits she files against the department. On the drive home Dallas "trie[s] to amuse herself by imagining what it would feel like to take Bowers on in a good sweaty match of hand-to-hand. The satisfying sound of bone against bone, the sweet scent of first blood." But Dallas is conscious of her responsibilities: "All the image managed to do was infuriate her [because] a superior officer couldn't go around whipping on a uniform, no matter how much she deserved it."[45]

She has less trouble restraining herself from lashing out when civilians injure her. She repeatedly sustains injury while breaking up fisticuffs. She takes an accidental fist to the face trying to stop a man from beating up a masturbating passenger on the subway.[46] A Minnesotan tourist clocks her with a massive purse when Dallas stops to assist at a fender bender.[47] A woman bites Dallas' shoulder when she intervenes in a scramble for a purse.[48]

In addition to these inadvertent involvements, Dallas sometimes courts violence. She does not hesitate to make herself a target in order to turn a murderer's attention from others—whether from those close to her or random victims—and she regularly puts herself in harm's way. Dallas relishes such altercations. She and Peabody are near the scene of a taxi accident when the drivers start to fight. Noting that "one of them just pulled out a bat," Peabody asks if she should "call for backup." "Rubb[ing] her hands together in anticipation," Dallas says no, "I can handle it."[49]

Dallas finds it satisfying to subdue witnesses or suspects who attack her. In one life-or-death struggle, "She smelled her own blood and indulged herself by bringing her elbow up to ram Selina's chin."[50] She sometimes overreacts or fails to curtail her violence once the threat has passed. She delivers knockout punches to subdued suspects after extended struggles where her life was in danger.[51] On other occasions, she holds back. Apprehending one of a pair of spree killers, she is not particularly careful to avoid hurting the suspect, but neither does she deliver additional physical injury for its own sake. "A dark part of her might have enjoyed rolling the murdering bitch right back over the glass shards, and maybe the boot that stepped down on the knife caught a couple of fingers." But whatever impulse to injure existed, "The cop kicked the knife aside, and yanked the spitting, screaming woman up, shoved her facedown on the bed," and declared, "You're under arrest."[52] Here, the dark part of her that appreciates and enjoys violence is distinct from the cop who exercises force only as needed to do the job.

On the other hand, Dallas periodically exercises power and violence in coercive, calculated, and unethical ways.[53] Sometimes her threats of violence are obviously over-the-top bluster, as when she "shouted at the messenger who'd nearly sideswiped her vehicle with his jet-board. 'Police property, asshole. If I had time I'd hunt you down and use that board to beat your balls black.' "[54] At other times, though, her threats are more credible, as when she threatens a drug dealer on the street.[55] Similarly, after parking in a rough area, she grabs a bystander and threatens him with dire physical consequences if her car is damaged.[56] She is casually brutal when she enters a notoriously violent area in search of an informant. A man is "down on his hands and knees, puking horribly," and Dallas asks if he's alright. When he responds with profanity, she—mindful of their sizable audience—"gave him a solid shove with her boot that sent him facedown in his own vomit."[57] She puts a knife to his throat, threatens him, and gets information, first from him and then from others. She threatens, though the reader is aware it is for show, that she doesn't care how many they put in the morgue.

She sometimes merges force and threats, including the threat to lie about her use of force. Again, while readers may know these are idle threats, those receiving them do not. In one scene, she has a suspect pinned down: "Slatter tried to roll out from under her boot. Eve merely increased the pressure. 'I can crack a couple ribs,' she told him, 'and say it happened during the game. Think about it.' "[58]

On another occasion, someone she wants to interview as a witness spots her and runs. Dallas identifies herself as police, orders him to stop, and then tackles him. She says, "I'm going to let you up so we can have a civilized conversation. When I do, if you run, I'll catch you—and I'm going to be really unhappy when I do. Understand?" And he says, "Yeah, yeah. I didn't do anything. Cops can't just go knocking people down." "File a complaint."[59]

On another occasion, she uses force fairly in an altercation with someone she's questioning. However, when the witness refuses to answer questions, protesting, "You broke my nose," and insisting that the law requires Dallas to call for medical help, Dallas replies, "Interesting, you refreshing me on the law. I think we can hold off on the broken nose a little while. Of course, the broken arm's going to need attention." When the woman replies, "I don't have a broken arm," Dallas utters a threatening "yet." Along with withholding medical care and threatening bodily harm, Dallas promises to overlook illegal activities in her effort to extract information. Another example of a threat occurs when Dallas, interviewing a sick witness, makes as if to remove his breathing tube. "She wouldn't actually rip it off—probably wouldn't—but he didn't know that. 'You want to take another breath?' " When he points out that his droid knows she's there, she asserts that she, "an officer of the law, sworn to protect and serve," would be believed—especially with Roarke present as a witness.[60]

If I get slapped . . . I've got it coming

Dallas is aware that her use of force must be proportionate to any threat, that excessive or unjustified police violence can have consequences.[61] She also occasionally provokes assault in order to have an excuse to arrest someone or threatens arrest to squeeze information from others.[62] Dallas' safety was never seriously threatened when she allowed a privileged woman to assault her after interrogation: "She turned away from the nail swipe so those long, pretty nails barely broke the skin under her jaw. And she took the first shove that bashed her into the wall. The rest would look better on the record that way. Eve stomped on Ava's instep, plowed an elbow into her gut, then finished with a solid uppercut."[63] Dallas knows she has overdone it: "I should've just knocked her back. If I get slapped for knocking her out, I've got it coming." Roarke insists that "she deserved each, and the rest [of the consequences] you've seen to she'll get."[64]

A similar awareness of consequences, the possible disproportion of her actions, and the possibility of administrative sanction arises in the case of Jess Barrow. Unlike Ava Anders, Barrow has not directly used violence against her, but he provokes her by manipulating her and Roarke's behavior through mental compulsions. Barrow was at their home for a session with Mavis when he uses mind control, causing Roarke to ravage Eve.[65] Dallas is hurt physically; Roarke is hurt emotionally. He is wracked with guilt, believing that he has raped her (which she denies), concerned that he is behaving like his violent and possessive father, and consumed with worry that he may have caused her to recall the repeated rapes she suffered as a child.[66] When Dallas figures out that Barrow was using compulsion, she calls him into her office at home, though she is not on duty, bringing Peabody, who had also been present. She questions him about potential connections between the mind control he is using and a series of apparent suicides she has been investigating that she believes, correctly, are linked to a similar technique.

When Barrow taunts her ("You want to sting me because I wired into your man. You should be thanking me. I bet the two of you fucked like wild minks"), she reacts: "Her hand was in a fist, her fist slamming into his jaw before her brain registered the act. He went down like a stone, face first, arms splayed, and sent her link flying." Whether permissible or not, the power dynamic here is somewhat different than if Barrow had been in police custody, although it was a formal interview. Dallas' spontaneous violent reaction is an ethical infraction, but far from the most significant or problematic one.

More troubling than the punch is the cover-up. After Dallas decks Barrow, Peabody leaps into cover-up mode. "Let the backup record show that the subject physically threatened the lieutenant during questioning. As a result, subject lost his balance and struck his head on the desk. He appears to be momentarily stunned." She destroys evidence: " 'Lieutenant Dallas, I believe your recorder has been damaged.' With a brush of her hand, Peabody tipped Eve's coffee onto the unit, effectively frying its chips. 'Mine is in working order and will be sufficient for reporting this interview. Are you injured?' "[67] This concealment of evidence of an assault on a suspect being interrogated illustrates the fragility of safeguards such as recording.[68] Barrow is far from a sympathetic character, so the reader has no predisposition to outrage on his behalf. At the same time, if outrage is deflected because of Barrow's despicable conduct, the reader becomes complicit in the logic of ends justifying means.

The issue becomes more complicated when Roarke arrives. Peabody leaves, and Roarke asks for—and Dallas reluctantly grants him—five minutes alone with Barrow. Dallas warns Roarke, "The record shows he's relatively undamaged. If there are marks on him, it's going to swing back on me and compromise my case against him." Roarke twists Barrow's penis and cuts off his air supply. " 'Now, let's talk,' he said pleasantly enough. 'About private matters.' " When Dallas enters five minutes later, she sees Barrow "unmarked" but not unharmed; Roarke admits that "he doubted Eve or the NYPSD would approve of the tricks he'd picked up in his more shadowy travels."[69]

Undue force

Prosecution or professional sanction for injuries sustained in police custody occasionally happens, as do questions about cover-ups via destruction of evidence and intimidation via threats. When Dallas goes to interrogate Barrow the next morning, she asks, "Feeling better today?" Barrow insists, "I could hang you on undue force. But I'm going to let it pass because before this is done, you'll be the top joke of your idiot department." Peabody says, "The subject's memory might be faulty due to the injury he received while assaulting an officer." Barrow starts to correct himself ("She struck me without provocation, then let that bastard she married come in and . . .") but trails off. He demurs when Dallas asks if he wants to "make an official complaint."[70] In a later installment, readers learn that Barrow and his attorney had tried to make much in the media of Dallas having hit him, but they were unwilling to explain what he had done to provoke it.[71]

Formal complaints and publicity are two weapons in the public's arsenal for opposing brutality. Pressure by other officers to adhere to certain standards of treatment, and the possibility for official reprisals not necessarily occasioned by civilian complaints, are others. Dallas mentions the latter when she talks of possibly getting "slapped for knocking [Anders] out."[72] Occasionally, police brutality and other forms of misconduct generate sanctions. On the other hand, suspects and witnesses sometimes raise groundless complaints. When a pompous witness demands "an explanation as to why I was removed from my home by two uniformed officers and shoved into the backseat of a police car," Dallas orders, facetiously, "Peabody, make a note to speak with said uniformed officers. No shoving." Peabody answers, "So noted, sir."[73] Another wealthy suspect says he was "manhandled" and plans "to file charges of police brutality." Yet he does not request an "examination to document any injuries [he] may have incurred during his arrest."[74] In context, his claim is frivolous, as is the shout of "Police brutality!" by a fleeing purse-snatcher whom Dallas tackles and restrains without excessive force.[75] A suspect, whom witnesses declare killed a woman by pushing her down the stairs, insists, "Cops tossed me down on the street. I'm gonna sue." The cop tells Dallas that the suspect "took a little spill" while fleeing the scene.[76] The untrustworthy suspect has lied about pushing the woman down the steps despite eyewitnesses to the contrary, so his account of police violence is not credible. Dallas sometimes jokes about police brutality as if it were only a myth: when a man with an intellectual disability fears that police are hurting his brother who is being questioned as a witness, she says, "Take him into Observation. Let him see his brother's not being beaten with our vast supply of rubber hoses and saps."[77]

Repeated baseless complaints and sarcastic dismissals make light of police brutality. The falsity and frivolity of most such complaints contrast sharply with complaints of sexual assault and harassment. Because the series repeatedly recounts rapes and other forms of sexual predation, false accusations can be acknowledged and condemned as "an insult to every woman who's ever been forced" without diminishing the horror of sexual violence.[78] With few counterbalancing examples of substantial or fatal violence by police against innocent people, the laughable, obviously fabricated, easily dismissed accusations of criminals or the privileged stand in for all such accusations.

That is not to say that Dallas and her colleagues discount the possibility of brutality. It is the main reason that, in addition to the safeguard of recording devices intended to ensure compliance with procedural regulations and documentation of any breach of protocol, more serious violations or use of lethal force require psychologically invasive Testing.[79] Dallas' investigation of a fellow cop's murder has her suspecting a detective who has "had a lot of disciplinary slaps, and a few marks for using undue force. He's got a temper." She later remarks, "I won't be surprised to hear at some point he's ordered to hand over his pieces and his badge."[80] Dallas is well aware that cops might exercise retaliatory violence toward suspects, especially suspects who have killed or attacked other police officers. Thus, she specifies that the officers guarding a suspect implicated in killing two officers must be capable of not harming him.[81] When planning the takedown of the serial killer who had badly beaten and nearly killed Peabody, Dallas accepts Baxter's point that "the suspect is a large individual with considerable muscle" and that "extreme measures" might be necessary in apprehending him, but Dallas also warns that she "want[s] him conscious for Interview" and that Baxter must not "let those measures get out of hand."[82] Even when Dallas turns Barrow over to Roarke briefly, she still considers herself "duty bound to protect the bastard."[83]

Sometimes the use of force or violence against a fellow officer is presented as unproblematic. Interrogating a corrupt cop, Dallas enters the room, shoves him, and then when he asks immediately for a lawyer, grabs him "one-handed by the collar and shove[s] him against the wall" while Feeney, McNab, and Peabody look on "with varying degrees of interest."[84] One of Dallas' detectives manages to be rough with an incompetent or corrupt colleague: she "caught him full in his fat gut with her elbow, knocked him flat, and then she gives him a big smile and says, 'Oops.'" Dallas approves ("I always liked Cartwright"), and Roarke says, "Darling, we really must send her some flowers."[85] In such cases, rough treatment against bad actors within the police is not merely tacitly approved but positively regarded.

Most instances of force, justified or not, are directed against civilians. As the incident with Barrow demonstrates, procedural safeguards have limits and misconduct may go unpunished. In this way, In Death shares a common feature of television police procedurals: as legal scholars Charles Ogletree and Austin Sarat observe, "Police misconduct can be overlooked as long as the 'bad guys' are caught and receive the punishments they purportedly 'deserve.'"[86] On other occasions, however, looseness in use of such tools gives suspected perpetrators a pass in the interest of justice. For instance, when Dallas is convinced of certain suspects' innocence or believes circumstances mitigate their guilt, she delays turning on her recorder so that she can advise them about how to behave in an interrogation.[87]

Going to put you in lockup

Dallas uses, at the very least, manipulative techniques in interrogation, often to avoid having suspects lawyer up. Threats of violence during apprehension or interrogation sometimes form part of the manipulation.[88] So, too, do threats about prison conditions. Although Dallas occasionally expresses remorse at employment of certain interrogation techniques, like dimming lights while questioning a suspect who is frightened of the dark, she never expresses regret for threatening suspects with custodial rape by guards or prisoners.[89]

Such threats help elicit confessions. Dallas tells a cop suspect that if he insists on a lawyer, he'll be put in lockup to wait: "I've got three witnesses here that're going to testify that you assaulted me. That's going to put you in lockup, where all the big, bad guys will be drawing straws to see who gets to be your date for Friday night. I bet you know what those big, bad guys do to cops in lockup, don't you, Vernon?" In the aftermath of the interrogation, when Vernon has provided information, both Feeney and Peabody approve of Dallas' actions and consider Vernon's reprehensible. Peabody says, "I love being a cop and he's made me ashamed of it."[90] There is no indication that Dallas' threats were unethical or that custodial rape might be a problem to resolve.

Dallas uses graphic threats of prison rape while interrogating a suspect in a string of rapes and murders. Repeated, brutal rapes by fellow prisoners are, she says, "your goddamn kismet, pal."[91] She tells a man who for half a century participated in annual gang-rapes (but insists, "It was just sex, it was tradition"), "You might just find yourself in the same situation in prison, for the rest of your life. And we'll see if you think of it as just sex."[92] Likewise, to obtain a confession from one participant in a ritual murder, she threatens to lie to ensure her harsh treatment in prison: "I will personally see that word gets out that you fucked with tiny little children. Do you know what cons like to do to people who fuck with tiny little children?"

When the woman protests that she's "never touched a child," Dallas replies that she'll lie. She hopes, though, that the woman will turn down the deal "so I can look forward to getting reports on how many inventive ways the other cons and the guards rape you over the next, oh, fifty years." She elaborates, "They find ways to get sharp, ugly tools into those cages, Leah. They'll slice and dice you, let them stick you up again so they can slice and dice some more." Only when the suspect relents does Dallas begin to record the interview.[93] Dallas uses similar threats of violence as well as sexual assault with the female, dominant partner in a string of brutal torture-murders. That unlikable suspect confesses in part out of "fear for herself at the idea of being in a place where someone could do to her what she had done to others."[94]

Early in the series, there are a few references to prison life. When *Glory in Death* opens, Nadine Furst is off planet doing an exposé on conditions at Penal Colony Omega, where it's "three people to a cage" and conditions are poor.[95] It is difficult to know whether her account of not being able to get any decent food represents snobbishness or genuinely bad conditions, but Dallas is unsympathetic: murderers *should* be treated like criminals. Still, for all that the series begins with an allusion to prison life—Dallas wakes to light slanting through her window, throwing shadows that look like cell bars—there is little discussion of what constitutes prison routines, populations, or penal practices, except when violence or the harshness of off-planet facilities is mentioned in trying to convince suspects to confess. Dallas is skeptical of purported rehabilitative programs.[96] While some prisoners work, the concern with prison jobs is not that they are exploitative but that the prisoners in question use the electronics access provided by their employment for their own nefarious purposes.

Carceral violence emerges repeatedly, usually in passing. Prison violence and corrupt guards usually affect unsympathetic characters. A few unlamented men die ugly deaths in prison.[97] More attention falls on prisoners who manipulate the system and bend guards to their bidding than on systematic violence of guards toward prisoners. Prisoners use guile, violence, or both to escape if they can—often using their access to medical treatment. A torture-killer escapes from an off-planet prison while being taken to the infirmary.[98] Serial rapist/

child abductor Isaac McQueen acts like a model prisoner, then kills a nurse to escape.[99] A patricidal Swede committed as an adolescent to an "Institute for the Criminally Insane" seduces her psychiatrist and convinces him to release her to a lower-security facility from which she then escapes. During her years in the facility she made a habit of "bartering sex for privilege." When "caught in intimate situations" with staff, "she claimed coercion . . . and the staff involved were fired."[100]

Guards admittedly act badly at times, and part of what makes threats, such as the ones Dallas delivers while interrogating suspects, effective is that suspects believe those threats. Yet In Death focuses on truly pathological prisoners rather than the regular prison population. Sleeping with and manipulating a guard to gain privileges is completely in character for misandrist serial killer Julianna Dunne, who, after an early release for good behavior, steps back on her murderous path.[101] Yet it also adds to the portrayal of sociopathic prisoners manipulating their way within the system and showcases exploitative relationships in which the prisoner seems to be in the position of power.[102] "Julianna Dunne, multiple murderer, waltzing her way through the system, stacking up privileges and favors, and conning, bribing, sweet-talking guards, staff, and other prisoners into doing whatever she needed or wanted to be done." Dallas rants, "Like they were goddamn servants . . . and this was her goddamn castle." Dunne's parole officer objects to the accusation that he is "having a sexual relationship with a client," but he never denies it. Assuming that Dunne and not Dunne's parole officer holds the power, Dallas tells him, "You'd have been child's play for her. . . . You can be grateful she just wanted you to help push her through, and didn't want you dead."[103] This narrative approach minimizes pervasive abuses of prisoner rights, including but not limited to physical and sexual abuse by other prisoners and guards.[104]

Violence during incarceration is by turns condemned, taken for granted, and used strategically.[105] The structural violence of incarceration itself is occasionally hinted at, with no attention to how it may affect communities differentially.[106] The consequences of imprisonment merit sporadic mention. Peabody says of a woman sentenced to a year and a half in Rikers' Minimum Security facility, "She's not the same person coming out as she was going in."[107] The susceptibility of people on parole to being hauled back to prison is acknowledged. Sometimes, Dallas uses this susceptibility as a lever to demand cooperation. "Applying a little pressure" to someone with previous smudges on her record, whose man has just been murdered, helps extract information.[108] At other times, she intervenes when someone on parole is being mistreated by others in the system. She interviews an unlikely suspect to check his alibi and hears his complaint that police harass him regularly even though he's "clean." Once she verifies his alibi, she gives him her card: "Cops come in giving you the fish eye, let me know."[109] These individualized interventions make a difference for specific people but do not acknowledge, let alone remedy, the broader system of which they are a part.

I just love police dramas

Dallas frequently uses violence in appropriate and measured ways to stop criminals or protect herself, colleagues, or civilians.[110] At other times, she abuses her power, or threatens to. Readers—like Dallas' colleagues—become complicit in these casual brutalities. Readers identify with Dallas and root for her. She has suffered traumatic violence herself and commands what P. D. James terms "reader identification and loyalty."[111] When Dallas threatens, readers are aware that she is unlikely to carry out the threats. Those she threatens cannot know this; that is why the threats are effective. Reader loyalty means that when she hurts people, especially but not only when they hurt her first, readers tend to be on her side.

This is the case even when she is in the wrong. In December 2060, Dispatch summons her early one morning to the scene of a murder in a run-down neighborhood. Roarke accompanies her. Before she enters the building, a bystander attracts her attention by making kissy noises. Rather than let the beat droid securing the scene handle it, she engages the man, asking, "Want a kiss?" In response, he insults her and invites her to suck his penis, boasting about its size. She suggests that he prove his claim. When he displays his penis, she grips it and twists hard; when his friend tries to intervene, she punches him in turn with her free hand. In obvious pain, the one whose genitals she's squeezing makes distressed noises and collapses to his knees. She twists harder. She threatens to "have your bruised and ugly dick hauled in along with the rest of you and your idiot friend there" if he doesn't cooperate. When he agrees, she asks a couple of questions, makes additional threats, and tells them to leave. She declines a beat droid's offer to write up the incident ("What incident?"), noting that the "droids looked as amused as droids could manage." She tells Roarke, standing nearby, that she feels better: "I needed that," she says. "Perked me right up." He agrees, "Everyone's entitled to a bit of entertainment now and again."[112]

This scene is, perhaps, the moral nadir of the series. Dallas' conduct is despicable. Rather than ignore, glare at, or verbally eviscerate the man—techniques she employs to good effect on other occasions—or let the beat droid on scene handle it (as it starts to do), she chooses assault. During her encounters with denizens of the underground, one could argue that violence is necessary to guarantee her own and Peabody's safety. In this instance, the only insult was to her dignity. One cannot even attempt to justify the violence on the grounds that it was necessary to extract information; it wasn't, and it didn't. If taken at face value, it merely entertains her and Roarke—and readers, who are meant to imagine the encounter in Dallas' place and not in that of her victim. Sexualized brutality toward a man whose offense was a rude overture, who displayed his genitals in response to her prompting, goes beyond any reasonable definition of acceptable conduct. In comparison, Roarke used similar violence on Jess Barrow after Barrow forced him into rough, barely consensual sex with Eve. Whether Roarke was justified or not, two things differentiate his very much in-character violence toward Barrow from Dallas' act toward the unnamed man on the street. First, Roarke is a civilian, not a cop. Second, Barrow's provocation was orders of magnitude greater than that of the loiterer. Dallas uses violence far disproportionate to the occasion against someone who presented no threat and then jokes about it. This egregious incident is unusual in the series, which often evokes and describes ugly, sadistic violence but in ways that clearly signal its wrongness. This callous conduct should spark reader unease at the very least; perhaps its inclusion is meant to provoke just that, by illustrating that even a largely admirable detective, granted too much discretion and too little accountability, may abuse her power.[113]

Fictional violence is, in large part, spectacle; the prospect of joy at seeing someone in prison as a means of justice being done is about a kind of connection to the punishment process.[114] Spectacles of punishment also inform how audiences conceptualize police, prisons, and imprisonment. Conventional wisdom about police procedure, courtroom processes and outcomes, and punishment, however, bears little resemblance to the reality. Crime shows on television—and, to a perhaps lesser extent, police procedural fiction—present neatly packaged dramas in which justice is, mostly, served. Film and television portrayals of the criminal justice system in operation shape to a significant extent the ways in which popular audiences perceive that system.[115] In a metacommentary in the novels, one older woman who "just love[s] police dramas" asks, "Could I ask, when the two of you interrogate—oh, wait, the term's 'interview' these days—when you interview a suspect, do you ever rough them up?" Peabody responds that it's unnecessary: "The lieutenant scares confessions out of them."[116] Others characters, however, who are familiar with police dramas from the screen and from the true crime book *The Icove Agenda* insist that it is different, and not nearly so exciting, in real life.[117]

In Robb's fictional future, as in the contemporary world, popular culture's depictions of crime, criminal justice, and punishment are influential in shaping ordinary people's ideas. For readers who glean "knowledge" of how policing and incarceration affect lives and communities solely through fictional descriptions, more accurate information as well as different sorts of fictional descriptions might lead to more critical engagement. Expanded sympathies are a necessary precursor to imagining change.

In Death rarely attends to how individual stories of crime and punishment fit into broader patterns. The structural elements of policing, court practice, incarceration, and parole are submerged in the series. Writing at the turn of the twenty-first century, sociologist Eduardo Bonilla-Silva notes that "blacks and dark-skinned Latinos are the targets of racial profiling by the police which, combined with the highly racialized criminal court system, guarantees their overrepresentation among those arrested, prosecuted, incarcerated, and, if charged for a capital crime, executed."[118] Readers of In Death never learn if these disparities have been acknowledged or corrected in Robb's fictional world. There is no acknowledgment that prisons have racialized effects: both in removing people from communities and then reverberating in individual lives, which in turn affects communities.[119]

"Fantasy," American studies scholar Sharon Patricia Holland writes, "can oscillate between delusion and creative hope."[120] One might read Robb's future nearly free of anti-black racism as a hopeful fantasy: writing into being a future free of its ravages, in which the criminal justice system is not a key institution in maintaining a racist order through police violence and discriminatory incarceration.[121] Or one might read it as fantasy in the sense of an obvious, persistent unreality. Perhaps readers are meant to imagine that racism has been eradicated. Yet big shifts are typically mentioned. Rather than the unexplained absence of guns, Robb writes of their (occasionally violated) ban; rather than the absence of prostitution, Robb writes of its legalization and regulation.[122] The series occasionally notes homophobia and returns regularly to an undercurrent of sexism.[123] Some "traditional values" types resist same-sex marriage, women's access to contraception, even women's participation in certain professions.[124] Such ideas are sometimes espoused by unlikable characters. Racial prejudices, by contrast, surface extremely rarely. One lazy and corrupt cop spews anti-Mexican sentiments and misogynist slurs; he harbors broader prejudices, including tempered bias toward a murdered black officer.[125] In this unusual passage, various sorts of prejudices are brought together, and the Mexican officer insulted by her coworker speaks about the "overfed white male"—their captain's words—who believes "the only real cop is male and white and hetero."[126]

While racial discrimination is mentioned once or twice, racist dimensions of police violence—the legitimate and illegitimate ways in which cops use force—never appear. Discriminatory policing and adjudication stand outside the scope of the stories told, which often end with confessions, sometimes with the death of the suspect in deadly confrontations. Dallas and her closest colleagues investigate murder, a crime for which few doubt long-term incarceration is the appropriate penalty. The overall shape of policing, criminal justice, and the carceral system appears only in vague outline. Dallas' semi-frequent interventions in routine street policing occur only when she personally witnesses crimes being committed (she apprehends pickpockets, muggers, and even a burglar when they break laws in her presence), unlike stop-and-frisk policies that routinely result in disproportionate charges against people of color. It is worth considering what the policing done by the fictional NYPSD of the mid-twenty-first century—its successes, its failures, and its unknowns—might lead readers to ask about policing in the contemporary United States.

CHAPTER

5

Perfection in Death

In December 2060, Dallas' detectives hang a sign over the squad's break-room door, joining a jumble of holiday decorations including a zombie Santa, a banged-up menorah, and ears of corn commemorating Kwanzaa:

> NO MATTER YOUR RACE, CREED, SEXUAL ORIENTATION, OR POLITICAL AFFILIATION, WE PROTECT AND SERVE, BECAUSE YOU COULD GET DEAD.[1]

Erected as a joke, the sign strikes Dallas' fancy. She decrees that it will remain after the sad Christmas tree and other seasonal debris are gone. It expresses a core truth: death equalizes. As Dallas thinks when a wealthy lawyer dies, "Money might drip . . . but death had no respect for it. It was a club without a class system."[2]

Not only is death universal, so is vulnerability. "Murder," Robb writes, "harbored no bigotry, no bias. It subscribed to no class system. In its gleefully, deadly, and terminally judicious way, murder turned a blind eye on race, creed, gender, and social stratum."[3] Despite the mention of race, as well as sexuality, gender, creed, and even political affiliation in these abstract affirmations of human worth, the form of difference to which the series attends most clearly is class.[4] Juxtapositions between rich and poor victims pepper the series. Its first installment juxtaposes the deaths of a wealthy woman from a prominent family working as a licensed companion and an older LC struggling to get by.[5] Another opens by contrasting two murders: in his lavish home, a rich man's "death had come to him on the luxurious sheets of his massive, silk-canopied bed." A poor young woman's death the night before had occurred "on the stained mattress tossed on the floor of a junkie's flop."[6] The surroundings diverge, but the end result is the same: hence the protecting and serving that the squad sign proclaims. The media might care more about some victims than others, but each deserves the best efforts of Dallas and her detectives. As Peabody declares, "Murder equalizes. . . . Our job is to stand for the dead—whoever they were in life."[7]

In insisting that all deaths matter, the series rejects claims by some privileged doctors and scientists to determine who ought to live, and how. Dallas foils a conspiracy to harvest organs from the dispossessed to create near-immortality for the wealthy and connected; she exposes a cloning ring that makes made-to-order women for elite clients. She emphatically rejects the claim that some people simply deserve better lives than others. Yet insidious, unexplored assumptions about human perfection, capacity, and worth undermine the series' proclamations about diversity and dignity and the power of its insistence that death remains the great equalizer.

No one called it homicide

If equality in death is a given—at least when murder is in play—in life it is not so. Despite Dallas' recognition that death eventually claims every human being, she is deeply aware of the class stratification of her city and its population. Rich and poor may die within the same period of time, but they occupy vastly different physical spaces, even if thriving professional neighborhoods and miserably poor ones are separated by a mere block or two.[8] "For some," she muses, "death wasn't the enemy. Life was a much less merciful opponent."[9] New York has an underground area, a "deep, dank world of unlicensed whores and doomed addicts." Intermittent police sweeps and sporadic mayoral attempts at cleanup do little to change the basic violent, unruly nature of the place. "She'd learned to accept that not everything could be changed, not everything could be fixed."[10] Hunger, inequality, and violence persist. New technologies do not prevent and may even facilitate illegal behaviors, including sale of newborns and human trafficking.[11] Despite technological progress, "human nature" is a constant: "As always, children went hungry, women sold their bodies, and men killed for a handful of credits."[12]

"The pain, the despair, and the terror" of the city's poorest feature prominently in *Conspiracy in Death*, set in early 2059. For addicts and "the mental defectives and physically flawed who slipped through society's cracks," "the city was simply another kind of prison."[13] It's not that no one notices. "There were social programs, of course. It was, after all, an enlightened time. So the politicians claimed." Liberals clamor for ambitious interventions but cannot fund them. Conservatives slash budgets while speechifying "on the quality of life and family."[14] Ineffectual government social programs persist despite technological advances: cars that go vertical, Auto-chefs dispensing prepared meals, and off-planet colonies, both penal and recreational. The poor are political Arena balls. Purportedly transformative government programs die with a whimper, caught in bureaucratic snags or political wrangling. It is not only public social engineering projects that garner Dallas' suspicion. Private charitable programs "designed to instill pride and self-worth" may also mask unsavory motives; one wealthy woman relied on those she perceived as underlings to do uncompensated favors for her, even to the point of manipulating a vulnerable participant into killing the benefactress' husband.[15]

Just as rich and poor victims are connected by death, poverty and wealth are connected in Dallas' own life. Despite her current circumstances, "she knew what it was to come from places such as this. Knew how much the same they were—city by city—in smells, and routines, in hopelessness."[16] Dallas' routine juxtaposes urban blight and decadent luxury. As she and Peabody arrive at a run-down crime scene to investigate the death of Snooks, a sidewalk sleeper, they discuss an East Washington gala Dallas attended the previous evening: "Save the moles or something. Enough food to feed every sidewalk sleeper on the Lower East Side for a year." The nation's political capital is the site of fancy charity events far removed from the real needs of human beings. Dallas' life with Roarke, bafflingly, puts her in such settings.[17]

Snooks' death would not normally have been a matter for a homicide detective. Given the January cold, "many slipped from life to death during those bitter nights. The city had killed them, but no one called it homicide."[18] Something unusual about this death led the ineffectual and surly cop on "stiff scooper" duty to request a homicide investigation. Snooks, it turns out, had not frozen to death. Someone had surgically removed his heart. His death becomes an event rather than mere background noise.[19]

Dallas estimates the victim was about one hundred years old and in poor health: "Even without murder, he'd never have attained the average twenty more years decent nutrition and medical science could have given him." Morris' autopsy discovers "first-rate major organ removal" but also damaged and diseased organs. Snooks had "six months, tops, before he'd have kicked from natural causes."[20] There is nothing natural, though, about one man's exclusion from the medical advances that can treat once-incurable diseases and extend human longevity to well beyond a century.[21] In the course of investigating Snooks' death, and the connected deaths and organ thefts of other vulnerable people, Dallas and her colleagues discuss unequally distributed health-care options and the social, economic, and personal factors that determine access.[22]

Some forms of biological and social engineering have become widely available, including "genetic testing [that] often weeded out the more violent hereditary traits before they could bloom."[23] Heart defects can be repaired before birth, but it is unclear whether undesirable tendencies to violence are corrected in utero via gene therapy or eliminated through selective abortion.[24] Organs can often but not always be salvaged by routine measures; sometimes "the poor or the disenfranchised" have allowed illness to progress too far and more radical measures, such as artificial organ replacement, must be used.[25] Dallas rejects cyborg longevity: she does not wish to live forever "with a bunch of interchangeable spare parts."[26] But unlike treatments for late-stage brain tumors, which require "the right insurance or bank account," these replacements are inexpensive and widely available; they are also key to *Conspiracy*'s plot.[27]

Recurrent cynicism about engineered shortcuts to perfect the human body arises partly from a fetishization of the real: those who can afford it prefer real coffee, "meat from actual cows," and natural fabrics including leather and cashmere.[28] Yet the real is not only about luxury commodities but also about rejecting purchased solutions: bodies should be sculpted by exercise rather than surgery.[29] It is precisely this insistence on the natural rather than the artificial that leads a group of doctors astray in *Conspiracy in Death*.

Conspiracy's doctors want to regenerate individuals' own organs rather than rely on cheaply available artificial organs. They need diseased human organs on which to experiment. To keep their illegal research secret, they must steal these organs, in the process killing those from whom they are taken. One doctor objected, and was herself murdered, when she learned her collaborators were killing people. When Dallas points this out, the mastermind retorts, "They're hardly people."[30] The project for organ regeneration has larger implications than just being "able to remake a human being, using his own body." It will dramatically extend life spans: "Death will essentially become obsolete." But as Dallas points out, he will choose to "remake" only some people, since there aren't "enough resources for everybody to live forever." The doctors, who consider themselves above others, think they have a right to decide who lives and who dies. Immortality will be for only a select few. Bad-guy surgeon Dr. Waverly aims "to create and mold and select." As he puts it, "Who needs more aging whores or sidewalk sleepers?" In his view, political leaders will appreciate his "mission" since, as he describes, "We've found a way to clean up the streets over the next generation, to employ a kind of natural selection, survival of the fittest."[31] Saving some bodies requires vampiric reliance on the bodies of a disposable underclass, who are phased out: the rich live nearly forever and in a "clean[ed] up" society to boot.

Waverly, full of "arrogance and pride" but "no ordinary madness," believes that his knowledge and experience justify his exercise of godlike powers over human bodies and, through them, the social body.[32] Vanquishing age leaves no room for the aged. Eliminating disease requires the absence of the diseased. Eradicating poverty becomes eradicating the poor.

A lot of money for a perfect woman

Similarly messianic hopes for a radically transformed society undergird the plot of *Origin in Death*, set in the fall of 2059.[33] A small group of doctors and scientists has been secretly cloning females and raising them to order.[34] Like the murderers in *Indulgence in Death* and *Seduction in Death*, the villainous Drs. Icoves, *père et fils*, believe they are above the law, that their privilege protects them from the consequences of their actions and entitles them to services from others. They are eventually proven wrong, though privilege does pose obstacles to the initial investigation.[35] A lawyer asks incredulously if Dallas is "seriously alleging" crimes including "human cloning, psychological imprinting, and the merchandising of women" against respected, wealthy institutions and individuals. The answer is yes.[36]

Conspiracy's plotters had aimed to extend the lifespans of already living individuals with sufficient wealth and power. In *Origin*, the conspirators' short-term goal is to create perfectible, reproducible ideal beings. Though originally aimed at replacing lost loved ones, the practice becomes cloning girls: incubated in tanks, raised in institutions, educated and trained for specific purposes. Some become spies; others—including those at the center of the story—are bred and sold to be ideal wives and mothers.

Perfection and (female) beauty are part of the story. Early on, readers learn that "unlike many of the patients of the Wilfred B. Icove Center, physical beauty wasn't one of [Dallas'] priorities."[37] Dallas and Peabody are visiting the reconstructive surgery center to interview a patient: a model, badly beaten, who has killed in self-defense. As they are preparing to leave, the clinic's founder and namesake is murdered in what seems to be a professional hit. His son, Dr. Will Icove, seeks Dallas' help.

In doing background research on the victim, who records present as "a fricking saint," Dallas discovers his motivation for going into his field. His do-gooder mother, a physician, had, decades earlier, been "running clinics in depressed areas and countries" when she "was severely burned attempting to save children from a building under attack. She lived, but was disfigured." Photos show that she was "a wowzer" and "pretty hot" before the explosion; afterward her appearance was "grim." Though "they were able to keep her alive, and do considerable work on her," they were unable to restore her looks, and "she self-terminated three years later."[38]

Beauty and physical wholeness are inextricably linked in Icove senior's work. His concierge describes his work as "beautifying people, helping them keep their youth." Then, backtracking, she adds, "I mean to say, he did amazing work with accident victims. Amazing." Indeed, his efforts in reconstructive surgery were battlefield innovations during the Urbans: Summerset, who knew him somewhat during that time, offers this encomium: "Victims who would have lost limbs, or gone through their lives scarred, were spared that due to his work."[39]

Having lost his mother years before, during this period Icove suffered another loss. His wife, pregnant with his daughter, was killed; he hoped to "preserve her DNA, and potentially recreate her," but arrived too late to harvest viable cells. His experiments with collaborators took a turn from reconstruction toward re-creation. He developed "Quiet Birth," in which children were gestated in artificial wombs so that "every moment of development [could] be monitored. Every developing cell [could] be engineered, adjusted, manipulated."[40] Although Dallas has no romantic idealization of reproduction or babies, and no sentiment attached to an idealized version of motherhood and maternity (she jokes about having Roarke undergo the process if it ever becomes possible), the books present artificial reproduction as monstrous, associating it exclusively with eugenic cloning. In sharp contrast, in the 1970s a few feminists such as Shulamith Firestone proposed radical reworkings of family, household, and reproduction that are, here, implicitly rejected, alongside the rejection of eugenic criteria.

Quality control was key. Not only could individuals be replicated, they could be tinkered with to create perfection.[41] "Deformed" fetuses, with failures or defects, were terminated and studied. Survival to birth did not necessarily entail a normal life span. Five-year-olds who failed to meet the standards of the program were also killed. Avril Icove—wife of Will Icove, also murdered in the course of the novel—exists in a set of three. There had been two more. "One died at six months," and Icove terminated the other when she was five: "we weren't strong enough, and our intellect wasn't developing according to the required levels. He killed us. He injected us as you might a terminally ill pet. We went to sleep, and never woke. And so, we're three."[42]

The three surviving Avrils, who married and loved Will, asked only one thing of their husband and their father-in-law: that "any children we would have together—would never be re-created. They'd never be used this way. They gave us their word." When the doctors broke their word and harvested cells from Will and Avrils' children, she/they turned against the doctors. Though the men's notes recorded it as "a precaution only, in case something happened to the children," the Avrils found it unacceptable. The children "aren't things to be replaced." The Avrils intuit that the notion of replacement-only will not stand up to human imperfection. "Do you see us? We're not allowed a flaw, no physical or biological flaw. This is the father's directive. Our children have flaws, as any child does, should. We knew they would take what they were and alter it."[43]

Ultimately, Dallas discovers that the Icoves' marketing of ideal females ("Some people would pay a lot of money for a perfect woman") was only one element of a long-term plan "to create a race of Superiors" using technology to "eliminate imperfections and genetic flaws, and eventually mortality. Natural conception, with its inherent risks and questionable success rate, could, and should, be replaced by Quiet Birth." Over the decades, they had "seed[ed] legislatures, state rooms," media, medicine, and government with cloned "graduates" from their programs. They intended to legalize Quiet Birth and then, within a century, "ban natural conception" since "natural conception means natural flaws. . . . Quiet Birth ensures human perfection, eliminates defects. . . . Acceptable parents are guaranteed that the kid will meet their specific requirements."[44]

Origin contains competing messages about perfection. Robb clearly condemns the Icoves' quest for perfection, with its intolerance of human flaws and frailties. Though physical beauty is not itself a failing, making beauty a priority is at the very least superficial. The destruction of children who are imperfect, who fail to attain certain levels of achievement, is loathsome. Yet in other places, acquired flaws or injuries, if not entirely overcome, are acknowledged to be unmanageable or intolerable. Trickier still, the books seem to presume that it is clear what precisely requires fixing.

An enlightened time of technological advancement

Medicine and science get mixed reviews in the books. Competent and reliable medical professionals abound, including Louise DiMatto and Charlotte Mira, along with harried and hurried others encountered along the way. Dallas' childhood left her wary of doctors and hospitals, but even she recognizes the worth and importance of doctors when people are injured or ill. But caring for the injured and ill differs radically from attempting to eliminate disease or mortality entirely. Like Waverly in *Conspiracy in Death,* or the Icoves in *Origin in Death,* other scientists become twisted by the possibilities they find. Greed and hubris lead to pathology.

The scientific community debates appropriate research and disagrees over how far is too far: programs are alternately critiqued and lauded. There are some clear limits: "reproductive cloning is illegal under the laws of New York, the laws of the country, and the laws governing science and commerce on and off planet."[45] Laws do not necessarily coincide with doctors' beliefs or popular opinion. Some unsympathetic characters defend illegal research and experimentation, including Jess Barrow, who had implemented "subliminal nudges" on unwitting subjects, including Dallas and Roarke.[46] Barrow had pointed to genetic engineering to make his point that currently accepted practices were once illegal; Louise similarly notes, "Birth control for women was illegal right here in the U.S. of A. less than two hundred years ago. Without research and underground movements, we might still be having kids every year and burning our bodies out by forty."[47]

Although they live in "an enlightened time of technological advancement," science has limits, both technical and moral.[48] People disagree about intervention during the "miracle" of gestation. Louise believes technology should be used to "ensure the health and safety of the mother and child. Eliminate birth defects and disease whenever possible. But crossing that line into designing babies? Manipulating emotions, physical appearance, mental capacity, even personality traits? That's no miracle. It's ego." Still, Louise admits that the science "fascinates" her: "Even bad science is seductive." The Icoves, Mira believes, "would consider the science, the medicine, the benefits and the possibilities more important than the law." She offers this assessment—and the acknowledgment that "often, they are"—before she learns of their cloning activities. The junior Icove insists, when confronted, that his "father's work was revolutionary."[49]

The line between eliminating a defect and manipulating mental capacity or personality traits is debatable, however. Dallas notes the "bans on gene manipulation that veer outside of disease and defect control" and segues from there to the fact that such bans are necessary because "people, and science, always want more. If you can cure or fix an embryo, why not make it to order? I'll have a girl, thanks, blonde, blue eyes, and give her a pert little nose while you're at it. People pay a hell of a lot for perfection."[50] While Dallas criticizes designer embryos, she assumes that it is self-evident what constitutes a defect to be fixed or a disease to be cured. The debates to which she alludes are not about ability but only about preferences—aesthetic preferences—within the spectrum of what is understood as normal.

In a follow-up conversation, Peabody sums up past generations' debates over eugenics and genetic manipulation. The arguments in favor were to increase intelligence and diminish propensities for violence. Peabody raises, briefly, the question of "who decides what's intelligent enough, or what violence is acceptable, even necessary for self-preservation and defense." She adds, "And while we're at this master-race crap, should we only breed white kids, black kids? Blondes?"[51] This brief aside on supremacist thinking raises a vital topic, though the flip equation of plots to breed "white kids" and "black kids" ignores the entrenched racism of eugenics. In theory, one could just as easily opt for a black master race as a white one; in practice, scientists have never done so.

The mental defectives and physically flawed

Other utopian attempts to use science to solve social problems—for instance, to chemically create youth or overcome addiction—end up causing greater harm. *Immortal in Death* centers on a drug that causes cells to regenerate, thereby giving the feeling of youth; its effects, however, are temporary because it causes addiction, a tolerance builds up, and ultimately the body cannot sustain its effects; early and horrible death follows. It is sold, however, more along the line of "illegals" (illicit drugs) than purported medical or scientific advances.[52] In the novella "Chaos in Death," a group of researchers struggles with the treatment of addiction. Illegals remain a troubling fact of life in mid-twenty-first century New York.[53] Youth dabble with Zoner; other illegals lead to violent rampages or users who slip further and further from functionality; rarely do individuals kick the habit and get their lives back on track.[54] "Chaos" begins with the death of three addicts. A scientist is working to create a serum to remedy the persistent unquiet that he believes lies at the root of addiction. An impatient colleague fiddling with the formula ends up poisoning himself, twisting into a Hyde-like creature, deluded and capable of murder.[55] His physical deformity mirrors his mental instability; both his appearance and his behavior are hideous. He kills four people before he too dies, unable to control his desire for the elixir that, far from strengthening him, makes him both physically and mentally unstable.

While *Immortal in Death* focuses on greed and vanity, "Chaos" grapples with normality, imperfection, and the social, psychological, and biological issues associated with illness, especially mental illness. These themes recur throughout the series. On the one hand, psychiatric support and medical interventions are important and presented positively. Dallas often refers survivors to grief counselors or recommends other therapeutic resources.[56] Through informal talk therapy, she herself often relies on Mira for support as she processes trauma. Characters occasionally seek treatment for chronic conditions such as depression and addiction, though the latter is seldom successfully treated. But mental illness frequently equals, or is associated with, criminality; difference from what is presumed normal raises concerns.[57]

Killers are sometimes—but by no means always—psychopaths, delusional, or simply "batshit crazy."[58] In some instances, traumatic experiences can lead people to snap.[59] Sometimes family history predisposes people to delusions or other forms of mental illness. But criminal behavior is often inexplicable. The novels frequently ask what causes evil, and why some people with traumatic and abusive pasts grow up to be ethical, responsible human beings while others with every advantage, including good parents and stable childhoods, end up doing awful things. One monstrous serial killer considers torturing people to determine the outer limits of human tolerance to be his life's work, but has perfectly normal parents who gave him guidance, discipline, advantages, love.[60] Mental illness causes even more uncertainty than any sort of physical illness in this regard since, as one doctor declares, even healthy minds are mysterious.[61] When Dallas questions Mira about responsibility if a suspect was "genetically imprinted toward sociopathic behavior," Mira is disdainful: "the branding at birth issue . . . is a cop-out, plain and simple." Instead, "Upbringing, environment, choices both moral and immoral form us into what we are. We are not born monsters or saints."[62]

Despite this emphasis on moral choice, Robb's retrograde jargon of "mental defectives" and "violent tendencies" suggests biological determinism and connects the future with the past.[63] (In another blast from the past, the panhandler licenses that beggars must display recall the poor badges of sixteenth- and seventeenth-century England.[64]) More broadly, in the vocabulary Robb selectively invents to estrange her universe from the present, sidewalk sleepers replace homeless people; licensed companions substitute for prostitutes; body sculpting takes liposuction's place. The terminology for illness is particularly noteworthy, though. This diagnostic lexicon of imperfection connects "the mental defectives and physically flawed" in the official discourse of the medical and psychiatric professions.[65] It treats difference as deviation, and deviation as defect, stigmatizing both physical and mental variation as shortcomings. Illustrating the presumption of certain universal norms, asexuality occasionally appears as a symptom of psychological deviance.[66] Such language echoes and feeds into popular assumptions about imperfection.

Specialist terminology connects to the unthinkingly ableist everyday language Dallas and others use. She favors the epithet ***moron***, and uses it routinely when speaking to and about incompetent colleagues as well as others she encounters.[67] When Roarke programs a hologram for her to test a weapon, she complains that it's not challenging enough: "You'd have to be a one-armed moron with a vision impairment to miss with this thing."[68] Such vocabulary choices are not mere reflections of Dallas' unrefined persona, like her salty language and her preference for pizza over fancy cuisine. Others use similar terms.[69] Nor does her use of such terminology translate into bad actions. Her few interactions with people with cognitive disabilities are models of propriety. Confronted with a witness who another detective describes as "you know, a little slow," she deals effectively and compassionately.[70] Such individuals are few and far between, however, in the books.

Disability of many sorts is simultaneously nearly absent from and hauntingly present in the series. People living with physical disabilities or differences seldom appear.[71] Even severe trauma leaves few physical effects. The populace is remarkably fit; technologies that compensate for infirmity or disability receive almost no attention. At the same time, the few references to injury, (temporary) disability, and the specter of a disabled future reveal deep anxieties about (dis)ability and (in)dependence.

Capable bodies are crucial for the series' main characters. Though Dallas does not denigrate those who use body sculpting—common among the wealthy—she approves when people earn their physiques, as she and Roarke do. Fitness is not a moral imperative; still less does an attractive body equal goodness. Excessively vain people, like a personal trainer whose murder Dallas investigates, garner disdain.[72] Dallas has little patience for Peabody's recurring semicomic body angst.[73] Bodies matter for what they do rather than how they look—a welcome, if only partial, departure from the culture's obsessive focus on women's looks and clothing. Dallas eventually tells Peabody that she "know[s] what it's like to look in the mirror and not really like what's looking back," but it was because she was "skinny" and "weak" and had to "build some muscle, get strong."[74] Dallas replaces perfectionist stereotypes about women's appearances with emphasis on strength and functionality. Physical prowess is a professional asset. She runs fast, punches hard, and fights dirty, confronting opponents who are often bigger and sometimes stronger than she is. Yet valuing ability, fitness, and power may inadvertently stigmatize bodies that do not function with ease and competence.

Age and illness disgusted him

Some characters conflate ability, youth, and attractiveness. Profiling an unidentified suspect who believes himself a vampire, Mira hypothesizes, "He'll be young . . . No more than forty. Most likely attractive in appearance and in good health. Who would want eternal life if they were homely and physically disadvantaged?"[75] The statement is uncharacteristic for the typically gracious and insightful Mira, whose profession requires perceiving beneath surface appearances.[76] Perhaps she intends it as an extrapolation of the killer's philosophy: ugliness, age, or physical disadvantage would make one want less life. The killer's first victim, a young, rich, beautiful woman, had assumed exactly this. Aged twenty-three and in peak condition, she allowed him to exsanguinate her so that he could transform her into a vampire before she began to age visibly and become decrepit. Investigating the crime, Dallas and her colleagues agree that the victim's ludicrous belief is "sheer stupidity"; though she does not deserve to die for it, it cannot be said to be the well-honed judgment of a thoughtful person.[77]

Another deeply unsympathetic character—neither victim nor (quite) a murderer—thinks similarly. Visiting his elderly grandmother in a cushy care facility, he extracts information about a hidden valuable, sparking a traumatic reaction from her. He abandons her in her distress, and it is only by chance that staff reach her in time to help. He can think only of escape: "The concept of age and illness disgusted him. There were *ways,* after all, to beat back the worst symptoms of the aging process . . . Looking old was, to his mind, a product of laziness or poverty. Either was unacceptable."[78] This vile character's opinion proves precisely how reprehensible he is. Yet, like Mira's comment, it presents aging and acquired debility as losses—losses that can be warded off with sufficient wealth. Though disability may be avoided and the signs of aging can, with sufficient care and resources, be at least partly masked, any future is always a future in which one ages.

Unless, that is, one becomes a vampire. Mira's comment assumes that if immortality were attainable without nefarious deeds, all "normal" people would want it. Rather than explore why a deranged individual would want eternal life, it excludes those who over forty, unattractive, or "physically disadvantaged" from the ranks of those who would want to live forever in their current condition. By implication, such lives deserve extension less than the lives of pretty, young, able people. It does not require such a large leap to intimate that such lives are not worth living at all. Unlike in *Conspiracy,* where the surgeon's belief that he is fit to determine which classes of people ought to live and which ought to die is obviously objectionable, this perspective—likely the murderer's, but not explicitly designated as such—is spoken by Mira. The observation that those who are defective will opt out of longevity might pass for common sense or psychoanalytically acute insight.

Ingrained ideas about the lesser worth of lives with disability surface, too, when stunner fire paralyzes McNab. The only possibilities he can imagine are complete recovery or devastating debilitation.[79] He is paralyzed from the waist down. One arm also sustained damage, meaning that "he wasn't just sitting [in the wheelchair], but strapped in. So he wouldn't slump down like a ragdoll, tumble out like a baby."[80] Unsure whether he will regain full use of his legs, McNab fears that he will "be strapped in a chair the rest of his life."[81] He is anxious, frustrated, and afraid of his new condition.

McNab's injury and those of other characters illustrate a profound truth: just as all human beings are subject to death and susceptible to murder, so all may acquire disabilities. Police work is dangerous and makes cops especially vulnerable. Characters get hurt frequently, sometimes badly, on the job. Dallas regularly sports bruises. She gets shot, stabbed, stunned, and concussed. She injures her shoulder badly enough to require physical therapy. Both she and Peabody are hurt, the former more seriously, in a boomer explosion at a bank branch.[82] Peabody gets hospitalized after being skewered by long-bladed scissors and again when badly beaten by a serial killer.[83] Maleness conveys no invulnerability to injury. Trueheart sustains a worrisome spinal injury in his first major confrontation.[84] Later, he is drugged and nearly killed by a deranged photographer. Not only cops but those accompanying them risk injury: Roarke gets stabbed in the course of an apprehension. Severe injuries, in other words, are par for the course, yet complete physical recovery occurs in each case, including from paralysis.[85] The usual alternative to full recovery is death. Even minor characters badly injured tend to heal completely or die.[86]

In injury's aftermath, physical prowess may suffer temporarily. Characters may need medical intervention, rest, and recuperation. No lasting impairments necessitate major life changes, though. Not only are there no people with visible disabilities populating the city, the physical ability of each of the main, secondary, and tertiary characters is safeguarded. This safeguarding of characters' physical ability is retroactive. Neither Dallas nor Roarke has facial scarring, missing teeth, or hearing loss as a result of the brutal beatings they suffered in their youth. Dallas did not lose her uterus from repeated childhood rapes.[87] Trauma, in other words, seldom leaves visible traces.[88]

People with visible disabilities have been written out of In Death's future, appearing as a spectral possibility invoked only to be surmounted. Disability tragically limits potential rather than creating new, different modes of life. Invisible disabilities, cognitive variation, and more are largely ignored; mental illness tends to surface only when it results in criminal behavior.[89] Physical disability prompts particular anxiety.

With no models for living differently, it is no wonder that McNab and others worry. Dallas speculates that if McNab does not regain use of his legs, "They'll bounce him on disability, or stick him in a cube doing drone work. He'll never feel like a cop again once that happens. He prances when he walks. . . . Now he's stuck in that chair. Goddamn it."[90] Even leaving aside adaptive technology, it stretches credulity to accept that half a century into the future an e-geek could not do electronic detective work while seated in a wheelchair.[91]

One exception to the complete recovery model imagines a similarly dismal result when loss, disability, and mental illness connect. In "Possession in Death," a dancer suffers a career-ending injury that also kills his beloved fiancée and dance partner. He is "lucky to live through" the accident, still able to walk and, after a fashion, dance—with the series of dancers he kidnaps, holds hostage, and eventually kills when they can no longer dance with him. He had been a "dynamic, intense, passionate man" with a "long, leanly muscled body" capable of impressive athleticism. His case prompts Dallas to ask how one deals with the loss of "that energy, that passion, that fierceness? It must be almost like death or losing someone to death"—as, of course, he also had.[92] His failure to recover completely from injury leads not just to self-harm but to outwardly directed violence.

In its attention to acquired physical disabilities—presuming other sorts of disability have been eliminated genetically or in utero—the series imagines heroic medical interventions but fails to ask what requires repair and what requires rethinking access and flourishing. To populate a future near-exclusively by those with normatively able bodies reflects a significant failure of imagination. Technology ignores accessibility: door security such as palm plates and retinal scans are never posted too high for someone in a mobile chair (because mobile-chair users are virtually absent); similarly, audio cues in security protocols make no provision for Deaf people. Readers encounter no visually impaired or Deaf characters; there is no accommodative technology, let alone acknowledgment of Deaf culture.[93]

The "enlightened time of technological advancement" excludes technology built with access in mind.[94]

Both by excluding persons living with physical disabilities and in how it treats those whose abilities are temporarily curtailed, In Death expresses deep anxieties around physical weakness. During McNab's recovery, Dallas cannot "help herself from checking the rhythm of his walk." She notes with pleasure that "there was no limp, no drag in the step."[95] She similarly despises any show of weakness in herself. Once, on her way to meet her commander, she helps subdue an out-of-control suspect and wrenches her knee. She conceals her pain for most of the meeting with her boss, but limps on exiting; she blames herself for the lapse.[96] On another occasion, when she must take time off to recover from an injury, "the weeks of disability" make her feel "edgy and useless. Weak."[97] Because the prospect of ongoing physical dependence is so frightening, even short-term injuries and temporary impediments occasion worry and "pity."[98] When Summerset breaks his leg and has his arm in a sling, Dallas empathizes: "She knew what it was to break bones and tear muscles—and how much worse the cure could seem to anyone used to doing for himself."[99] Puzzlingly, this disdain for physical dependence on others in contrast to self-sufficiency stands in contrast to the desirability of interdependence in other areas.[100]

The series celebrates individual competence, especially as manifested in physical prowess. Dallas typically rescues herself and does not depend on Roarke to come to her aid. Yet she depends on him in countless other ways, as he depends on her. She sleeps better when he is around; he wants her with him when he confronts his past in Ireland. Allowing others to help, and acknowledging that one needs others in these ways, signals not weakness but emotional maturity. At the same time that accepting others' love and care is praiseworthy, physical incompetence and dependence are despised. From Summerset's stint in a wheelchair to McNab's worry that he will remain paralyzed, the indignity of requiring bodily assistance remains a concern.

Alive was better

In Death is by no means unique in presenting a future void of physical disabilities; Marge Piercy's utopia *Woman on the Edge of Time* is, as disability studies scholar Alison Kafer notes, similarly "populated by peoples of all skin colors, genders, and sexualities, [but] it is almost completely devoid of people with disabilities: advances in medicine have led to the elimination of most illnesses, and genetic 'aberrations' have been eradicated or can easily be corrected."[101] In Death imagines disability only as limiting and hence never explores the lives of persons with disabilities. Citing Susan Wendell's argument that "living with disability or illness 'creates valuable ***ways of being*** that give valuable perspectives on life and the world,'" Kafer argues that "to eliminate disability is to eliminate the possibility of discovering alternative ways of being in the world, to foreclose the possibility of recognizing and valuing our interdependence."[102] Instead, it is assumed without debate that "a 'good' future is one without disability, while a 'bad' future is overrun by it."[103]

Though the series firmly insists on the worth of all lives, recurrent anxieties about physical impairments suggest that some lives are far more desirable than others. The devaluation of lives with disability is most obvious where longevity—the projection of the self into the future—is at issue.[104] Dallas insists that being "alive was better" than being dead—even after suffering rape or witnessing one's family murdered.[105] With life, hope. Temporary suffering, physical or emotional, can be overcome. Nevertheless, though it is never explicitly stated, physical functionality and even beauty seem necessary for a valuable life. Dr. Icove's "wowzer" physician-mother cannot be returned to her previous appearance, so she self-terminates; the loss of her looks becomes the loss of her life.[106] In contrast, Mira describes a friend who became a client of Icove's after a brutal rape and beating by an ex. "She was lucky to live through it . . . a medley of pain and potential disfigurement." Physical recovery to the status quo ante seems a sine qua non of post-injury flourishing: "He gave her her face back, and that—along with several years of therapy—helped her get her life back."[107] This is unlike Icove's permanently disfigured mother, who, like Humpty Dumpty, could not be put back together again. Those who only wish to live forever while young, rich, and beautiful are ridiculed; those who declare that the poor and ill should not have the same chances are condemned. Yet underlying anxieties about difference and disability undermine these affirmations of equality.

In contrast to the series' persistent unease about physical debility and its resulting constricted way of thinking about living with (acquired) disabilities, Robb thinks expansively and creatively about flourishing in the wake of other changes, challenges, and upheavals: the families of choice in which many series characters participate. Dallas, Roarke, and others come from profoundly damaged and damaging families. They find surrogate parents and make colleagues into friends and friends into family. They are informally adopted into existing families. Rediscovery of biological relatives is sometimes disastrous, as with Dallas' mother, and sometimes wonderful, as when Roarke in short order learns of his true parentage, his mother's death, and the existence of an extended clan including his Aunt Sinead, his mother's twin sister. When they encounter each other, they recognize and mourn loss. At the same time, they celebrate newly developing connections.

Child survivor Nixie Swisher presents another instance of explicitly negotiated familial ties outside of biological relation. She suffered tremendous loss when revenge killers slew her family and also her safety net: because Nixie's best friend was mistakenly killed in her place, her friend's parents, who ordinarily would have taken Nixie in, believed themselves incapable of doing so. Dallas and Roarke provide temporary refuge, then arrange—through individual connections outside the auspices of social services—for her to be fostered, and then eventually adopted, by Elizabeth Barrister and Richard DeBlass, who had lost their own adult daughter to murder. (Sharon DeBlass was the victim whose death brought Eve and Roarke together.) They had already adopted another child, a boy whose mother was alive but neglectful and abusive. Dallas acknowledges Nixie's loss: "You got kicked hard." She reminds her that the "good people" who want to take her in "know about getting kicked hard." They are proposing to give her "a place" and "a family." Nixie will have a mother, father, and brother, connected not by blood but by love. They will not replace the ones she lost. "It's never going to be what it was, but it can be something else."[108]

You could get dead

In contrast to those who devalue human life, or who believe that they ought to be able to determine who lives and who dies, equal care for the dead serves as the bedrock for Dallas' ethical practice. She stands for all the dead assigned to her. When an informant named Ratso seeks justice for a murdered underworld contact, he wants Dallas on the case: "How much you figure most cops gonna bother with someone like Fixer?" She insists, "There are plenty of cops who'll . . . work their butt off trying to close the case." Ratso stands firm, insisting that she'll "work harder."[109] He is probably right; examples abound of lackadaisical police work. Once, Dallas arranges for good detectives in another branch to reinvestigate the murder of a (reluctant) witness' husband.[110] Dallas cares about the deaths of the poor and disenfranchised as well as the wealthy and connected; she seeks justice for the innocent and beloved as well as the guilty and the jerks.[111] As she explains, "If they're not people to me, what's the point?"[112]

Although the deaths of those she stands for engage her emotions, she keeps a tight rein on herself.[113] Others sometimes mistake her composure for lack of caring.[114] Instead, it is a defense mechanism. As she explains, "When you stand over death you stay cold so it can't get inside you."[115] It does, though, and those close to her realize that her ability to imagine the murders makes her excel at her job but also takes its toll.[116]

Dallas combines "a basic dislike of people" with "unstinting and bottomless compassion for them."[117] The root of this compassion is a recognition of shared mortality. The corollary to the sign's proclamation "you could get dead" is "I could get dead." Yet as philosopher Martha Nussbaum points out, "Our society is full of refusals to imagine one another with empathy and compassion, refusals from which none of us is free. Many of the stories we tell one another encourage the refusal of compassion, so not even the literary imagination itself is free from blame."[118] Individuals and institutions in Dallas' orbit sometimes laud and often act on these values of compassion, as the sign commands. Those who fail to do so—uncaring cops, scheming physicians, elitist murderers—fail to recognize others as fully human..

Creators and scholars alike often appeal to imagination as a vital tool for remedying harmful exclusions that replicate contemporary patterns of unhealthy and oppressive structures.[119] Futuristic fantasy authors decide what to keep, what to jettison, and—vitally—how to explain, explicitly or implicitly, these choices. The squad-room sign proclaiming the equal significance of all human deaths and, therefore, all human lives is one of the few places where racial discrimination appears as a possibility, invoked only to be immediately rejected. Such gestures alert the attentive reader that there is more at play than the continual invocation of the mixed-race category suggests. Some exclusions persist, unnamed and unrecognized. The overwhelming whiteness of Dallas' female friends and the near-total absence of people with disabilities from her beloved city appear as natural and normal, unquestioned. Yet it matters when such choices appear *as choices*. Rationales for cloning or organ theft or widespread social engineering are exposed to the scorn they deserve. Readers rightly despise the man who, disgusted by his aged and disabled grandmother's debility, leaves her to die. The more insidious—because never explicitly stated—assumption that physical dependence and acquired disability might make life not worth living can best be decisively rejected when the assumptions that undergird it are brought, explicitly, to the fore.

Conclusion
Ending in Death

It is fall 2060. A disgruntled descendant of an Urban War–era cult leader has unleashed a deadly chemical weapon in two New York City eateries, inducing violent delusions that cause grisly massacres. His motivation is personal, born of resentment rather than zeal. He has no qualms about killing hundreds or thousands to settle his petty grudges. Dallas must find him before he strikes again. During a brief respite from the manhunt, she wakes in her husband's arms with her cat cuddled nearby. She reflects, "The world's so fucked up, Roarke, but right here? It's all just exactly right."[1] At that moment, cozily ensconced in her palatial home, Dallas has attained the stereotypical romantic fantasy: everlasting hot monogamy and egalitarian partnership with "her ridiculously sexy husband."[2] She cannot rest on her happily ever after, though. Outside her gates, everything is far from alright. She will eventually capture the mass murderer threatening her city, cage him, and allow the flawed justice system to take its course. She will bypass formal channels and use personal resources to keep tabs on a secretive government agency, ensuring that the killer's deadly formula does not fall into the wrong hands. But there are limits to what she can do. She can neither single-handedly fix the broken world nor abandon her duty to serve and protect.

In Death celebrates the possibilities and acknowledges the limits of human endeavor. Just as the books mix romance, crime, and science fiction elements in varying proportions, so its characters balance the intimate and the societal, personal happiness and professional responsibility. Content in her complicated, committed relationship,

Dallas still encounters unspeakable evil, mundane wrongdoing, and sheer unpleasantness in her daily life.[3] Her loving partnership does not erase bad feelings but buffers them, enabling her to do her work effectively for the long term. Roarke and a community of friends and colleagues sometimes provide respite from the world's brokenness. At other times, they struggle alongside her to repair it or at least stave off further devastation. They cannot resurrect the dead, but they can find answers, seek justice, and promote healing.

In Death does not seek to make the world anew. Through Dallas, Robb critiques elements of the society she depicts: relentless consumerism, lingering sexism, sexual violence, police and corporate corruption, and old-moneyed white guys who think they can get away with anything. Dallas harbors no hope of eradicating humanity's violent inclinations or transforming society wholesale. She distrusts wide-eyed idealist movements for radical social change. Dallas is skeptical, too, of political reforms; she holds low opinions of both politicians' morals and their effectiveness. Though leery of invasive government surveillance, she accepts it, evading at times without ever challenging outright. She works within the system despite its serious failings. In Dallas' estimation, the criminal justice system, like all government programs, is imperfect but not irremediably broken.[4] With her connivance, Roarke bends or bypasses rules in service of her goals. She, too, frequently finesses procedures or finagles exceptions.

Similar patterns emerge beyond her professional activities when she engages in ad hoc, impulsive generosity.[5] She acknowledges seemingly intractable large-scale poverty and accepts that it sucks.[6] Neither she nor Roarke suggests overhauling or privatizing the overburdened, dubiously effective foster care system. Neither succumbs to the neoliberal temptation to propose market solutions to poverty. In In Death's fictive world, the only ones who espouse grand theories and advocate sweeping reforms are ineffectual politicians and delusional megalomaniacs.

Robb has a point in treating utopian projects with skepticism. In the nonfictional world, those who want to make society better have often been willing to sacrifice many along the way. Good intentions can lead to terrible outcomes. After all, people who cared about the well-being of those sentenced for crimes promoted the prison as a contemplative space of retreat more conducive to reform than the brutality of corporal punishment.[7] Ending institutionalization of people living with mental illness was prompted by important concerns, but without adequate supports at the other end, homelessness (and addiction, and more incarceration) have often resulted.[8] Small-scale initiatives and individual acts of charity may be more appealing than big-picture change, though they leave too many people in need. At the same time (and as the books recognize), legislative changes can have important repercussions: a stipend for stay-at-home parents clearly represents a utopian hope and, perhaps, a minimum legislative goal.

The series is at its best when it raises difficult questions without endorsing solutions. It often stages clashes of perspectives, allowing each argument's merits to emerge. The system provided an (imperfect) refuge for Dallas, while Roarke was sustained by personal connection outside of it. Many who mistrust the system have good reasons. Vigilante justice is wrong—except when it isn't. Divergent perspectives on the law receive explicit, ongoing discussion, as do difficult questions about the source of seemingly inhuman violence. Even when the books tend to present one notion as obvious, such as the necessity of long, unpleasant prison sentences for those convicted of crimes, references to exceptional situations (a wrongful conviction, a woman whose sentence was disproportionate to her crime, fatal prison violence) allow for reading against the grain. Robb presents the police positively overall but seeds plentiful exceptions of corrupt, ineffectual, and abusive cops. Her repeated, passing references to grinding poverty and dangerous, violent neighborhoods could be read as a mere sop to noir atmosphere. The ways in which desperate poverty fades quickly from the forefront of storylines might also be read as an acknowledgment that privileged audiences tend to shift attention from long-term structural obstacles to well-being toward urgent, seemingly isolated incidents of violence.

Readers must navigate and negotiate these perspectives.[9] Recent debates over diversity in literature have tended to focus on the author's responsibility to reflect the world, not necessarily in straightforwardly representational ways—art can effect transformations less easily accomplished in life—but by avoiding harmful exclusions and caricatures on the page. A writer who depicts characters and communities beyond her experience must strive to do so in nonstereotypical ways.[10] Absolutely true. But the weighty burden of changing and challenging representations must be shared by readers. This means buying books about diverse characters by authors who come from those groups and voting with one's wallet for more inclusive fictional worlds. It also means, with series like In Death, engaging more appreciatively and critically—engaging fully—with the societies and characters they present.[11]

Fictive worlds are not direct analogues for contemporary society. Some lessons learned by paying attention are transferable, however. Readers can become attuned to the ways an author conjures whiteness while rendering it invisible or depicts policing as race-neutral, as though racism suddenly evaporated in the early twenty-first century, leaving no notable traces. Readers can notice—and perhaps emulate—effective mentoring strategies while perceiving how continual expectations of availability for work have become normalized and consider how platitudes about work-life balance may or may not help make sense of their own lives. Readers can appreciate how characters build relationships across differences of experience and temperament, and they can observe the diverse approaches powerful women take to cultural norms of femininity. Recognizing continuities and discontinuities with present-day realities allows readers to read their social worlds afresh. They can notice when acceptable choices taken individually become troubling in the aggregate. They can notice when dominant scripts about female nurturing are outmoded and inadequate; they can perceive attractive alternatives. They can parse both novels and the news with attention to the story not told. Skills for assessing a literary world—evaluating, admiring, and criticizing—apply also to making sense of flesh-and-blood reality.

If imagination is part of the writer's toolkit for social transformation, the reader's more modest but also powerful tool is thoughtfulness. At its most basic, thoughtfulness is the rejection of thoughtlessness, the failure of the privileged to listen to or to consider others' experiences or perspectives.[12] Ethnic studies scholar C. Richard King offers "the cultivation of thoughtfulness" as a potential antidote to the "various mechanisms embedded in U.S. society that encourage Americans not to know, not to remember, and not to think." Reading thoughtfully can serve as precursor and adjunct to living thoughtfully.[13] Cultivating more inclusive and more just societies requires recognizing what currently exists. Thoughtful engagement with fictive worlds, like the one Robb so richly depicts, is a place to begin that essential work.

Notes

The notes cite Robb's novels and novellas by shortened title. Scholarly sources appear in full on first occurrence. The bibliography contains full publication details for all cited works.

Introduction

1 Lauren Collins offers an accessible profile of Roberts (Collins, "Real Romance: How Nora Roberts Became America's Most Popular Novelist," *The New Yorker*, June 22, 2009). Roberts began to publish under the pseudonym Robb partly out of concern about saturating the market with her novels (Denise Little and Laura Hayden, eds., *The Official Nora Roberts Companion* [New York: Berkley, 2003], 16, 26, 59). In addition to the scores of novels she has published as Roberts, since 1995 she has published two In Death novels yearly and sometimes a novella as well; more are due to appear. An Goris discusses the relationship between Roberts and Robb as authors in her PhD dissertation, "From Romance to Roberts and Back Again: Genre, Authorship, and the Construction of Textual Identity in Contemporary Popular Romance Novels" (Leuven: University of Leuven, 2011). I use "Robb" when referring to the author of the In Death novels.

2 Goris, "From Romance to Roberts," 411; John Lennard, *Of Modern Dragons and Other Essays on Genre Fiction* (Penrith, UK: Humanities-Ebooks, 2007), 56. Additionally, the novellas, beginning with "Haunted in Death," gesture toward the paranormal. The genre fluidity of the series is such that its audiobook narrator, Susan Ericksen, won awards in sequential years for "Science Fiction & Fantasy" (2009's *Promises in Death*) and "Mystery & Suspense" (for 2010's *Fantasy in Death*).

3 Pamela Regis terms romance "the most popular, least respected literary genre" (Regis, *A Natural History of the Romance Novel* [Philadelphia: University of Pennsylvania Press, 2003], xi). Eric Selinger and

Sarah Frantz call it "the despised and rejected 'other' of modern literary writing" (Selinger and Frantz, "Introduction," in *New Approaches to Popular Romance Fiction*, ed. Sarah S. G. Frantz and Eric Murphy Selinger, 1–20 [Jefferson, N.C.: McFarland, 2012], 3). Diana Gabaldon writes, humorously as well as denigratingly, on negotiating herself out of the romance genre (Gabaldon, *The Outlandish Companion* [New York: Delacorte, 2015], 2:434–41). It has become de rigueur to observe critical disdain for romance novels (e.g., Laura Vivanco, *For Love and Money: The Literary Art of the Harlequin Mills & Boon Romance* [Penrith, UK: Humanities-Ebooks, 2011], 11–17); Maya Rodale makes pointing out such criticism a centerpiece of her *Dangerous Books for Girls: The Bad Reputation of Romance Novels Explained* (Middletown, Del.: n.p., 2015); Smart Bitches, Trashy Books website founders Sarah Wendell and Candy Tan discuss it in their smart and sassy *Beyond Heaving Bosoms: The Smart Bitches' Guide to Romance Novels* (New York: Fireside, 2009). Jayashree Kamblé discusses "a fake genre" she terms "Media Romance," which "exists as a kind of metafiction in the public imagination" (Kamblé, *Making Meaning in Popular Romance Fiction: An Epistemology* [New York: Palgrave, 2014], 21). Selinger notes that although "undisguised contempt" no longer reigns unchallenged, "disdain for popular romance fiction remains a way to demonstrate one's intelligence, political bona fides, and demanding aesthetic sensibility, even in circles where resistance to such orthodoxies is the norm" (Eric Murphy Selinger, "Review: Rereading the Romance," *Contemporary Literature* 48, no. 2 [2007]: 307–24 at 310, 308). It is not incidental to this derision and denigration that women dominate romance publishing, writing, and readership. Although critical skepticism exists about genre fiction as a whole (Lennard, *Of Modern Dragons*, 10–13), the "habitual contempt of men and literati" applies especially to romance—as Lennard acknowledges before falling into the same dismissive trap (59, 61–62). According to Romance Writers of America, men constitute just under a tenth of romance readers (Hsu-Ming Teo, *Desert Passions: Orientalism and Romance Novels* [Austin: University of Texas Press, 2012], 283; also Catherine M. Roach, *Happily Ever After: The Romance Story in Popular Culture* [Bloomington: Indiana University Press, 2016], 5). My secondhand copy of Robb's *Big Jack* illustrates this disrespect while revealing its gendered nature. One reader wrote "good book!!" on the inside cover. A later, presumably male, reader crossed out "good" and wrote "silly womans [*sic*] book," demonstrating his critical acumen by adding a frowny face. Critical distaste for romance means that "the scholarly community has consistently turned a cold shoulder to one of the world's most massively read authors" (Goris, "From Romance to Roberts," 12). There is strikingly little scholarship on Roberts and even less on Robb. Goris' dissertation and articles as well as a few chapters (Regis, *Natural History*, 183–204) or parts of chapters (Laura Vivanco, *Pursuing Happiness: Reading American Romance as Political Fiction* [Penrith, UK: Humanities-Ebooks, 2016], 90–91, 93–103) in monographs or anthologies (Christina A. Valeo, "The Power of Three: Nora Roberts and Serial Magic," in Frantz and Selinger, *New Approaches*, 229–40) are supplemented by snippets in other analyses of romance. Roberts' influence goes beyond her impact on readers; Goris, "From Romance to Roberts," 85, notes that in key ways "Nora Roberts has decisively influenced the common practices of the genre as a whole." Writing of Roberts' books (not Robb's), Valeo argues that "the message of empowerment permeates all of them. Her stories are peopled by powerful women and so suggest that women are powerful" (Valeo, "Power of Three," in Frantz and Selinger, *New Approaches*, 238); similarly, Hsu-Ming Teo considers Roberts "one of the most progressive and politically liberal romance novelists writing in the United States today," a "liberal, progressive, feminist" and "antiracist writer" (Teo, *Desert Passions*, 228–29). Mary Ellen Snodgrass, whose *Reading Nora Roberts* (Santa Barbara, Calif.: Greenwood, 2010) orients the lay reader to Roberts' oeuvre, calls Roberts' work feminist and declares Eve Dallas a feminist heroine. She values Robb/Roberts' literary merit and strong characterization, drawing a sneering contrast to other, stereotypical romance writing. Snodgrass' chapter "J. D. Robb Novels" (69–89) covers the series until 2009 but draws most of its analysis from the first novel, *Naked in Death*. Goris' dissertation focuses on Roberts' romance novels but discusses In Death as well (Goris, "From Romance to Roberts," esp. 402–32. (I read this dissertation only once this book was essentially complete. There are similarities in our analyses, especially of the courtship narrative, and salient disagreements as well, which I indicate in the notes.) Two other books devote some attention to Robb: the chapter "Of Pseudonyms and Sentiment: Nora Roberts, J. D. Robb, and the Imperative Mood," in Lennard's *Of Modern Dragons*, and a section of Kamblé's *Making Meaning*, 49–57.

4 Writing of black cultural production, feminist cultural critic bell hooks distinguishes "between hostile critique that is about 'trashing' and critique that's about illuminating and enriching our understanding" (hooks, *Yearning: Race, Gender, and Cultural Politics* [Boston: South End Press, 1990], 7). She argues for "critiques that offer critical insight without serving as a barrier to appreciation." See also hooks, *Writing Beyond Race: Living Theory and Practice* (New York: Routledge, 2013), 124. Some writers strongly separate serious or literary works from popular, pulp, or junk writing (hooks, *Writing Beyond Race*, 161), while others acknowledge such differences but recognize genre "blurring" (Annie Dillard, *Living by Fiction* [New York: Harper & Row, 1983], 80–81). In his *An Aesthetics of Junk Fiction* (Athens: University of Georgia Press, 1990), Tom Roberts argues that genre demands reading strategies that differ from those appropriate to literary fiction. On the attempt to discourage readers from bringing literary-critical methods to bear on romance novels, consult Selinger and Frantz's "Introduction" and Selinger's chapter "How

to Read a Romance Novel (and Fall in Love with Popular Romance)," in Frantz and Selinger, *New Approaches*; and also Wendell and Tan, *Beyond Heaving Bosoms*, 197–99.

5 *Kindred*, 1.

Chapter 1

1 *Naked*, 5. Readers never learn when or why "Security" was added to the mandate of the NYPD, founded in 1845. For a history of the NYPD, with particular attention to its use of violence, consult Marilynn S. Johnson, *Street Justice: A History of Police Violence in New York City* (Boston: Beacon, 2003).

2 As Annamarie Jagose notes, "Sex has often been the ambivalent focus of quotidian and utopian projects of sociopolitical transformation" (Jagose, *Orgasmology* [Durham, N.C.: Duke University Press, 2013], 177). On sex work as work, consult Melissa Gira Grant, *Playing the Whore: The Work of Sex Work* (New York: Verso, 2014). Gira Grant insists that "under criminalization, sex work *is* regulated—by the criminal and legal system, by cops" (131, emphasis in original). The police remain involved in In Death's system of government licensure, where those operating without licenses, or with the wrong type of license, remain subject to arrest or fine. As Gira Grant writes, "Forced registration just looks like policing by a different name to sex workers" (132). The system neglects something Gira Grant deems vital: "Sex workers' ability to share information among themselves is essential for supporting all sex workers in negotiating their work, and in turning down work that is unsafe, underpaid, or undesirable" (29). In In Death, elite sex workers individually scrutinize clients, at times extensively, and may communicate informally with each other, but there is no collective organization. There is a clear hierarchy—but also a continuum—between "street-level prostitution" (54; *street level* is also a term used in In Death) and its more exclusive counterparts. Sex clubs exist, but there is no real concept of sex work. LCs are licensed, trained, and certified, and they work at different levels (*Origin*, 80–81); disturbed people are prevented from getting licenses (*Devoted*, 306; *Festive*, 224). Robb's program of sexual and social hygiene, progressive on the face of it, coexists with ongoing and regular victimization of (mostly female) sex workers, ranging from street violence, including rape, and harassment by clients and cops (*Creation*, 123; *Ceremony*, 222; *Imitation*, 74 [which extends to strippers]; *Calculated*, 153 [also giving an example of an LC who routinely offers "freebies to cops, and firefighters, when I can. To show my support."]; *Delusion*, 147; *Thankless*, 143; *Obsession*, 130; *Judgment*, 186; *Holiday*, 277–78) up to murder (*Naked*; *Imitation*; *Indulgence*). As one parole officer observes when an LC assigned to her gets murdered: "Cops, emergency and health workers, prostitutes. Dangerous professions with a high mortality rate" (*Imitation*, 18). On "widespread police misconduct toward sex workers and people profiled as sex

workers" in New York, see Grant, *Playing the Whore,* 4–5; for a much earlier example, see Johnson, *Street Justice,* 22. Readers of the series will recall one recurring character who is an LC, Charles Monroe, introduced in the first book. While he works as an LC, he becomes involved with doctor Louise DiMatto. He eventually abandons sex work for a career as a sex therapist. Though Dallas overcomes her early hesitations about him (*Holiday,* 244), it is difficult to imagine a female LC becoming part of her social circle. (Gira Grant points out that in the "prostitute imaginary" [4], "men who work in the sex trade are rarely considered members of the same occupation" [19].) At the most exclusive level, there are twice as many male as female LCs (*Indulgence,* 101), though overall more women than men work as LCs (*Origin,* 112).

3 Regis posits eight essential elements in the romance novel: society defined, the meeting, the barrier, the attraction, the declaration, point of ritual death, the recognition, and the betrothal (Regis, *Natural History,* 30–38). These elements are spread throughout the first three books of the In Death series. Jan Cohn discusses obstacles and antipathy throughout her *Romance and the Erotics of Property: Mass-Market Fiction for Women* (Durham, N.C.: Duke University Press, 1988).

4 *Naked,* 54.

5 *Loyalty,* 16 (reprised in *Brotherhood,* 286). Roarke's literary forebears include Rhett Butler, "the first important hero of romance fiction to be allowed and valued for economic aggressiveness" (Cohn, *Romance and the Erotics of Property,* 148). Like Butler, Roarke "carries the distinguishing marks of conventional villainy. He is dark, marked with power rather than aristocratic languor, charged with sexuality" (147). On the shift to busyness and industriousness as moral goods, see Judy Wajcman, *Pressed for Time: The Acceleration of Life in Digital Capitalism* (Chicago: University of Chicago Press, 2015).

6 *Naked,* 43.

7 Robb vacillates a bit (or Roarke mentally rewrites history): at first he says, "I didn't make you for a cop. . . . I saw a woman. I saw *the* woman" (*Reunion,* 99, emphasis in original). Later (*Fantasy,* 204) he says, "I knew you for a cop the moment I laid eyes on you." What doesn't change is his certainty that she will change things. Recognizing her was "annoying" (*Ritual,* 154).

8 *Naked,* 83. It also presumes heterosexuality; though Dallas has never met the officer before, she assumes his fiancée is female.

9 *Betrayal,* 238.

10 Scholars tend to treat the hero's journey to emotional vulnerability as the crux of romance; his "I love you" is the "money shot" (Roach, *Happily Ever After,* 102). Although Roarke coming to love Dallas matters, In Death focuses on her accepting emotional vulnerability (Goris, "From Romance to Roberts," 404–5), inverting the typical script. Lennard

connects their clashing "imperatives" to the clash of genres: "Crime going to the woman, Romance to the man" (Lennard, *Of Modern Dragons*, 73).

11 *Naked*, 55; also *Kindred*, 76. He eventually gives her diamonds, starting with a massive pendant. She first rejects it, not only as tangible wealth but as a symbol of his emotions. She accepts it when she acknowledges his love for her and her love for him (*Glory*, 122). Robb refers to this "baby-fist-sized diamond" and what it symbolizes repeatedly (e.g., *Rapture*, 82; *Seduction*, 159; *Treachery*, 8; other diamonds appear as well: e.g., "Ritual," 130). Diamonds play a central role in *Big Jack* (e.g., 286). (*Big Jack* was originally published in *Remember When*, a one-volume pairing of Robb's *Big Jack* and a Roberts novel, *Hot Rocks*.) Diamonds also play roles in "Haunted"; *Innocent*, 295; and *Memory*, 321–22. Dallas dislikes the usual male-apology presents; one of her colleagues insists to Roarke, "A sack of diamonds from the Blue Mines on Taurus I wouldn't work, unless you knocked her in that block of wood she calls a head with them" (*Divided*, 247).

12 Later, she expects jewelry but gets chocolate: "I know the way to your heart, Lieutenant" (*Witness*, 203). Her predilection for coffee becomes a running joke that she married him for it (e.g., *Naked*, 55; *Judgment*, 87; *Ceremony*, 287).

13 Dallas reminisces about Roarke's gift to her in a way that likens him to the criminal who tricked sixteen-year-old innocent Deena MacMasters into a relationship before raping and murdering her. Dallas acknowledges that she ignored her better judgment to get involved with Roarke—and "got lucky" (*Kindred*, 76). Perhaps this is Robb's belated acknowledgment that Roarke crossed a line with that courtship ploy.

14 Kamblé's *Making Meaning* analyzes how traits of heroes change over time. Even "inspirational" romances aimed at evangelical Christian readers "provide models of marriage that resonate more with the contemporary companionate and egalitarian secular ideal of marriage than with traditional marriage espoused by socially conservative Christians" (Rebecca Barrett-Fox, "Christian Romance Novels: Inspiring Convention and Challenge," in *Romance Fiction and American Culture: Love as the Practice of Freedom?*, ed. William A. Gleason and Eric Murphy Selinger, 347–68 [Burlington, Vt.: Ashgate, 2016], 347). There has been, perhaps, a bit of a backlash to the taming of the alpha male, with dominance springing up in paranormal romances—where creaturely heroes' jealousy and controlling instincts can be justified as part of their nature—and kinky erotic romance. Although E. L. James' *Fifty Shades of Grey* (New York: Vintage Books, 2011), based on Stephenie Meyer's *Twilight* (New York: Little, Brown, 2005) with its vampire hero, seems to bridge the two, a flourishing erotic subgenre focused on dominance and submission already existed; in contrast to *Fifty Shades*, much of that literature deals thoughtfully with consent and power. On negotiations of masculinity in popular romance, consult also Ananya Mukherjea's "My Vampire

Boyfriend: Postfeminism, 'Perfect' Masculinity, and the Contemporary Appeal of Paranormal Romance," *Studies in Popular Culture* 33, no. 2 (2011): 1–20.

15 *Betrayal*, 173. Names are a big deal in the In Death universe; in our world, too, politics matter in deciding what names to use. Strict symmetry is impossible, given that Roarke goes by a single name. I mostly use Dallas throughout, but I use Eve when the context seems appropriate, especially when it is her relationship with Roarke.

16 The idea that marriages or courtships fall flat because women ignore men's power features in the 1970s best-seller *The Total Woman* (see Kristin Celello, *Making Marriage Work: A History of Marriage and Divorce in the Twentieth-Century United States* [Chapel Hill: University of North Carolina Press, 2009], 128–30) and numerous more recent books such as *The Surrendered Wife* or *The Rules*.

17 Scholars have debated whether popular romance novels are conservative, liberating, or a mix. Early scholarship on the genre argued that the novels helped dissatisfied women tolerate their lot. Romance fiction, in this analysis, functions as a pressure valve: rather than sowing the seeds for new forms of satisfying relationality beyond the prescriptive marriage plot, it sublimates and diverts dissatisfactions. More recent scholarship has recognized the complexity of popular romance. Selinger notes that "at the start of the 1990s, the anger at patriarchy and longings for comfort, communication, and egalitarian relationship that feminist scholars like [Janice] Radway and Tania Modleski had seen as unconscious *subtexts* in romance fiction were often freely espoused, not just by the genre's heroines, but also by their authors" (Eric Murphy Selinger, "Editor's Introduction: Nothing But Good Times Ahead: A Special Forum on Jennifer Crusie," *Journal of Popular Romance Studies* 2, no. 2 [2012], emphasis in original). (For another recent brief overview of "inquiry into the genre," consult Eric Murphy Selinger and William A. Gleason, "Introduction: Love as the Practice of Freedom?" in Gleason and Selinger, *Romance Fiction and American Culture*, 11–15.) Pamela Regis critiques early critics of the genre in her *Natural History* and offers a strongly positive notion of how romance texts model freedom and liberation for women. Roach acknowledges conservative as well as "transgressive and empowering" (Roach, *Happily Ever After*, 11) elements at play. Drawing on the notion that romance "offer[s] a fantasy safe space that addresses these anxieties and has them all work out" (15), she considers this good rather than bad, ultimately arguing that it "functions . . . as a reparation fantasy about the end of patriarchy itself" (17). Writing about speculative fiction, attending to the material constraints of publication and circulation, André Carrington observes that "genre fiction" is "both deeply invested in market imperatives that buttress the existing social order and, occasionally, more imaginative or diversionary than texts that present realistic treatments of

everyday life" (Carrington, *Speculative Blackness: The Future of Race in Science Fiction* [Minneapolis: University of Minnesota Press, 2016], 14).

18 *Glory*, 112; *Reunion*, 173.

19 *Conspiracy*, 31.

20 Little and Hayden, *Official Nora Roberts Companion*, 438, 448, 441, 408. Roarke also features in Sarah Wendell's list of best romance heroes (Wendell, *Everything I Know about Love I Learned from Romance Novels* [Napervlle, Ill: Sourcebooks Casablanca, 2011], 78–80). Personal communication in 2nd Edition Booksellers, Raleigh-Durham Airport, June 15, 2015.

21 After the first three courtship novels, which collectively cover about six months, each installment covers less time. Using novels published through 2007, Lennard calculates about "2,300 pages per calendar year" (Lennard, *Of Modern Dragons*, 72); using all publications to date, I calculate at least twice that (15,664 pages total in the editions I list in the bibliography). For comparison, Sue Grafton's Kinsey Milhone novels began as contemporary detective novels but became, quickly, period pieces; her detective has no cell phone, for instance. Amanda Cross' Kate Fansler novels and Ian Rankin's John Rebus novels stay roughly in sync with the times. Walter Mosely's Easy Rawlins novels, set in the mid-twentieth century, span two decades but have become set more closely together as they approach 1970.

22 bell hooks, *All About Love: New Visions* (New York: William Morrow, 2000), 181.

23 Much grappling over romance fiction's ethics and aesthetics focuses on the so-called Happily Ever After, or "HEA." Goris notes that the "HEA" is "not simply an optional or convenient ending to the popular romance narrative, but a generic must" (Goris, "From Romance to Roberts," 27). A recent study argues that the ending—in which "the woman always wins"—matters most: "By the end, the heroine is happy, safe, financially secure, well loved, sexually satisfied, and set up for a fulfilling life (as is the hero). A warm circle of friends supports her; bad guys have been brought to justice; families are reconciled" (Roach, *Happily Ever After*, 26). Roach emphasizes the central role of the ending and its eschatological function in the love story as a kind of American cultural religion: "What is most important about the romance story is this ending toward which it moves" (173). Laura Vivanco suggests that the insistence on "happy endings" is particularly American; drawing on psychologist Dan McAdams, she suggests they are "redemption narratives" (Vivanco, *Pursuing Happiness*, 19–21). Others downplay the significance of the ending: it is formally necessary but not necessarily representative of the full significance of what has been worked out along the way (Regis, *Natural History*, 9–12). Jonathan Allan suggests scholars should focus on heteronormativity, "continuity and futurity" in romances (Allan, "Reading

the Regis Roundtable: An Outsider's Perspective," *Journal of Popular Romance Studies* 3, no. 2 [2013]: 4).

24 On serialization, consult An Goris, "Happily Ever After . . . and After: Serialization and the Popular Romance Novel," *Americana: The Journal of American Popular Culture (1900 to Present)* 12, no. 1 (2013). Roberts is strongly associated with serialization (Goris, "From Romance to Roberts," 231–32). John Lennard suggests that crime fiction is well suited to striking "the commercially requisite balance between the episodic, satisfactorily concluding within the volume, and the ongoing drive of a series in exploring the continuing lives of people and place" (Lennard, *Of Modern Dragons,* 14). Goris suggests that "Eve's and Roarke's post-HEA consists of a repetitive partial re-enactment of the core dynamic of the romance courtship—they run into and overcome barriers time and again—in a process that is represented as consistently strengthening their romantic union" (Goris, "From Romance to Roberts," 420).

25 *Portrait,* 190–91; *Treachery,* 48, 92. "Marriage, to Eve's mind, was a kind of obstacle course. You had to learn when to jump over, when to belly under, and when to stop your forward motion and change direction" (*Survivor,* 98). Kristen Celello explains that communication has become increasingly central to notions of marital success (Celello, *Making Marriage Work*).

26 Once, Roarke inadvertently undermines her professional authority (*Reunion,* 304–6, 312–13). He later approaches a similar situation differently, saying, "One tries to learn by one's mistakes" (*Imitation,* 323).

27 *Portrait,* 49.

28 Cohn, writing in 1988, argues that the hero "come[s] to recognize that the heroine's career is of value and that, in fact, she is the woman he loves precisely because of her competence and commitment" (Cohn, *Romance and the Erotics of Property,* 113). Far from being the essential transformation here, this is Roarke's starting point.

29 *Survivor,* 153; *Celebrity,* 34. Roarke seldom uses "baby" or other diminutive endearments, except when she emerges from a terrible nightmare or on similarly charged occasions (e.g., *Portrait,* 186; *Betrayal,* 171; "Taken," 75).

30 Kamblé notes, "The single-mindedness with which Eve discharges her professional duties, even after she takes on the new role of a wife, is a distinguishing feature of the series and is a crucial component of its appeal. From the beginning, her world is the center of the narrative, one into which Roarke enters as her partner rather than requiring her to enter his to play the role of corporate wife. . . . Roarke accepts the segueing of his narrative into hers" (Kamblé, *Making Meaning,* 50). As for the possibility of reciprocity, Roarke has to do some of his own work, but offers, "If you're still at it when I'm done, I'll give you a hand." When she repeats the offer, he replies, "That's a very nasty threat" (*Portrait,* 57; similarly, *Purity,* 333). On her interest in his work, see *Imitation,*

170–71; *Calculated,* 108–9; and *Vengeance,* 279: "I stay out of his business, which is more than he does for me."

31 *Reunion,* 151. Kamblé points out, "Her dashes across continents and Roarke's freedom to accompany her undeniably rest on his independence of a time clock, and on the assurance of comforts on the journey as well as the protection and upkeep of the home in their absence" (Kamblé, *Making Meaning,* 52). Judy Wajcman (*Pressed for Time,* 11, 61–62, 164) insists on "temporal sovereignty"—control over allocating one's time—as an element of life satisfaction. Roarke recognizes control over time as "a benefit of being in charge" (*Seduction,* 207); on Summerset's role in caring for the home, see *Origin,* 307.

32 Quote from *Salvation,* 197, 209; similarly, *Born,* 12.

33 *Purity,* 22. Similarly, *Vengeance,* 24: Roarke applies the same standard to both of them.

34 *Visions,* 5. Also *Innocent,* 39; *Imitation,* 48–49; *Vengeance,* 17.

35 He refers to this as when "we work together, or, more accurately, when I contribute to your work" (*Creation,* 42).

36 Alan Derickson discusses this "tradition of heroic manly sleeplessness" in his *Dangerously Sleepy: Overworked Americans and the Cult of Manly Wakefulness* (Philadelphia: University of Pennsylvania Press, 2014), 26. Laura Vivanco suggests it may apply to romance heroes in her blog post "Sleepless Masculinity," December 23, 2014, http://www.vivanco.me.uk/blog/post/sleepless-masculinity. *Twilight* vampire Edward Cullen is, in Stephenie Meyer's defanged reimagining, a literally sleepless hero. Kamblé describes Roarke as a "larger-than-life symbol of global capitalism" (Kamblé, *Making Meaning,* 50). On elite men, especially entrepreneurs, as "paragons of wakefulness," see Derickson, *Dangerously Sleepy,* 1–26. Roarke fits Derickson's category of the "elite short sleeper." When Dallas asks, "How come you can look sexy and relaxed after a couple hours' sleep and I feel like my brain's been used for Arena Ball practice," he replies, "Enormous strength of will and lucky metabolism" (*Creation,* 192).

37 *Immortal,* 242. Also *Vengeance,* 249; *Visions,* 301.

38 *Betrayal,* 179. Roarke's fatigue often connects to difficult emotional circumstances (e.g., *Portrait,* 178; *Judgment,* 297; *Divided,* 81).

39 Readers of the series will recognize this pattern from many novels. It figures prominently in *New York to Dallas,* where nightmares enter the equation. Others get into the act of encouraging her to rest in *Seduction in Death* (132, 280–83, 285, 319). Other examples include *Visions,* 170–71; *Loyalty,* 307.

40 *Purity,* 333. Jonathan Crary has noted that questions of "the reciprocity between vulnerability and trust, between exposure and care" coalesce around the question of sleep (Crary, *24/7: Late Capitalism and the Ends of Sleep* [New York: Verso, 2013], 28).

41 *Naked,* 100. Also *Conspiracy,* 89: "He hated seeing marks on her."

42 *Creation,* 40.

43 *Conspiracy*, 37; similarly, *Rapture*, 293–94. Her commander ensures that she gets professional treatment for an injury she calls "a scratch" and he calls a "knife wound" (*Indulgence*, 160–62). Lennard observes that male pressure to accept medical treatment is a "recurrent topos" in works by Robb and Roberts (Lennard, *Of Modern Dragons*, 68).

44 *Creation*, 297.

45 *Seduction*, 169; also related, *Rapture*, 187–89. A doctor friend says as much to her in the wake of a fairly serious set of injuries: "Don't be a hero" (*Reunion*, 255).

46 *Delusion*, 17.

47 *Fantasy*, 45; also *Imitation*, 173; *Purity*, 113.

48 E.g., *Indulgence*, 177.

49 E.g., *Survivor*, 287; *Creation*, 87. Summerset, too, schemes to pair green beans with her steak (*Born*, 255).

50 *Fantasy*, 94.

51 *Betrayal*, 151. On their relative scores in the taking-care-of-each-other category, see *Promises*, 139. Roarke sometimes inverts the usual pattern to take care of Summerset (e.g., *Delusion*, 193), who then reminds him to tend to Dallas (197–98).

52 *Seduction*, 58.

53 *Betrayal*, 172; similarly, *Rapture*, 279.

54 *Betrayal*, 174–75. Dallas objects to the term "wifely" (*Portrait*, 55; similarly, *Loyalty*, 139). When he watches her dress, declares, "You won't be warm enough in that," and hands her a sweater, she retorts, "You're a nag, Roarke" (*Conspiracy*, 116, also 163). Though he does much more "nagging" than she does, they think of it as a female-gendered trait. When Roarke urges her to eat or sleep, Eve says to him, "You're such a wife" (*Witness*, 291; similarly, *Portrait*, 63; *New York to Dallas*, 292; *Origin*, 137, 155 [where stereotypically "female and fussy," "wifely" behavior serves as a clue]). When Dallas cares for a very sick Feeney, he says to her, "You're turning into a woman on me, fussing and nagging." She's insulted and responds with the threat of bodily harm. He answers, "That's better" (*Strangers*, 102).

55 The erosion of boundaries between workplace and home (which themselves have a historical origin point), including Dallas' occasional decision to work with her team at home in addition to solo after-hours work at her home office, depends on seamless technology. Constant connectivity, presciently futuristic in 1995 when the first In Death book was published, seems ordinary two decades later. As everyday technology has caught up to that described in the series, some of Robb's terminology has shifted to more closely resemble present-day usage. Goris makes a similar observation in "From Romance to Roberts," 410n21. On the role of technology in the reconfiguration of "work-life boundaries," see Wajcman, *Pressed for Time*, 137–50.

56 *Survivor*, 74.

57 *Imitation*, 50. Similarly, when Roarke works for an hour on Christmas morning and Dallas wants to, she says, cheerfully, "We're really sick people, aren't we?'" Roarke replies, "I prefer thinking we're very healthy individuals who know what suits us best" (*Memory*, 327; also *Indulgence*, 80, 233). On their shared penchant for working at home, see *Memory*, 196; on working together, see *Memory*, 211; on what's normal for other people, see *Memory*, 279.

58 Readers frequently ask Roberts when the pair will have a child. She insists in interviews and her website FAQ that this will not happen anytime soon as it would alter the dynamic too greatly.

59 *Strangers*, 68. On the ways in which time pressures affect people differently based on gender as well as class, consult Wajcman, *Pressed for Time.*

60 *Survivor*, 151, 242, 259–60; *Imitation*, 118; *Promises*, 156; *Born*, 166, 241–42.

61 *Indulgence*, 117. Also *Calculated*, 185. The concerns Dallas expresses about character, blood, and destiny (e.g., *Delusion*, 109) might serve as a proxy for thinking about race. Roarke jokes about "family traditions." "Which will ours be, I wonder? Crime, of course, but which side of the spectrum?" (*Seduction*, 224). On reproduction and whiteness, consult Kamblé, *Making Meaning*, 141; Sharon Patricia Holland, *The Erotic Life of Racism* (Durham, N.C.: Duke University Press, 2012), 75. One might write a great deal about good, bad, absent, and surrogate mothers (and fathers) in In Death and Roberts' fiction (e.g., in her Chesapeake Bay Saga, where the heroes' biological mothers are abusive and their loving, strong, adoptive mother has died; and in the Bride Quartet, where one heroine's wonderful mother has died, another is indifferent, one is emotionally abusive, and one is lovely and solid).

62 *Imitation*, 120, 175–76. Childcare facilities presumably exist but are rarely if ever mentioned.

63 "Interlude," 43–44; *Brotherhood*, 69. Evelyn Nakano Glenn notes, "Too often, low wages for care workers are rationalized on the grounds that care work offers intrinsic rewards that compensate for lack of material rewards or even, especially in the case of family caregivers, that too much monetary compensation would undermine altruistic feelings" (Glenn, *Forced to Care: Coercion and Caregiving in America* [Cambridge, Mass.: Harvard University Press, 2012], 198). A few nonparental paid caregivers in In Death are abusive (in *Memory in Death*, a previous foster mother fostered only for the stipend; a nasty woman raised the murderer in *Imitation in Death*), while others are lovely ("Taken in Death," *Survivor in Death, Fantasy in Death*)—in other words, just like parents.

64 Celello chronicles the rise of "the idea that marriage required work—and that wives, in particular, should do most of it" (Celello, *Making Marriage Work*, 43). New expectations for companionate "marriages based on love, sexual gratification, and equality" did not eliminate gendered

expectations that women would perform housework and childcare while men would support them and head the household (22). On the gendered organization of household labor, see Wajcman, *Pressed for Time,* 116–18.

65 *Imitation,* 44.

66 Celello notes that "assumptions about gender have never ceased to be the basic factor in how Americans think about who benefits from marriage and who should perform the most marital work" (Celello, *Making Marriage Work,* 164). *Brotherhood in Death* uses the notion of marriage as work frequently (e.g., 115, 121).

67 *Judgment,* 338.

68 *Judgment,* 346. Similarly, *Rapture,* 269; *Origin,* 320, where they suit up for an op rather than go out to a club.

69 *Loyalty,* 15. Dallas does not know how much exactly Roarke's worth or to whom he's willed it (*Loyalty,* 80). Also *Immortal,* 3; *Strangers,* 176, 272, 355; *Memory,* 123–24; *Imitation,* 175. On household help, see *Seduction,* 54; *Purity,* 85. Kamblé notes that "as the series progresses, Eve is grudgingly accepting the benefits of being married to the richest man in the world" (Kamblé, *Making Meaning,* 52). "His love for Eve and his good works serve to justify the fact that her response to his money is changing from suspicion to annoyance and then to grudging acceptance. The progression also exonerates her—and the reader—of unquestioning submission to capitalism" (Kamblé, *Making Meaning,* 53). Dallas uses Roarke's wealth in the pursuit of her duties. Peabody asks, "What's it like being with a guy who can snap his fingers and get you pretty much whatever you need?" Dallas replies, briskly, "Convenient" (*Survivor,* 254; similarly, *Kindred,* 215). Yet Dallas recognizes, and the reader can as well, that wealth is seductive and that it requires tremendous effort to resist becoming accustomed to luxury (e.g., *Reunion,* 102, 264; *Strangers,* 172; *Kindred,* 218; *Fantasy,* 205–6) or jaded about money (e.g., *Memory,* 172, 272).

70 *Innocent,* 254. Though some wealthy people she encounters have personal assistants, Dallas vehemently rejects the notion that she might employ one (*Obsession,* 61–62).

71 *Kindred,* 2. Similarly, *Strangers,* 59; *Promises,* 159. Galahad "had very genuinely saved her life. Twice" (*Calculated,* 83). Dallas names him after he first plays the role of her "white knight" (*Naked,* 304); he also saves her by distracting the villain (in *New York to Dallas,* 364). He helps bring her out of nightmares (e.g., *Visions,* 72) and serves as a therapeutic resource for others (*Survivor,* 21, 41).

72 *Innocent,* 86.

73 *Salvation,* 43. Examples of Summerset's disdain: *Naked,* 290–91; and *Vengeance,* 15.

74 He is the only one allowed to be "less than solicitous" to her. Roarke explains why (*Immortal,* 88–92, quote from 89).

75 *Immortal,* 84.

76 *Immortal*, 90; *Portrait*, 197. In *Survivor* (130), "beaten half to death" is qualified: "More than half, come to that."

77 *Concealed*, 201.

78 *Treachery*, 34; *Origin*, 107–8; *Portrait*, 197; *Innocent*, 272.

79 This concern rears its head most directly in *Vengeance in Death*, where a killer targets people Roarke had used to take his own vengeance for another killing years earlier; questions of trust and competing loyalties arise (e.g., 77). Summerset and Eve are the only ones Roarke "trusted without reservation" and therefore the only people besides himself who were allowed in the room with his "unregistered and illegal" computers (*Witness*, 235). Viviana Zelizer explains the relationship between trust and intimacy: "Positively, trust means that the parties willingly share such knowledge and attention in the face of risky situations and their possible outcomes. Negatively, trust gives one person knowledge of, or attention to, the other, which if made widely available would damage the second person's social standing" (Zelizer, *The Purchase of Intimacy* [Princeton, N.J.: Princeton University Press, 2005], 15).

80 *Innocent*, 107, 186; *Memory*, 313.

81 *Brotherhood*, 139.

82 *Conspiracy*, 106. Summerset provokes Dallas similarly on other occasions, e.g., *Reunion*, 177. At other times, he recognizes her distress and contacts Roarke to intervene (*Ceremony*, 186; *Salvation*, 99; *Devoted*, 290). (Eve uses him to provide for Roarke's emotional needs, as when she mentions that Roarke could use a call from his aunt in Ireland [*Salvation*, 229].)

83 *Portrait*, 175, 186 (similarly, *Rapture*, 186; *Ritual*, 139).

84 *Portrait*, 139–41.

85 *Portrait*, 65. Zelizer defines a household narrowly as "two or more people who share living quarters and daily subsistence over substantial periods of time" and notes that "households in this narrower sense still include paid caregivers, foster children, lovers, and relatives, just so long as they share bed and board." As she points out, "Whatever pains and pleasures it brings, living in a household almost always engages household members in intimacy" (Zelizer, *Purchase of Intimacy*, 213).

86 On their quasifamilial relationship, see *Betrayal*, 288. When Peabody remarks that Roarke and Summerset being "like family" "makes [Eve] sort of like Summerset's daughter-in-law," Dallas is horrified (*Betrayal*, 293–94).

87 *Portrait*, 25.

88 *Portrait*, 175, 7, 51, 92. *Portrait*, 52, 92, discusses individuals lashing out at those close to them when they are unhappy.

89 *Portrait*, 139–41, 178. On another occasion, despite their mutual dislike, they cooperate when Roarke is in need (*Betrayal*, 144).

90 *Portrait*, 187. Similarly, *Fantasy*, 323–24.

91 *Portrait,* 198. However, Roarke sometimes pushes for personal life as a priority (e.g., *Thankless,* 251).

92 *Portrait,* 210, 269.

93 Glenn distinguishes between caring tasks and caring feelings. Drawing on an array of theorists, she defines "care" as "a practice that encompasses feeling (caring about) and activity (caring for). 'Caring about' engages both thought and emotion . . . 'Caring for' refers to the varied activities of providing for the needs or well-being of another person. These activities include physical care . . . emotional care . . . and direct services" (Glenn, *Forced to Care,* 186). Both caring work and caring feelings are often gendered feminine.

94 Zelizer, *Purchase of Intimacy,* 16, 14. On secrecy, intimacy, and "the possibility of betrayal," see Gabriella Turnaturi, *Betrayals: The Unpredictability of Human Relations,* trans. Lydia G. Cochrane (Chicago: University of Chicago Press, 2007), 23.

95 Zelizer notes that "fully intimate relations involve some degree of mutual trust" (Zelizer, *Purchase of Intimacy,* 14, 15).

96 hooks points out that "communities sustain life—not nuclear families, or the 'couple,' and certainly not the rugged individualist" (hooks, *All About Love,* 29).

97 *Vengeance,* 220 (similarly, "Interlude," 109; *Witness,* 177); *Purity,* 38.

98 *Loyalty,* 214.

99 *Portrait,* 174. Also *Innocence,* 140.

100 *Portrait,* 174.

101 *Reunion,* 124. Mira shares that she and her husband also fight and especially did so when they were first married (*Memory,* 295–96).

102 *Ritual,* 161. The character is Isis.

103 *Reunion,* 315; *Judgment,* 126 (also 19).

104 *Fantasy,* 102; similarly, *Purity,* 187.

105 *Reunion,* 315.

106 Romance conventions once demanded virginal heroines and incorrigible heroes. Now, most subgenres allow women to have had lovers, sometimes including long-term partners, before their involvement with the hero, who is typically more discriminating than he would have been in earlier decades. Yet Roarke has still "had a lot more anyones" than Dallas has (*Witness,* 290). Apart from a brief reference to her first (voluntary) experience of sex (*Concealed,* 106), the only one of her past lovers mentioned is Detective Don Webster, formerly Homicide, now Internal Affairs, with whom she spent a "single night" (*Purity,* 24).

107 *Immortal,* 123–24. "I never made love before him. I had sex, but I never felt anything but basic release" (*Naked,* 161: sex had been "simple, straightforward, and, yes, impersonal"). Also *Ceremony,* 295; *Calculated,* 101.

108 *Seduction,* 288.

109 *Witness*, 290; *Glory*, 104; *Vengeance*, 138, 175; *Immortal*, 20; *Origin*, 9 (one of Roarke's former lovers tells Dallas, "Holy God, that man's got stamina"). On Roarke's past more generally, see *Divided*, 105–6.

110 *Innocent*, 238. Additionally, *Reunion*, 173; *Born*, 113; *Imitation*, 190; *Seduction*, 286; *Conspiracy*, 111.

111 *Big Jack*, 181; *Reunion*, 98–99.

112 Jagose, *Orgasmology*, 176.

113 *Naked*, 162.

114 *Brotherhood*, 358. Goris explores the mind/body connection in Roberts' work in "Mind, Body, Love: Nora Roberts and the Evolution of Popular Romance Studies," *Journal of Popular Romance Studies* 3, no. 1 (2012). In Robb's novels, the body also tells the truth about evil and danger (e.g., "Eternity," 46).

115 Although Eve desires and initiates sex frequently, their exchanges often suggest that Roarke has stronger desires; she accuses him playfully of wanting sex relentlessly (which he accepts, e.g., *Strangers*, 173). Sometimes, there is a sense that he has to talk her into sex, though it's mostly played for laughs: "Half-naked, already breathless, she levered herself on her elbows. 'All right, just get it over with' " (*Betrayal*, 75). She sometimes offers sexual favors for help (e.g., *Devoted*, 109, 111) or he jokes about taking payment (e.g., *Calculated*, 87, 89).

116 *Born*, 205. Similarly, *Ceremony*, 169: "I don't want to be taken, unless I take back." "Heterosexual intercourse continu[es] to figure, however ambivalently, the optimistic expression of a sexual ideology whose privileged ethical terms are equality and mutuality" (Jagose, *Orgasmology*, 194).

117 *Naked*, 161.

118 Similarly, *Innocence*, 340–41. Ananya Mukherjea notes the difficulty of holding "a fantasy of stable and secure gendered expectations without fundamentally compromising or relinquishing hard-won and necessary but also sometimes challenging feminist rights and responsibilities" (Mukherjea, "My Vampire Boyfriend," 1).

119 *Immortal*, 128. She's got "a healthy competitive streak" (*Vengeance*, 20).

120 *Imitation*, 44–45. The bouts end, predictably, in sex.

121 *Fantasy*, 110. Dallas and Roarke have similar parity in martial arts and swimming: *Survivor*, 267; *Vengeance*, 218; *Kindred*, 203.

122 *Imitation*, 98. Similarly, *Devoted*, 295.

123 *Imitation*, 168 (also *Rapture*, 90; similarly, *Portrait*, 187; *Creation*, 353). Roarke carries Dallas when she is ill or injured (e.g., *Witness*, 287) and when she has fallen asleep (e.g., *Seduction*, 159) or is about to do so (e.g., *Immortal*, 37). They discuss whether his doing so is "masterful" (*Immortal*, 40), "manly" (*Vengeance*, 18), or "macho" (*Divided*, 80; he says, instead, that it's "expedient"). In a 1985 Roberts novel, the couple debates whether carrying is emblematic of "male dominance," as the heroine wonders, or "romance," as the hero insists. The heroine declares that

she isn't "looking for romance or dominance" (Nora Roberts, *Boundary Lines*, republished in Roberts, *Engaging the Enemy* [New York: Silhouette Books, 2003], 401). Masculinity norms are at play: "benevolent but incontestable male dominance continues to be widely socially approved and desired" (Mukherjea, "My Vampire Boyfriend," 12). Lennard investigates what he terms "the imperative mood" in Robb's writings, comparing it to the strictures of romance norms; he proposes that Dallas and Roarke, written pseudonymously, "must have been an explosive liberation for Roberts from the generic imperatives of female objectification and male discourtesy with which she was struggling" (Lennard, *Of Modern Dragons*, 71). Here, Lennard reveals his unfamiliarity both with the range and depth of popular romance fiction and its scholarly analysts.

124 *Immortal*, 123. Also *Purity*, 121.

125 Perhaps the only example where Roarke outright rescues Dallas is *Glory*, 293–95, following which she claims to have been about to gain the upper hand. He also comes close in *Survivor*, 357; *Calculated*, 330; and "Chaos," 92–95.

126 *Loyalty*, 354–55; Roarke remembers that act in the context of Dallas' importance to him in *Witness*, 177.

127 *Ceremony*, 110–11.

128 *Divided in Death*, 218.

129 *Memory*, 68.

130 *Vengeance*, 233; similarly, *Portrait*, 210–11; *Survivor*, 258. Mukherjea notes "the dissatisfaction that many heterosexually involved women would like to see their male partners feel about their own gendered dominance and the ways in which they benefit from an unfair, sexist social system" (Mukherjea, "My Vampire Boyfriend," 12).

131 *Naked*, 165.

132 *Promises*, 166. When Dallas resists the car, Roarke points out the illogic in refusing the vehicle but allowing him to bribe functionaries "with cases of brew and sports tickets," convincing her to use it by saying it will be a favor to him since he'll know she's safe.

133 For instance, *Conspiracy*, 13; *Innocent*, 178–79; *Memory*, 287; *Imitation*, 91; *Creation*, 195; *Treachery*, 7. Dr. Mira's absentminded but insightful husband Dennis, of whom Dallas is very fond, also gives her a fuzzy hat with a pompom and soft gloves (*Devoted*, 121).

134 *Fantasy*, 338, 339, 161. This love also makes Dallas deeply vulnerable (*Fantasy*, 333–34).

135 As bell hooks writes, "All relationships have their ups and downs. Romantic fantasy often nurtures a belief that difficulties and down times are an indication of a lack of love rather than part of the process. In actuality, true love thrives on the difficulties. The foundation of such love is the assumption that we want to grow and expand, to become more fully ourselves" (hooks, *All About Love*, 181). With Roarke, Dallas is able to continue to confront the violence she sees in her work: "I don't know

how long I could have kept looking, kept caring, if I didn't have someone to come home to who'd look with me when I needed it" (*Salvation*, 275).

136 *Portrait*, 135. Roarke also explains to an old girlfriend who wishes to resume their affair that "I'm completely in love with my wife" (*Innocent*, 90).

137 Eve: "I've remembered more in the past year than I could in all the years before. Because you were there, and I could face it" (*Reunion*, 224). Also *Reunion*, 271.

138 *Rapture*, 27. On community and its links to romance, consult Vivanco, *Pursuing Happiness*, 90.

Chapter 2

1 Gabriella Turnaturi argues that betrayals, considered sociologically rather than ethically or philosophically, reveal the shaky ground on which all interpersonal relationships stand: "With betrayal, we are faced with the greatest tragedy of human relations: the fact that the other is unknowable" (Turnaturi, *Betrayals*, 2, 5; quote from 2). One might argue that this unknowability is precisely what romance seeks to remedy; certainly, among the romantic declarations Dallas makes to Roarke is "God, you get me" (*Big Jack*, 286). Betrayal cannot be understood without its opposites, and indeed, as Turnaturi notes, "To speak of betrayal requires previous expectations of loyalty" (Turnaturi, *Betrayals*, 9). Betrayal and its opposites, loyalty and connection, are a major theme in the series (series titles include *Betrayal*, *Treachery*, *Loyalty*, *Devoted*, *Kindred*, and *Brotherhood*). Turnaturi suggests that because "betrayal involves the rupture of a pact, the negation of the principle of cohesion," it is "a threat to the possibility of *all* relations" (28, emphasis in original).

2 *Immortal*, 5. Dallas told Roarke about it in *Kindred*, 95.

3 *Naked*, 223.

4 *New York to Dallas*, 44–45. Feeney eventually becomes a sort of father to Dallas (*Ceremony*, e.g., 207).

5 *Visions*, 276. Roarke follows up: "Friendship, partnership. They aren't just about trust, Eve. They're about affection. Even love" (*Visions*, 277).

6 Louise "was pretty as a strawberry parfait, classy as a crystal flute of champagne, and a born reformer who lived to fight in the trenches" (*Visions*, 50; *Memory*, 175).

7 Introduced in *Immortal*, Trina has wild hair, a revealing outfit, and speaks with "the vocal equivalent of rusted iron" (*Immortal*, 4, 150–51). Dallas denies that Trina is a friend but ensures that she is protected when a stalker seeks to target those close to her (*Obsession*, 268). In *Kindred* (241), the list Peabody gives of "the usual" people to be invited to a gathering is "me, Mavis, Nadine, Trina. Maybe Reo if she can make it."

8 Reo is professionally "hungry" and ambitious, feminine but forceful: "Despite the sunny sweep of silky hair, the baby-doll blue eyes and curvy pink lips, Cher was known to be a piranha" (*Origin*, 102; similarly,

Brotherhood, 301; *Memory*, 53). She becomes included in the friend circle in *Festive*, figuring also in *Obsession* and *Brotherhood*, where, for the first time, she accompanies Dallas as part of an investigation.

9 *Kindred*, 148.

10 *Judgment*, 30. Also *Rapture*, 202; *Devoted*, 215.

11 *Creation*, 170.

12 Contemporary shifting public opinion and laws on same-sex marriage, culminating in the U.S. Supreme Court's 2015 ruling that states could not ban same-sex marriage, have, perhaps, obscured how significant a change this would have seemed in the mid-1990s when the first In Death books appeared.

13 *Naked*, 53.

14 *Vengeance*, 6.

15 *Origin*, 180.

16 Dallas' declaration to Peabody that "women are the worst" critiques dominant cultural norms that promote women trying to change the men they choose, then finding themselves no longer attracted (*Imitation*, 257). She worries when her own behavior is "embarrassingly *female*" (*Innocent*, 92, emphasis in original; also *Creation*, 186). An Goris reflects on the commonalities among Dallas' friends and the ways in which "their feminine identities are implicitly differentiated from and even opposed to Eve's" (Goris, "From Romance to Roberts," 413–14). Goris concludes that these depictions demonstrate "the underlying development of Eve's more traditional feminine identity" and "her becoming part of a happy feminine community." She argues that contrary to "romance stereotypes" Dallas' "journey is not one of increasing independence, but one of increasing feminization and emotional co-dependence" (415). I would argue, instead, that femininity remains contested and ambivalent and that what is "empowering and positive" (414) about Robb's treatment of this community of women is precisely the ways in which women are to be let alone to accept or reject dominant cultural norms of womanhood. I disagree about "increasing feminization," though I do think there is a move from some elements of independence to emotional *interdependence*.

17 In *Concealed in Death* (55), Peabody and Dallas encounter a reconstruction artist who is enormously pregnant with twins. When the babies move and the woman puts a hand on her belly, Dallas retreats while Peabody steps closer. Discussing childbirth classes with Mavis, Peabody notes, "Childbirth's natural," and Dallas replies, "Not when I'm involved" (*Memory*, 177).

18 *Indulgence*, 166; *Born*, 166.

19 *Imitation*, 27; *Reunion*, 285. Other professional women play up their femininity (*Purity*, 138–39). Deputy Mayor Jenna Franco and Dallas have an explicit conversation about use of enhancements: Franco, who subscribes to the notion that "fashion and cosmetics were valuable tools for

a woman to get what she wanted," declares in frustration, "I don't think of lip dye as a tool of Satan." Related to this issue, see Jo B. Paoletti, *Sex and Unisex: Fashion, Feminism, and the Sexual Revolution* (Indianapolis: Indiana University Press, 2015), 44. Franco and Dallas come to explicit agreement that both do their jobs well while using "vastly different methods" (*Purity*, 156–57). Dallas has a similar exchange with Cher Reo: "You've got the badge and the bad attitude, I've got the legal heft and Rock 'Em Red lip dye" (*Brotherhood*, 302). On the use of face enhancements, see *Indulgence*, 310–11.

20 *Origin*, 180; *Ceremony*, 254. Also *Memory*, 138; *Portrait*, 158.

21 *Indulgence*, 332.

22 Winifred Gallagher explains that purses convey meaning and symbolize identity. She tells the stories of several women who collect, enjoy, and appreciate purses, and one who does not. The latter, an army major, chooses not to wear the optional purse with her uniform, believing, like Dallas does, that it is an unnecessary encumbrance (Gallagher, *In the Bag: What Purses Reveal and Conceal* [New York: HarperCollins, 2006], 87).

23 *Betrayal*, 5.

24 *Indulgence*, 327–38; *Fantasy*, 244, 248; similarly, *Calculated*, 313.

25 *Fantasy*, 124; *Witness*, 101; *Portrait*, 172; also *Big Jack*, 79.

26 *Holiday*, 7. Also, on Dallas' aversion to shopping, see *Portrait*, 71; *Ceremony*, 75; *Born*, 39; *Promises*, 196. She does not shop but rather picks things up (*Memory*, 35).

27 *Salvation*, 176.

28 *Treachery*, 119.

29 *Innocent*, 23.

30 *Born*, 34. On serving as matron of honor for Louise, see *Strangers*, 214 and passim.

31 *Born*, 46. Robb frequently sets up dichotomous options: Dallas would rather do X dangerous and difficult thing than Y sedate, conventional thing. For example, in *Innocent in Death*, she "would rather have been stalking through an abandoned tenement in search of a psychotic chemihead juiced on Zeus than striding down the pristine hallways of staunchly upper-middle-class Sarah Child Academy" (2). Similarly, see *Strangers*, 15; *Survivor*, 18; *Salvation*, 172; *Born*, 125.

32 *Kindred*, 6.

33 *Immortal*, 4.

34 *Memory*, 228. Nadine says the opposite, gushing about an event "so completely female" (*Promises*, 255).

35 Peabody's offhand remark (*Obsession*, 36) about needing a "bestie gay guy" aside, the series generally does not traffic in these stereotypes. This is unlike the increasingly offensive deployment of racist stereotypes presumably meant to be funny in Janet Evanovich's Stephanie Plum bounty hunter series.

36 As hooks observes, "Whiteness is rarely overtly named" (hooks, *Remembered Rapture: The Writer at Work* [New York: Henry Holt, 1999], 148). Coco Fusco writes, "To ignore white ethnicity is to redouble its hegemony by naturalizing it" (Fusco, "Fantasies of Oppositionality: Reflections on Recent Conferences in Boston and New York," *Screen* 29, no. 4 [1988]: 91). Though Ruth Frankenberg sought to explore the implications of the ways in which "white people are 'raced,' just as men are 'gendered,'" well over two decades ago, whiteness remains largely "unmarked and unnamed" (Frankenberg, *White Women, Race Matters: The Social Construction of Whiteness* [Minneapolis: University of Minnesota Press, 1993], 1). hooks points out the problem with "sentimental books that focus on cozy female bonding that just happens to cross race, class, and sexuality," eliding the real differences that separate women (hooks, *Writing Beyond Race*, 55). Though In Death does not fall neatly into the category of sentimental books, it too gets some laughs out of the "world of funky fun sisterhood."

37 In theory, one need not assume that characters whose skin color is not described are white. Yet Robb typically signals darker skin while rarely describing whiteness. A martial arts hologram program has three combatants: the (presumably white) woman is described by size and hair color, while the black and Asian males are given ethnic identifiers (*Survivor*, 265). More to the point, Roarke's "Irish white skin" (*Creation*, 6) appears once or twice but every book mentions his black hair and blue eyes. Peabody is described as white once, in *Visions in Death* (196), where race, including whiteness, has slightly increased visibility because a serial killer is targeting white women with long brown hair (e.g., 263). Louise (*Conspiracy*, 99), Charles (*Holiday*, 52), Mavis (*Promises*, 167), and McNab ("Wonderment," 78) have light/white skin that Robb seldom mentions, describing them with hair and eye color instead. An exception to the rule that non-white characters are given racial identifiers and/or skin tones is Detective Santiago, introduced when he transfers into her department as "a young, broad-shouldered man" (*Indulgence*, 303). Neither he nor his female partner Detective Carmichael (or male detectives Reineke or Jenkinson) is given a first name, skin color, hair color, or ethnicity. Officer Carmichael's skin tone is mentioned only when "his face [was] pink from the cold" (*Calculated*, 56). E-detective Callendar is "dark" with "burnt honey skin" (*Creation*, 72); unusually, descriptions of her typically emphasize her curvaceous body or her wacky clothing and omit skin color. Detective Baxter is given a first name and some character traits but no physical description.

38 *Promises*, 38; *Devoted*, 324; *Survivor*, 352.

39 A few examples: *Salvation*, 85; *Visions*, 182; "Wonderment," 59; *Strangers*, 91, 114; *Purity*, 152; *Innocent*, 3, 7; *Born*, 35. White skin is occasionally likened to milk or cream.

40 In addition to those she encounters through her work, Dallas knows a few interracial couples, including Leonardo and Mavis. Her superior officers are also dark-skinned men married to lighter women: Commander Whitney's wife Anna is blonde (*Glory,* 68) and Chief Tibble's wife Karla is "the shade of the well-steeped Irish tea Roarke occasionally enjoyed" (*Strangers,* 181).

41 *Conspiracy,* 150.

42 *Conspiracy,* 300–301. In doing so, Dallas learns that Roarke had opened an account for her when they married; she seldom refers again to it, but considers drawing on it for a person victimized as a child, as she was, by a foster mother they shared (*Memory,* 233).

43 Roarke periodically asks Louise to treat Dallas for on-the-job injuries (e.g., *Reunion,* 246–49).

44 *Promises,* 89, 303.

45 Angelo is introduced in "Interlude in Death," 29–30 (where her voice suggests "hot desert nights"), visits New York during *Treachery in Death,* and appears in *Salvation in Death.* DeWinter connects her own Asian and black "heritage" to that of just-discovered skeletal remains (*Concealed,* 13).

46 Introduced in *Concealed in Death,* DeWinter figures in *Festive in Death, Obsession in Death,* and *Devoted in Death.* In *Devoted in Death,* a prickly exchange results in both Dallas and DeWinter acknowledging that they "really need to learn how to communicate better" (170). (Later, *Devoted,* 303: "Yeah, she definitely owed DeWinter that drink.") DeWinter is absent from the most recent book, *Brotherhood in Death,* in which the tertiary character who helps Dallas is hair-and-fiber expert Harvo, elsewhere described—in an exception to Robb's typical pattern—as *very* white (*Visions,* 256; also *Memory,* 178). Dallas responds to information from her with "Harvo, you're my new best friend" (*Brotherhood,* 335). Though obviously a joke, it is one Dallas does not make with any non-white woman. Indeed, though Dallas likes "exotic" psychic Celena Sanchez (*Visions,* 31), a high-society bred friend of Louise DiMatto's who consults on a case, she tells Peabody she has no room for new friends (243). It turns out Sanchez used her visions to arrange the murder of her ex-lover's new love; though Dallas "still [likes her] on some level," there is no danger they will become friends (354).

47 *Obsession,* 268.

48 Morris has an "exotic" face and eyes (e.g., *Imitation,* 20, 23; *Salvation,* 21; *Promises,* 14; *Fantasy,* 17; in *Origin,* 44, he has a "sharp face and avid eyes"; in *Memory,* 97, his eyes are "slanted and oddly sexy"). Morris' personality, too, is "bohemian, exotic, artistic" (*Promises,* 13). A minor character, Agent Teasdale, gets similar descriptions: "dark brown eyes tipped up in the corners," in *Delusion,* 12; "cool, enigmatic Asian eyes," in "Taken," 45.

49 Santiago's name implies Latinx heritage, as does the slippage in *Delusion in Death, Calculated in Death,* and *Thankless in Death* to calling him Sanchez rather than Santiago; he makes a brief reference to thinking in Spanish (*Devoted,* 310). Robb's audiobook narrator voices him with a Latinx accent. Nonetheless, like most of his detective colleagues in Dallas' squad, he gets neither a first name nor much of a description.

50 *Immortal,* 20. Leonardo's skin is "coppery gold" (*Visions,* 131; similarly, *Born,* 6, and *Memory,* 81) or caramel (*Divided,* 195). His and Mavis' daughter Bella has "blond curls" (e.g., *Kindred,* 367) and blue eyes (*Treachery,* 163); her skin tone is left unspecified (unless "pink" counts—*Creation,* 166). In *Promises,* 167, she is "pink and white and gold," a "pink-and-gold doll" with a "pink and full and fluffy dress," while Leonardo is "copper-skinned" and Mavis "rosy pale."

51 *Glory,* 37. Though Crack identifies himself as the bouncer (also *Origin,* 279), later books identify him as the club's owner (e.g., *Thankless,* 366). This could be a continuity error, a change in his role, or his misdirection of a not-yet-trusted cop early on.

52 *Glory,* 39.

53 Men who call a colleague a "girl" illustrate "an innate lack of respect for females in the workplace" (*Delusion,* 190).

54 Paradoxically, this infantilization of adult black males coexists with deadly violence (toward, to give only three recent and well-known examples, Trayvon Martin, Tamir Rice, and Michael Brown) justified by its perpetrators as an appropriate response to adolescents and teenagers understood as threatening *men.* As the poet Claudia Rankine puts it, "Because white men can't/police their imagination/black men are dying" (Rankine, *Citizen: An American Lyric* [Minneapolis: Graywolf, 2014], 135).

55 *Betrayal,* 138.

56 *Promises,* 112.

57 *Immortal,* 139; *Treachery,* 83. In *Origin* (280), Crack calls Dallas "skinny white cop girl." She doesn't reciprocate. Similarly, *Holiday,* 223.

58 *Glory,* 38.

59 Later, Crack is discussing dancers at his club and compares Dallas to them: "All you white girls look alike" (*Immortal,* 140).

60 bell hooks discusses the ways black male bodies are rendered both dangerous and erotic (hooks, *Art on My Mind: Visual Politics* [New York: The New Press, 1995], 205). In a much later encounter, Dallas seeks a very large suspect who uses a gym to maintain his physique. She looks at Crack and comments, "You're a big guy." He sexualizes it, "patt[ing] his crotch. 'I got written testimony to that effect' " (*Visions,* 190). On naked men at the club, see *Immortal,* 141, 279.

61 Also *Immortal,* 139. Some of these characteristics apply to other large men: Leonardo has "uncanny grace for a man topping six-five" (*Judgment,* 145; also *Immortal,* 8, 20).

62 *Immortal,* 25. "Dark": *Salvation,* 91; *Creation,* 44; *Promises,* 33; *Origin,* 54; *Memory,* 165. "Cocoa": *Survivor,* 61. "Coffee": *Born,* 97. "Glossy oak": *Divided,* 125.

63 *Glory,* 236; *Visions,* 197; *Origin,* 216. When introduced in *Glory in Death,* Tibble is described in ways that play up his size. In later installments (e.g., *Visions in Death*) he is still tall but "lean."

64 *Treachery,* 83.

65 Urban poverty crosses racial boundaries in Robb/Roberts' works. Three culprits in a convenience store robbery-murder are located playing basketball at a neighborhood court. One is white, one mixed race, and one black. (The surviving store owner describes them as "the white boy," "the black one," and an "Asian mix" [*Treachery,* 5].) Yet in a stereotypical rendering, "from his rhythm, his moves, Eve judged [the black youth] had a little game in him" (11). Roberts gives one of her white heroes a violent inner-city childhood, shot at age thirteen on "Baltimore's bad streets" where he lays "pouring blood over the used condoms and crack vials in the stinking gutter" (*Inner Harbor,* 1). When the character briefly dies on the operating table, readers learn that he is a "tall blond boy" (3). Philip Quinn shares an abusive and rough background with his three foster brothers and fellow heroes in Roberts' Chesapeake Bay saga, in which his story is the third installment.

66 *Glory,* 36. Also *Immortal,* 141; *Origin,* 279; *Promises,* 113; *Visions,* 188, 190; *Betrayal,* 139. On crack cocaine and its connection with the war on drugs as part of a strategy for "law and order" replacing explicitly segregationist/racial logic, consult Michelle Alexander, *The New Jim Crow: Mass Incarceration in the Age of Colorblindness,* rev. ed. (New York: The New Press, 2011), 51–54.

67 As Frankenberg notes, "Whiteness, as a set of normative cultural practices, is visible most clearly to those it definitely excludes and those to whom it does violence. Those who are securely housed within its borders usually do not examine it" (Frankenberg, *White Women, Race Matters,* 228–29).

68 *Betrayal,* 139.

69 *Conspiracy,* 8; *Born,* 276; *Thankless,* 11; *Brotherhood,* 179; *Innocent,* 215. Trueheart is "clean-cut, kindhearted" (*Calculated,* 33).

70 *Conspiracy,* 45.

71 "Taken in Death," 38; similarly, *Strangers,* 291. For Trueheart's paleness when upset, see *Witness,* 238; *Conspiracy,* 15–17. On greenness, a record search on a young Topeka-born woman "comes up clean and green as a Kansas wheatfield" (*Divided,* 60). Trueheart is occasionally "gold"—but not for skin tone (*Calculated,* 35).

72 *Conspiracy,* 7; *Creation,* 101 (similarly, *Innocent,* 145); *Purity,* 41.

73 *Witness,* 248.

74 *Brotherhood,* 73, echoing *Purity,* 190.

75 *Purity,* 27.

76 *Witness*, 190; *Concealed*, 298; *Survivor*, 62.

77 *Witness*, 258.

78 *Origin*, 164; *Memory*, 16; *Promises*, 239, 287; *Fantasy*, 231; *Indulgence*, 209; *Promises*, 295; *Indulgence*, 164; *Memory*, 334.

79 *Betrayal*, 138; *Visions*, 188; *Survivor*, 322 (similarly, *Conspiracy*, 17, and "Taken," 50).

80 *Witness*, 236; *Devoted*, 73; *Purity*, 7 ("All-American" appears for another young white man in *Portrait*, 40); *Strangers*, 340; also *Seduction*, 290. In this calculus, white=attractive and black=ugly. Dallas jokes to Roarke that Commander Whitney is "pretty studly if you go for the big-shouldered, careworn type," but she "like[s] 'em pretty" (*Memory*, 201). Holland notes that "aesthetic preference" is embedded in a broader racial/racist order and has "moral" weight (Holland, *Erotic Life of Racism*, 41; broadly, 41–64).

81 Toni Morrison, *Playing in the Dark: Whiteness and the Literary Imagination* (Cambridge, Mass.: Harvard University Press, 1992), 47.

82 Holland, *Erotic Life of Racism*, 29–32; for a qualification, see Eduardo Bonilla-Silva, *Racism without Racists: Color-Blind Racism and the Persistence of Racial Inequality in America*, 4th ed. (Lanham, Md.: Rowman and Littlefield, 2014), 306, 310–12. At the same time that blackness and (invisible) whiteness are central to both contemporary American reality and the In Death universe, other racial and ethnic identities play a key role. C. Richard King points to the central role of anti-Indian racism in the constitution of American racial identity in ways that trouble the notion of a binary black/white division (King, *Redskins: Insult and Brand* [Lincoln: University of Nebraska Press, 2016], 74–90).

83 *Thankless*, 367.

84 *Visions*, 188.

85 *Holiday*, 223; *Immortal*, 279.

86 *Immortal*, 141.

87 *Portrait*, 295, 287.

88 *Portrait*, 288. On the way "a mélange of signs for African heritage" decorate Lt. Uhura's quarters on the Enterprise, and how these might reflect the Star Trek actor's performance, see Carrington, *Speculative Blackness*, 74–75. Africa gets occasional and typically stereotypical mentions in Robb's books (*Calculated*, 170, 197; *Rapture*, 214; and, at somewhat more length, *Concealed*, 324 and passim). Apart from Ireland and, to a lesser extent, Scotland, mentioned fairly frequently, Europe also gets short shrift. It would be an interesting exercise to compare the way Ireland is discussed (e.g., "Wonderment," 30) with the way Africa is discussed. Also of interest: the seemingly scant role global politics play in the novels.

89 *Portrait*, 288.

90 One read of Crack's code-switching would suggest that he is most comfortable in standard English: in distress, he resorts to it, just as Roarke's

language becomes more Irish when his emotions run high (*Portrait*, 289). Later, when Dallas asks about Crack's plans for Thanksgiving dinner, he responds, "Gobble Day. I got me a fine-looking female." When Dallas extends an invitation to him and his guest, an almost comically formal tone replaces "the street jive": "I'd appreciate that. I'd be pleased to come and bring my lady friend" (*Origin*, 281; note, though, a few formal phrases in their original encounter [*Glory*, 37–38]). Also *Visions*, 188–91, when after encountering Dallas, Crack speaks primarily in standard English. He greets her as Dallas, though he later uses "white girl," "hot stuff," and "Sweetcheeks" as sexualized endearments. Morrison observes "how the dialogue of black characters is construed as an alien, estranging dialect" and how "it is used . . . to reinforce class distinctions and otherness as well as to assert privilege and power" (*Playing in the Dark*, 52).

91 *Portrait*, 291, 293.

92 Recapped in *Visions*, 188. Notably, Dallas offers comfort more readily here than she does when actual babies are involved; she remains wary of Mavis and Leonardo's daughter Bella.

93 *Origin*, 280; *Visions*, 189–91.

94 "Possession," 13; *Festive*, 225; *Promises*, 155; *Origin*, 281.

95 *Strangers*, 181–82.

96 For example, "Chaos," 52–53, 66.

97 *Ceremony*, 255–56; *Concealed*, 143; *Treachery*, 145, 152–53.

98 *Imitation*, 276–80, 288.

99 *Immortal*, 123; also *Immortal*, 45. Roarke says, "She needs you, Eve. She needs a friend, and she's going to need a good cop" (*Immortal*, 64).

100 *Immortal*, 96.

101 Respectively, *Loyalty in Death*, *Brotherhood in Death*, *Divided in Death*, and *Vengeance in Death*.

102 *Festive*, 5.

103 *Immortal*, 86; "Chaos," 35–36.

104 *Indulgence*, 179; also *Imitation*, 54–55; *Rapture*, 56.

105 *Judgment*, 128; *Creation*, 55, 71; *Witness*, 37; *Purity*, 108. Earlier in their relationship, Dallas had said, "Don't push me on this Nadine. You're almost a friend" (*Immortal*, 210).

106 *Conspiracy*, 168.

107 *Imitation*, 250; also *Purity*, 347; *Imitation*, 57; *Portrait*, 199 (where the murderer is in regular contact with Nadine).

108 *Ceremony*, 133; *Brotherhood*, 89.

109 *Kindred*, 243; *Fantasy*, 250; *Survivor*, 157; *Origin*, 96. Nadine describes mutual assistance as what "really good cops and really good reporters" do (*Obsession*, 120). Johnson, in *Street Justice*, mentions the crucial role of journalists in exposing police brutality (13, 131–32).

110 *Ceremony*, 173.

111 *Reunion*, 118–25. Dallas sometimes tells Mira before she tells Roarke, as with the memory/dream of her mother in *Imitation*, 151–53. Their

sharing of confidences is not parallel, even though Mira discloses to Dallas that she herself was raped by her stepfather when she was young (on this, see *Divided,* 304–6).

112 *Rapture,* 105. At that point "Eve was unaware" of those feelings. Also *Judgment,* 178: "I look on you as a kind of surrogate daughter." Dallas admits awkwardly, "The, um, mother thing? That was weird. But nice" (*Judgment,* 182). Mira's daughter makes a similar point, calling Dallas the daughter of Mira's "heart and her spirit" (*Imitation,* 89). For a more fraught encounter where Dallas and Mira are annoyed with each other, see *Origin,* 273. *Delusion in Death,* in which, with Mira's assistance, Dallas grapples with the recent death of her own mother, juxtaposes her mother and Mira in potentially productive ways (e.g., 222).

113 *Memory,* 83.

114 *Immortal,* 167–70. Dallas' memory is of having killed her father years earlier in self-defense.

115 *Conspiracy,* 313. Mira also helps Dallas to realize that she is capable of emotional growth, "friendship, loyalty, compassion, humor. Love" (*Immortal,* 174).

116 In *Visions in Death* (249–52), Dallas confides her past history to Peabody because "a partner's got a right to know things" (*Visions,* 249).

117 *Ceremony,* 301.

118 *Purity,* 75–79. Dallas agrees to coach Mavis' labor even though the prospect horrifies her (*Visions,* 134–36). *Born in Death* recounts numerous such details.

119 *Seduction,* 148.

120 Robb plays with the chick-lit trope at the end of *Imitation in Death* (328, 331), when Peabody is nervous about the results of her detective exam and must prepare for a high-stakes stakeout.

121 *Obsession,* 95. On teen girls, see *Seduction,* 28; *Concealed,* passim.

122 *Obsession,* 4.

123 Similarly, Julianne Dunne imagines "a true bond" between herself and Dallas (*Reunion,* 264).

124 Mick thinks it's money at issue and says, "It's not like it was *your* money I'm after putting in my pocket" (*Betrayal,* 308). Unbeknownst to Mick, however, the people he is working with have attempted to murder Summerset to make Roarke more vulnerable.

125 *Seduction,* 57.

126 The serial-spree killing lovers in *Devoted in Death* are, unlike these pairs of male friends, not wealthy.

127 *Indulgence,* 177 (and "Possession," 7–8). Similarly, *Brotherhood,* 263, 375.

128 *Seduction,* 66 (also discussed at 32–33, 41–42, 61, 89, 135). These drugs include various compounds with a range of effects, from lowering inhibitions to affecting memory to removing the ability to consent to arousing. With the exception of fully informed and consensual uses of the last,

all right-thinking people condemn the use of such drugs as particularly abominable (*Innocent*, 150, 155; *Festive*, passim; *Brotherhood*, 347).

129 *Seduction*, 70, 96, 228–29, 340.

130 *Indulgence*, 315; similarly, 222. One might argue that Robb opposes those who place other forms of intimate companionship alongside or above monogamous coupledom. I think a more persuasive reading is that the twisted selfishness of this friendship (just like that of the married murderers in *Devoted in Death*), which treats outsiders as unworthy of basic human consideration, makes the participants morally blameworthy.

131 On monogamy and the possibility that others might arrive at different arrangements, see *Strangers*, 99, and *Ceremony*, 145. In the former case, the murderous wife who claims she and her husband opted for an open relationship is lying to shift suspicion away from herself. In the latter, the same people who "find [monogamy] limiting and foolish" are involved in occult murders.

132 *Imitation in Death*, *Festive in Death*, *Innocent in Death*.

133 *Strangers in Death*.

134 P. D. James, *Talking about Detective Fiction* (New York: Knopf, 2009), 169.

135 Dallas hypothesizes that Roarke differs from these men due to growing up deprived and to having made good friends. He does not consider those with less wealth beneath him (*Indulgence*, 191–92). In *Calculated in Death*, discussing a wealthy suspect as they finish dinner, Dallas remarks that it "only takes a minute" to put one's dishes to wash. Roarke notes that "a lot of people at a certain level of privilege wouldn't think of doing something so simple for themselves as cleaning a table or making their own coffee. Maybe taking care of a few small, basic tasks helps keep a person from sliding too deep into any of those seven deadly [sins]" (which they'd been discussing earlier as motives for murder; *Calculated*, 189–90).

136 *Indulgence*, 117.

137 Race and social prestige are not precisely coextensive. The killers in *Indulgence in Death* (207) prefer a possibly Asian or part-Asian man (David Su) with "bluer and truer blood" than Roarke's when they make up a foursome for golf.

Chapter 3

1 *Kindred*, 249; *Origin*, 274, 278; *Brotherhood*, 262. On another occasion, Dallas says of a modern-day Fagan who oversees street girls, "He has a code—it's screwed up, but it's a code" (*Concealed*, 234). Dallas claims, "Cops don't make the rules," but Roarke argues, "You may not write them, but you edit them every day to suit the situation. You have to because if the law, the rules, the spirit of them doesn't adjust and flex, it dies" (*Origin*, 290). On the other hand, "We [cops] uphold the

law. We are not allowed to nor are we equipped to judge and sentence" (*Judgment*, 203).

2 Similar sentiments emerge in Nora Roberts' novels. Her Bride Quartet—interlocking novels featuring heroines who are also partners in a wedding business—centrally addresses the connection between professional satisfaction and personal happiness (e.g., Roberts, *Happy Ever After*, 227).

3 Regis, *Natural History*, 12; Wendell, *Everything*, 43. Recent historical romance heroines such as those written by Sarah MacLean and Courtney Milan in their respective Regency series often have some sort of avocation or occupation even if their class status militates against paid employment. In detective novels, too, it is long since the case that "even the women who played a subsidiary part in the triumphs of the male hero should have some kind of job in their own right rather than sit at home ministering to the needs of their spouse" (James, *Talking about Detective Fiction*, 70).

4 *Salvation*, 41; Father Lopez also appears in "Possession." In a dream conversation with a murder victim who had been posing as a priest, Dallas rejects sin as out of her "jurisdiction," telling him, "Murder is my religion" (*Salvation*, 143). Religion is a thin thread weaving through the novels: in characters' choices of profanity (Roarke favors "Christ Jesus") and oaths (Peabody offers thanks to "Jesus, Buddha, and the goddess Morgana" after a particularly scary car trip ["Wonderment," 78]); in the symbolism and pathology of some criminals; and, less commonly, as a resource for spiritual life. Dallas believes in God but has no religious affiliation or recognizable religious practice, though she does occasionally discuss the relationship between earthly and supernatural justice (e.g., "Possession," 16). Catholicism figures most prominently, especially in *Salvation in Death* and *Vengeance in Death*. Roarke has a Catholic background (*Salvation*, 46, though he describes himself as "not precisely" Catholic [354]) and eventually gives her a protective medallion featuring the patron saint of cops. Summerset characterizes himself as "Unitarian. Mildly" (*Vengeance*, 82). Occult religions figure from time to time, seldom positively ("Eternity," "Ritual," *Ceremony*). Wicca appears periodically, and more positively, through recurring character Isis, a witch; one of Mira's daughters is Wiccan (*Ceremony*, 181), and many teen girls "dabbl[e] in Wicca" ("Eternity," 32). Peabody's Free-Ager background and beliefs are an ongoing theme (e.g., *Ceremony*, 275). Medical examiner Morris "was raised Buddhist," but "organized" religion "didn't stick." (*Promises*, 217). There does not seem to be a single practicing Jew, Muslim, or Hindu in the series—a very unusual rendering of New York.

5 *Indulgence*, 290. The place of work is an ongoing theme in many of the novels; in *Reunion*, characters who discuss it include Peabody's mother (33), serial murderer Julianne Dunne (83), and Dallas and Roarke (53).

6 *Fantasy*, 253.

7 *Celebrity,* 4. One might speculate that this is Robb's metatextual intervention: she is able to address the place of fiction—her own work—in the world. For a similar reflection on the difference between entertainment and real life, see *Indulgence,* 269.

8 Of the torture-killer known as The Groom: "For him, death was a vocation" (*Creation,* 1). Julianne Dunne "really enjoyed killing. It was such interesting work" (*Reunion,* 83). Some of the considerations that apply to ordinary careers also apply to death-dealing. The killers in *Survivor in Death* think of their killings as work and take pride in them (e.g., 161). In considering the possibility of a team of killers in a case, Dallas asks Roarke rhetorically, "How do you get good at anything?" He replies, "Innate ability and true interest lay a foundation. But it's practice, isn't it, that hones a skill." Thus, they are able to conclude that the team doing the killing had not begun with the victim assigned to Dallas, but had a history of other murders (*Devoted,* 93).

9 Or, "who and what we come from go a long way to forming who we are" (*Promises,* 144).

10 *Seduction,* 152. Dallas comments on a female LC's choice of profession in much the same way that she reflects on women's work generally (*Indulgence,* 125).

11 *Calculated,* 63.

12 In an interesting confluence of idealized structures, such notions have been occasionally shared by others. In the 1970s, short-lived solidarity between "hookers and housewives" ("two classes of women who earn their living from men's waged work") presented both as providing labor that ought to be compensated. Their opponents would argue that "caretaking and sex should be offered freely . . . with genuine affection and out of love" (Gira Grant, *Playing the Whore,* 112). On privatization, sanctification, and production as they relate to wages for housework, consult Kathi Weeks, *The Problem with Work: Feminism, Marxism, Antiwork Politics, and Postwork Imaginaries* (Durham, N.C.: Duke University Press, 2011), esp. 124–25.

13 *Ritual,* 143.

14 *Immortal,* 124. Mira insists that "as horrible as those eight years were, and as obscene, they formed you. They helped you build your strength, your compassion for the innocent, your complexity, your resilience" (124–25). Peabody, too, after learning of Dallas' story, says, "It's made you a better cop. . . . You use what happened to you as a reason to find justice for people who've had it taken away from them" (*Visions,* 251).

15 The trauma rears its head from time to time, and Dallas worries that it will affect her capacity to do her job (e.g., *Survivor,* 146). Peabody (*Imitation,* 109), Roarke (*Delusion,* 208), and Feeney (*Holiday,* 256–57) notice that murders with sexual violence affect Dallas more than others. Other situations, too, can temporarily impair her ability to function, as when she encounters a small girl with a broken arm at a shelter Roarke

funds (*Visions*, 65) or first sees the blood-covered Nixie Swisher, where for "one hideous moment, Eve stared at the child and saw herself" before regaining control (*Survivor*, 9–10, quote from 9).

16 *Brotherhood*, 284.

17 *Reunion*, 7. On romance heroines surviving rape/abuse (including by the hero), consult Teo, *Desert Passions*: "She may be abused, but ***she never remains a victim***" (159, emphasis in original). Pavla Stefanska's dissertation in progress investigates abused heroines in Roberts' novels; Lennard (*Of Modern Dragons*, 58) and Goris ("From Romance to Roberts," 356–57) touch on the topic.

18 *Reunion*, 64.

19 *Immortal*, 32. Similarly, *Seduction*, 116. Peabody's motives included the desire to live in New York (*Visions*, 176).

20 *Reunion*, 32, 297.

21 *Treachery*, 264.

22 *Big Jack*, 8.

23 *Calculated*, 159–61.

24 *Reunion*, 366–67.

25 *Creation*, 150. Similarly, *Kindred*, 199.

26 *Calculated*, 57.

27 Robb does the same to some extent, although she makes numerous references to Dallas having testified in court.

28 *Visions*, 21. Dallas frequently points out that she's not Roarke's cop but the NYPSD's cop. (Similarly, she's "not his cop bitch. . . . I'm my own cop bitch" [*Reunion*, 101].)

29 *Big Jack*, 254; *Imitation*, 129.

30 *Reunion*, 101. Threats such as these receive fuller consideration in chapter 4.

31 Dallas appeals to women's professionalism and power to taunt a misogynist serial killer (*Visions*, 122) and to interrogate a sexist suspect (*Delusion*, 269ff.); *Glory in Death*'s killer targets powerful, outspoken women.

32 Robb briefly mentions a few female detectives in the squad: Dallas says, while unjustly suspended, that Peabody should be assigned to Detective Cartwright if Dallas does not get her badge back (*Conspiracy*, 343); Detective Carnegie (*Salvation*, 78) chooses a doughnut with rainbow sprinkles. Since neither appears again, one or both might be continuity errors for Detective Carmichael, a regular fixture about whom readers nonetheless learn little. Although Carmichael shares a surname with a male uniformed officer, Dallas does not refer to them as male Carmichael/female Carmichael but by rank: Uniform Carmichael and Detective Carmichael, or simply Carmichael. Detective Jannson, who was in Dallas' bull pen but was not explicitly identified as part of her squad, appears in *Survivor in Death* (e.g., 160). Like Dallas, Feeney opts to refer collectively to his subordinates as if all were male: "The fact that Callendar had

breasts and no Y chromosome didn't make her any less one of Feeney's boys" (*Salvation*, 83).

33 *Creation*, 29.

34 *Immortal*, 26, 116.

35 *Big Jack*, 76. At one point, Dallas advises a female cop from someone else's squad: Detective Martinez notes Dallas is "not [her] commanding officer," but Dallas offers "advice from someone who's been on the job longer" (*Judgment*, 137). She offers solidarity as well to a detective in a corrupt squad who is being harassed by one of her colleagues (*Treachery*, 217).

36 *Reunion*, 91; *Innocent*, 145; *Survivor*, 297; *Devoted*, 59, 99.

37 Every so often readers learn that Dallas has commended Peabody's or Trueheart's work in her reports or has been tracking Baxter's evaluations of Trueheart's performance (e.g., *Imitation*, 157–58).

38 When someone suggests that she's molding Peabody, Dallas replies, "Peabody's a cop . . . not a lump of clay" (*Ceremony*, 122; *Reunion*, 27; *Strangers*, 129; *Witness*, 118). She models her "stony stare" on Feeney's (*Strangers*, 249; also *Creation*, 200).

39 *Ritual*, 179; *Seduction*, 6; "Haunted in Death," 310 (similarly, *Indulgence*, 305); *Big Jack*, 129 (with follow-up advice to be confident and less self-conscious at 132–33); *Salvation*, 326 (similarly, *Imitation*, 128).

40 *Ceremony*, 12; *Portrait*, 130–31; *Portrait*, 300.

41 *Reunion*, 20.

42 *Imitation in Death* discusses Peabody's readiness to take the exam—and Dallas' role in guiding and supervising her—throughout, including at 193–94, 203, 262, 282, 322–23, 306, 326, 339, and 341–42.

43 *Treachery*, 8. Regarding appointing Peabody as primary when Dallas will not be "right there," Dallas reassures, "You've got a shield for a reason" (*Devoted*, 277–78). In *Divided in Death*, Dallas had made Peabody primary on a case that "was pretty much connect the big, pulsing red dots" (*Divided*, 8). In *Memory* (3), Peabody remains anxious about serving as primary.

44 *Visions*, 198–99; *Strangers*, 113.

45 *Devoted*, 59. Similarly, Dallas tells Peabody not to question her instincts and competence (*Imitation*, 58–59).

46 "Haunted," 310.

47 McNab deals more effectively with Peabody's insecurities in *Salvation*, 335, when he reminds her of "all the bad guys you helped put away" and that it's not her job to serve as PA, judge, or jury.

48 Dallas uses a similar tone with McNab when he is having difficulty at a crime scene (*Celebrity*, 44); with Trueheart in *Witness*, 239; and with Nadine ("stop being a big baby") when Nadine is having an uncharacteristic attack of nerves (*Fantasy*, 155). Dallas reassures Nadine (sort of) first by saying her book "doesn't suck" and then elaborating a little bit and complimenting her on having made it accurate while also making it

"human and important." At times Dallas reassures Peabody more traditionally (e.g., *Judgment*, 68).

49 *Imitation*, 25. Similarly, *Devoted*, 333.

50 For example, *Reunion*, 150, when Peabody asks for advice about questioning a suspect. Dallas: "Wait until I'm back, but you're not going to screw up. I don't work with screw ups." Caro thinks it's that Dallas "know[s] what tone to take with victims and survivors, witnesses, or suspects. You were brisk, even brusque with Reva. That's the sort of tone she responds best to when she's stressed. You're very intuitive Lieutenant." Caro is perceptive about the attitude but wrong about the cause; Dallas simply uses that tone with everyone where possible (*Divided*, 222).

51 *Imitation*, 29.

52 *New York to Dallas*, 93. She also rejects "madam" (*Witness*, 44).

53 *Portrait*, 10; similarly, *Kindred*, 110–11; *Calculated*, 213ff.

54 *Divided*, 61 (also "Midnight," 181); *Imitation*, 203. Dallas grumbles when an interview subject calls her "miss" (*Seduction*, 215). Names are powerful: Roarke almost jettisons his father's name, but Summerset had said (as Roarke recalls), "Keep it, the name's yours as much as his" (*Portrait*, 199). Also, about acquired rather than birth names, see *Big Jack*, 217.

55 *Betrayal*, 105–9. Note the hyperdeferential language used by this immigrant store owner.

56 *Imitation*, 224, 227.

57 On Baxter, see *Imitation*, 218–19; on Carmichael and Santiago, see *Obsession*, 214.

58 *Devoted*, 240. Similarly, *Strangers*, 114.

59 *Devoted*, 156. On profanity, see *Brotherhood*, 364, and *Survivor*, 274.

60 *Treachery*, 20; also *Fantasy*, 48, and *Born*, 300. When, while angry at Roarke, Dallas says, "I'm not talking to you" and he responds that the silent treatment is "a clichéd and female weapon," she switches to a physical attack and tells him, "Just be careful who you call a female, ace" (*Seduction*, 169–70). Less jokingly, she despises female weakness, e.g., in the face of a man's abuse of a woman and her children (*Strangers*, 303).

61 "Haunted," 272. Similarly, *Memory*, 36.

62 "Haunted," 327. A Roberts' novel offers a similar discussion of baseball fielding (*Savor the Moment*, 133).

63 *Visions*, 182.

64 *Visions*, 50.

65 *Strangers*, 105.

66 *Divided*, 207.

67 *Strangers*, 235.

68 *Witness*, 166. Similarly, *Memory*, 141; *Brotherhood*, 287. Feeney tells Dallas something similar (*Ceremony*, 208–9).

69 *Creation*, 109; *Born*, 93.

70 When Mavis advises Dallas about a conflict with Roarke in which he's holding back, she says, "Girls are good at this, Dallas." Dallas demurs: "I'm not good at being a girl." Mavis replies, "You're your own kind of girl." Then Mavis advises Dallas to use her professional skills: "Think of it as . . . drilling him in Interview until he confesses" (*Portrait*, 158).

71 *Ritual*, 118.

72 *Reunion*, 179, 201.

73 *Treachery*, 264; *Conspiracy*, 7.

74 *Witness*, 183.

75 *Treachery*, 264, also 37–38.

76 Paoletti, *Sex and Unisex*, 57.

77 Mavis' outrageous style is partially a response to her mentally ill mother's abusive control (*Concealed*, 213).

78 Jo Paoletti's observation about children's clothing holds, too, for adults: "The dressier the occasion, the more gendered the clothing" (Paoletti, *Sex and Unisex*, 100).

79 *Fantasy*, 182. Also, on the torments of fancy shoes, see "Ritual," 114–17; on the fact that women have so much to say about them, see *Origin*, 180. One could write an entire dissertation on how the series treats shoes, gender, sexuality, and patriarchy. A fabulous pair of high-heeled shoes is not, as Peabody speculates, the product of "the shoe god" but rather, to Dallas' way of thinking, "the product of a man, a devious flesh and blood man, who secretly hates all women. By designing shoes like this he can torture them for profit" (*Visions*, 14).

80 *Judgment*, 129; *Visions*, 123.

81 *Treachery*, 112.

82 Although Dallas "had a weakness for leather and bold colors that she could rarely indulge" (*Naked*, 18), mostly readers learn that she does not spend a lot of money on clothes, does not like to shop, and does not like uncomfortable clothes.

83 "Eternity," 82. Baxter notes Dallas' lack of interest in fashion to Trueheart, but adds, "Not that she doesn't always look hot. Especially since somebody with taste's buying her threads these days" (*Portrait*, 307). For a rare example of Baxter less than fashionable, see *Conspiracy*, 251. Beauty consultant Trina insists that "if cops put more thought and creativity into fashion and grooming, it might improve public relations" (*Creation*, 195).

84 "Eternity," 81; similarly, *Concealed*, 298.

85 *Indulgence*, 132.

86 *Seduction*, 151.

87 *Calculated*, 272–78; *Holiday*, 122–25 and passim; *Fantasy*, 150; *Ceremony*, 32–33; also *Indulgence*, 328.

88 *Big Jack*, 96.

89 Dallas is proven right in *Reunion*, 244.

90 *Origin*, 144.

91 *Treachery*, 8; on pink as feminine, see Paoletti, *Sex and Unisex*, 96–98, 104.

92 *Indulgence*, 192.

93 *Treachery*, 7–8; *Delusion*, 7.

94 *Celebrity*, 193. Earlier, she "resisted wearing [another luxurious new coat] on the job. No way in hell was she going to get blood and assorted body fluids all over that fabulous bronze-colored cashmere" (*Conspiracy*, 13).

95 *Treachery*, 132.

96 *Celebrity*, 262–63.

97 *Calculated*, 112.

98 *Immortal*, 183; *Imitation*, 185; similarly, *Reunion*, 68.

99 *Origin*, 197; *Obsession*, 83.

100 *Strangers*, 71. Similarly, *Big Jack*, 122.

101 *Celebrity*, 262. Roarke is frequently concerned with the physical and dangerous aspects of Dallas' job. When he gives her the leather trench lined with protective armor, she loves the coat and is appreciative that it is not too delicate (*Origin*, 72). Peabody appreciates the fashion elements (*Celebrity*, 187), as does a fashion blogger who wants to showcase the coat along with "Lieutenant Dallas, Fashionable Cop" (*Festive*, 101). Roarke also knows Peabody: when Dallas decides to get Peabody a "magic coat" of her own (*Festive*, 222), Roarke has it made in pink. The coat conveys quite a few things, including care and protection; Dallas remarks that she can't have such a coat when her partner doesn't. The coat also reflects the way wealth allows Dallas, and those in her circle, more resources to do their job than others. Dallas has a similar coat made for Roarke and puts "stash pockets" in it "for carrying things even an expert civilian consultant isn't supposed to carry" (*Festive*, 330, 329). (The previous Christmas, she had Feeney help her design a comp/holo game: "I figured since you don't get to steal in real life anymore, you'd get a kick out of virtual" [*Memory*, 319]. Roarke replies, "The best present is having a woman who knows me.")

102 *Innocent*, 119. When Peabody compliments Dallas on her outfit later, she asks, "Roarke, right?" (*Innocent*, 121).

103 *Treachery*, 62–63, 63, 64.

104 Similarly, *Salvation*, 225–26. Other men concerned with fashion include Baxter, Leonardo, and a male fashion designer in *Glory in Death* who finds Dallas' clothing woefully lacking.

105 *Treachery*, 43.

106 For example, *Kindred*, 311; *Survivor*, 314, 324.

107 Roarke points out "'the difference between a strong, intelligent, and—though you won't like the word—sensitive leader and one who aims to lead only for gain' . . . She'd have preferred intuitive to sensitive, but let it go" (*Treachery*, 187).

108 *Judgment*, 107, and, more broadly, 101–7.

109 *Judgment*, 292.

110 *Promises*, 194.

111 *Judgment*, 66.

112 *Treachery*, 117. Detective Jacobson is presumably a continuity error for Jenkinson, as in "Chaos in Death."

113 Dallas manages well. She manages more efficiently than the killer in *Witness in Death*. In *Calculated* (149–50, 153) she profiles a killer in terms of how she'd write "an eval report," and she compares his "half sloppy" work to her subordinates' ability to "tie up the details" and "adjust as the situation called for it." What Dallas expects from her squad is fully in line with the post-Fordist model Kathi Weeks analyzes. It is not enough merely to enforce conformity, since "profits in the service- and knowledge-based economy depend increasingly on simultaneously activating and controlling, on releasing and harnessing, the creative, communicative, affective, and emotional capacities of workers" (Weeks, *Problem with Work*, 56). Weeks notes, "Whereas Fordism demanded from its core workers a lifetime of compliance with work discipline, post-Fordism also demands of many of its workers flexibility, adaptability, and continual reinvention" (70).

114 *Betrayal*, 279.

115 On another occasion, "Eve would wear captain's bars one day, but damn if they'd drag her off the street by them" (*Judgment*, 237). Also *Born*, 150–51.

116 *Witness*, 318.

117 *Survivor*, 173 (additionally, *Purity*, 292; *Treachery*, 279–80; "Interlude," 20–21, 23). They revisit the issue in *Thankless*, 51–53; with Roarke's receipt of a medal for civilian efforts, political obstacles disappear. Dallas is offered a captaincy but declines it, preferring to continue to work cases herself (see also 95–97, 178–79, 269). Promotion had been a higher priority for her when work was all that mattered to her (*Brotherhood*, 285).

118 *Treachery*, 72. Male and female officers overly concerned with promotion turn out to be murderous. In *Immortal* (136, 207), Lieutenant Jake Casto is also angling for a captaincy.

119 *Treachery*, 90. Oberman did have a solid trainer, however (*Treachery*, 188).

120 *Obsession*, 27.

121 *Treachery*, 41. On these contrasts, see *Treachery*, 53, 134. On fathers and their children, see also *Promises*, 297, 302.

122 *Imitation*, 127. Some cops abuse their wives and/or children, as in *Obsession*, 125—an officer who was also "on the take"—and *Concealed*, 204.

123 The only IAB detective who gets significant page time, including in *Treachery in Death*, Webster explains how he can work with IAB (*Promises*, 117–18). The books frequently discuss "the blue line" that leads

cops to cover for cops; ***Reunion in Death*** (181) mentions a "white wall" serving a similar function for doctors covering for other doctors.

124 Webster says as much (*Judgment*, 33). On dirty cops and one detective's reluctance to turn against another cop—"I'm fifth generation. . . . We have to stand up for each other"—Dallas replies with a request for him to "think. Not every one of us respects the badge" (*Judgment*, 138). Similarly, see Detective Renfrew in *Seduction*, 315–19. Feeney says, in another context, "Cops back up cops. That's the job" (*Ceremony*, 195; also *Conspiracy*, 21). Historian Marilynn Johnson defines police brutality as "the lawless and unnecessary or excessive use of force by police," police violence as "a more general term to encompass the police use of physical or deadly force that may or may not be justified under the law," and police misconduct as "an array of illegal behaviors that includes brutality but also encompasses police corruption, as well as illegal searches, false arrest, coercion, perjury, etc." (Johnson, *Street Justice*, 10).

125 *Conspiracy*, 42. Similarly, *Promises*, 52.

126 *Conspiracy*, 370.

127 *Naked*, 236. Dallas ultimately passes the information to Nadine Furst.

128 This includes bypassing certain protocols for recording, and fabricating an informant (*Treachery*, 74). An IAB supervisor, Captain Bayliss, operates outside acceptable channels in ***Judgment in Death***.

129 Dallas expresses skepticism about violence exercised by HSO agents and by Special Ops but not by the police. In ***Survivor in Death***, the killers are former spec-ops with "termination grade" ratings (232). Dallas is sarcastic: "Get them . . . Train yourself a killer, then ooops, he's no longer secure." With "sociopathic tendencies" and "suspected ties to Doomsday" as well as Cassandra terrorist organizations, their ringleader is a frightening figure (290).

130 *Divided*, 114. The obvious analogue is the Department of Homeland Security formed in the United States after the 9/11 attacks. The books say relatively little about surveillance beyond cursory mentions of Compugard and a few references to police practices, such as the use of surveillance goggles (*Immortal*, 237) and a Privacy Law prohibiting satellite surveillance (*Thankless*, 128).

131 *Divided*, 203, 100, 104, 122.

132 *Divided*, 107, 114, 115.

133 *Divided*, 124. Feeney reflects on the relevant issues in conversation with Roarke (*Divided*, 165).

134 *Divided*, 217. Dallas recognizes that his "rage . . . covered so skillfully with elegance and style" is part of what makes Roarke who he is. But "what would she do if he killed a man over her? How could she survive that?" Perhaps more importantly, "How could they?" (*Divided*, 220). As to their full acceptance of each other, see *Divided*, 236. However, when a serial killer thinks to avoid a long stint in prison by pursuing a duly authorized self-termination plan once he is caught, Dallas asks Roarke to

"make his self termination clearance disappear," which he does (*Creation*, 344; revisited in *Salvation*, 311).

135 *Divided*, 269. In another case, a murderer has tortured and murdered several people close to Roarke. Dallas tries but fails to apprehend him alive. Roarke is pleased that he is dead: "Justice, Eve, is weak and thin without the underpinning of retribution" (*Vengeance*, 357).

136 *Delusion*, 317.

137 For instance, quickly accepting the use of the unregistered equipment, Dallas employs "illegal means to try to find out if" murdered cop Amaryllis Coltraine "was tangled in something wrong" (*Promises*, 86). In *Seduction*, "Because she thought it slightly tacky for a member of the NYPSD to watch a civilian severely bend the law, she rose and wandered closer to the wall screen" (*Seduction*, 99). Similarly, *Seduction*, 123: "Do what you're going to do . . . But for right now I'm going with the pretense that I don't know about it." She is not the only one. McNab steps out so Roarke can fake a warrant (*Witness*, 181). For other examples, see *Ceremony*, 226.

138 *Fantasy*, 100.

139 She refuses (e.g., *Born*, 65; "Haunted," 298) when lives are not immediately on the line; in *Creation*, 91, where they are, she accepts the use of the unregistered equipment. Similarly, see *Seduction*, 225.

140 *Treachery*, 206.

141 *Conspiracy*, 328, 398.

142 *Survivor*, 174.

143 *Conspiracy*, 111. However, Roarke reacts with horror when Dallas tells him he'd make a good cop (e.g., *Visions*, 141).

144 *Promises*, 159. Roarke's divestment from one such opportunity and his unwillingness to explain that he's done it for Dallas' sake leads to suspicion falling on him in *Immortal in Death*.

145 *Betrayal*, 128, and *Promises*, 83, present slightly different takes on the sex trade; see also "Missing in Death," 238; *Salvation*, 53; *Creation*, 96.

146 *Fantasy*, 173.

147 *Salvation*, 304.

148 *Born*, 110.

149 *Creation*, 72.

150 As P. D. James notes, "The detective story is the novel of reason and justice, but it can affirm only the fallible justice of human beings, and the truth it celebrates can never be the whole truth any more than it is in a court of law" (James, *Talking about Detective Fiction*, 165). All must play a part; Dallas recognizes defense attorneys are also doing their job (*Innocent*, 219; *Obsession*, 53).

151 For instance, *Reunion*, 94; also *Visions*, 153–54, where she asks him to break into a consultant's apartment to verify an alibi.

152 "Missing in Death," 238.

153 *Strangers*, 371. Distinct from bribery, Morris does make a request as a friend for tickets to an event (*Witness*, 49, as Nadine does in *Betrayal*, 215).

154 *Immortal*, 112–13; *Betrayal*, 137; *Witness*, 100; *Indulgence*, 66; *Creation*, 56. Another colleague gets Mavis' concert tickets (*Born*, 184–87) rather than "sports or booze," while Roarke's resources are used to provide real chocolate for another incentive (*Seduction*, 194).

155 *Visions*, 98. When Peabody asks, "Who's going to perform the sexual favors, should it come to that?" Dallas tells her, "You, Detective. I outrank you."

156 *Divided*, 271.

157 *Treachery*, 51; also *Ceremony*, 150.

158 When Roarke suggests, "It's hard for you going after one of your own," Dallas responds, "She stopped being one of my own the minute she went on the take" (*Treachery*, 58). Similarly, former police officer Gina Tortelli insists that her skimming was common and not a big deal. Dallas insists that breaking the rules once means "you're done" (*Obsession*, 221–23).

159 *Judgment*, 289. On the connections between corruption and brutality, consult Johnson, *Street Justice*, 6–7 and passim; she refers specifically to an individual officer's involvement in both on 288.

160 Roarke cannot understand why Summerset never blamed him or made him leave after Marlena's murder. Summerset asks, "You were mine by then, weren't you?" (*Portrait*, 197).

161 *Vengeance*, 118–19.

162 *Portrait*, 222.

163 *Treachery*, 49.

164 *Divided*, 219: "Standing not just over the victim, but for the victim, and working to find whatever balance the system allowed. Even hating the system from time to time when that balance did not meet her own standards." Similarly, see *Obsession*, 141.

165 *Vengeance*, 116. Also, when Mavis is falsely accused of murder and Dallas assures her that she will clear her, Mavis says, "I thought it was 'innocent until proven guilty.'" Dallas replies, "That's just one of the bigger lies we live by" (*Immortal*, 52).

166 *Vengeance*, 117. Dallas defines a good cop as "someone who respects the badge and what it stands for, and doesn't stop until they make a difference" (*Reunion*, 32).

167 *Vengeance*, 124–25. They revisit the topic in *Salvation*, 105.

168 *Immortal*, 163–66.

169 *Immortal*, 171. Her commander likewise refuses to entertain the possibility of any formal or informal investigation (*Immortal*, 191). Dallas later compares herself to Nixie Swisher, who by chance survives the massacre of her family: "She had murder done around her. I did murder" (*Survivor*, 146). Mira corrects her. Later, Dallas says, "I've killed and I know

I've got the violence in me that makes me capable of it. Then. Now. But murder's got a different face. I don't see that in my mirror" (*Memory,* 371).

170 "Midnight," 128. Similarly, *Witness,* 68, 177.

171 *Judgment,* 36. Also *Seduction,* 131: "Even for Roarke, who'd been desperately poor, achingly hungry"—he tells, elsewhere, of "having rooted through alley garbage for food" (*Fantasy,* 57)—"it wasn't about the money so much as it was about the game of compiling it, *having* it, using it to make more of it" (emphasis in original). Also, of course, "wielding the power of it." Similarly, see *Reunion,* 51, and *Ceremony,* 88, where Roarke insists, "It's the money . . . and the making it."

172 *Fantasy,* 96. There is a danger here in that Roarke is able to get around and live by his private conduct rules precisely because he has massive amounts of money and impressive skills and therefore power.

173 *Kindred,* 236.

174 *Divided,* 9. Cohn writes that "contemporary heroes are frequently portrayed as giants of the marketplace, now accepted in popular romance as the arena for male acquisition of power" (Cohn, *Romance and the Erotics of Property,* 110). On heroes as enterprising capitalists, see Kamblé, *Making Meaning,* 31. This is not true for period romances with dukes and earls, nor for military heroes, but otherwise it is true (esp., e.g., Harlequin Presents and similar series). Courtney Milan offers a billionaire hero who breaks the mold in *Trade Me.* Benton, in Patricia Cornwell's Kay Scarpetta series, has inherited wealth; his dangerous job compensates for what would otherwise be effete masculinity.

175 Kamblé notes that the novels "explicitly address the hero's personal life and his business ethics and find both disturbing—and disturbingly inseparable" (Kamblé, *Making Meaning,* 53).

176 *Judgment,* 6.

177 *Loyalty,* 88.

178 *Loyalty,* 93. Other rhetoric: "The NYPSD is nothing but a soiled tool used by the hands of the right-wing bureaucrats and demigods to crush the will and freedom of the common man" (*Seduction,* 106). Also *Delusion,* 348.

179 Kamblé, *Making Meaning,* 53.

180 A salvo in her ongoing war with Summerset: he provokes her by using one of those shirts to polish the newel post (*Reunion,* 176).

181 *Visions,* 133. Roarke answers, "Retail conspiracy."

182 *Witness,* 295–97, 313.

183 For example, *Thankless,* 25.

184 *Indulgence,* 140.

185 Kamblé, *Making Meaning,* 31.

186 Dallas calls Roarke "the king of stuff" (*Betrayal,* 8) and "Mr. Buys the Entire World and Its Satellites" (*Brotherhood,* 23).

187 *Portrait,* 57. Also *Witness,* 221.

188 *Seduction*, 184, 187.

189 *Creation*, 148.

190 Examples include *Thankless*, 87; *Judgment*, 268–70; *Reunion*, 337; and "Ritual," 146.

191 *Seduction*, 177.

192 *Thankless*, 157–58.

193 Weeks, *Problem with Work*, 60–61.

194 *Brotherhood*, 169; *Obsession*, 97, 146; "Eternity," 51. In *Thankless in Death*, 235–39, Dallas arranges a new opportunity with Roarke's companies for a girl—barely adult—who reports illegal activity, despite her boss telling her not to do so. The girl is effusive in her thanks.

195 Weeks, *Problem with Work*, 43, 46, 48, 54.

196 On the lack of separation between the personal and the professional, see *Delusion*, 104. On balancing a career and a personal life (or living with imbalances), see *Reunion*, 53; *Innocence*, 174; *Ceremony*, 6; *Witness*, 204. On colleagues as family, see *Promises*, 220.

197 At one point, Dallas says, "This isn't the time for a family picnic," and Roarke replies, "Think of it as a combination family and company event" (*Divided*, 200).

198 *Seduction*, 334; *Divided*, 92; *Fantasy*, 89.

Chapter 4

1 James, *Talking about Detective Fiction*, 111 (also 11, 165).

2 Dallas draws a causal link between actual or feared violent or criminal behavior on the part of residents and the city's refusal to provide services such as recycling (*Conspiracy*, 71) or snow removal (*Obsession*, 200); in the latter case, McNab observes that this neglect makes life difficult for ordinary citizens to work or perform basic activities. Dallas presents the city's withdrawal of public services as a response to bad behavior, but McNab's comment accords better with history: public services are spotty or absent in poor areas in the first place, and the lack of, or poor quality of, services is what is likely to spark any significant protest by residents.

3 *Loyalty*, 98, 101.

4 Also *Vengeance*, 119, with discussion of links to police corruption.

5 *Delusion*, 195.

6 *Loyalty*, 56. Also *Betrayal*, 83–84; "Midnight," 232.

7 *Immortal*, 23; Dallas finds it more disturbing in the morgue.

8 For instance, *Immortal*, 123.

9 *Rapture*, 27. Also *Vengeance*, 107.

10 *Devoted*, 96.

11 Mira and Dallas discuss this incident of Testing much later (*Visions*, 195); Dallas recounts this origin story to Peabody in *Brotherhood*, 286–87.

12 *Rapture*, 106. Also *Immortal*, 124–25.

13 *Reunion,* 227. Similarly, *Delusion,* 237–38. When a woman who runs a rape clinic tells Dallas, "I believe in violence," she replies, "Hey. Me too" (*Brotherhood,* 263).

14 *Rapture,* 176–77; also *Witness,* 199. It is the fact that Roarke accepted an old flame sleeping with a mark when they were working a con that reassures Eve that her own position is secure: "She wasn't yours" (*Judgment,* 237). For a similar situation, see *Strangers,* 62–63, after Peabody makes a similar point about McNab (*Strangers,* 14). In *Immortal,* jealous of Casto, Roarke acknowledges, "It goes both ways," before admitting to being "very territorial," and Eve is pleased (*Immortal,* 235). On a reaction, after that, see *Judgment,* 160, 181, 195; *Treachery,* 203; *Innocent,* 178; *Salvation,* 127. The marriages of murder victims become fictional foils or mirrors for Dallas and Roarke's marriage in *Innocent in Death* and *Divided in Death.*

15 *Divided,* 79; *Brotherhood,* 121–22. For related passages, see *Origin,* 139; *Imitation,* 261–62; *Delusion,* 78; *Calculated,* 198; *Loyalty,* 20, 67. In *Rapture in Death,* Eve inadvertently experiences orgasm through a VR program. Roarke does not object; he only demands flesh-and-blood fidelity (*Rapture,* 173–77). Consult also Cohn, *Romance and the Erotics of Property,* 120. A quiz to determine if one is "an Eve, a Mavis, or a Peabody" gives wildly differing answers to a range of questions, but exactly the same violent response to any infidelity by their respective partners ("Bonus quiz," in *Origin,* 349–56).

16 Some cases that seem like jealousy are not. In *Loyalty in Death,* a wife discovers her husband having an affair and murders him and his mistress/her best friend; it turns out to be an elaborate set-up. Jealousy is a plot point in other cases, but the murderer is more often female (e.g., *Festive in Death*).

17 When Dallas and Roarke are on the outs because of a different view about an ex trying to worm her way back into Roarke's life, Roarke thinks, "He could bear the anger between them . . . Tempers were part of what they were" (*Innocence,* 162).

18 *Reunion,* 227.

19 *Divided,* 235; *Immortal,* 94, 129.

20 Eve and Roarke joke about violence between them, but though they have tempers and fight, he never hurts her that way (*Judgment,* 41, 51, 298).

21 *Judgment,* 94, 98.

22 *Ceremony,* 6.

23 *Loyalty,* 131; *Salvation,* 261. Dallas beats up droids (e.g., *Ceremony,* 188; *Obsession,* 155) or wishes she had time to do so (*Kindred,* 66). Zeke, Peabody's Free-Ager brother, notes that Dallas' aura is "strong" and that "the heart of it had been bright with compassion and loyalty" (*Loyalty,* 131–32).

24 *Survivor,* 268.

25 Examples include but are not limited to *Reunion, Treachery, Strangers, Festive, Witness, Visions* (in addition to a male serial killer), and *Devoted* (the woman is one of a duo).

26 *Treachery*, 207.

27 *Vengeance*, 194. Roarke reflects that his father "had met someone meaner, someone quick enough to jam a knife in his throat" (*Reunion*, 212). Roarke seems neither to know nor suspect Summerset's involvement. Dallas does not feel it's her place to tell him (*Thankless*, 274).

28 *Portrait*, 236.

29 *Purity*, 133–34. (How this death would be explained during Testing is not explored; perhaps Testing is only required for terminations using one's service weapon.) Jamie is determined to join the police force (e.g., *Ceremony*, 124), but Roarke hopes to lure him to private industry.

30 *Purity*, 22; *Kindred*, 142, 156; *Promises*, 119.

31 Testing searches out seeds of doubt or uncertainty in the officer being examined (*Purity*, 23), which would discourage introspection or critical reflection in favor of certainty about one's actions. Historical precursors to such Testing include the NYPD's Firearms Discharge Review Board. See Johnson, *Street Justice*, 277–78.

32 The clinical terminology of "termination" is more honest, perhaps, than the "officer-involved shooting" in use in the contemporary United States, which effaces any agency (compared, for instance, to "shooting by police"). On another occasion, while speculating about whether a fellow officer was involved in a "businesslike" death, Dallas observes, "Killing's business for cops" (*Promises*, 273). To remain on the force, Oberman either misled or bribed the psychiatrist responsible for testing her and her handpicked team members, but because "she's never wounded or terminated a suspect or any individual on the job . . . she's never been through Testing, required of any officer who terminates" (*Treachery*, 100). Bowers used substances to pass routine testing, but never went through the more intense Testing required after a termination.

33 *Promises*, 286.

34 *Purity*, 8–9.

35 *Treachery*, 179–80.

36 Prime examples include Ellen Bowers in *Conspiracy in Death* and Renee Oberman in *Treachery in Death*.

37 *Survivor*, 187.

38 *New York to Dallas* gives the backstory as well as the denouement: Dallas finds her mother's freshly murdered body. The incident returns in her dreams, with her mother accusing her of killing her. Throughout *Delusion in Death*, and periodically thereafter, she processes the associated events far more easily than she did those surrounding her father.

39 *Survivor*, 352.

40 Captain Jonah MacMasters, whose daughter was murdered, is similarly tempted (*Kindred*, 336, 343). Dallas remarks on other occasions about

being tempted to violence (e.g., in taking down a dirty cop), but not to killing (*Promises*, 302).

41 *Survivor*, 359; *New York to Dallas*, 355–56. Dallas confronts a parallel dilemma while possessed by a Romany "speaker for the dead" ("Possession," 47, 68, 77).

42 *Survivor*, 187; *Reunion*, 231.

43 *Portrait*, 217–23.

44 *Divided*, 325. Similarly, Roarke forgoes retaliation against an abusive former foster mother of Dallas' (*Memory*, 130–31). Also *Ceremony*, 296.

45 *Conspiracy*, 49. Dallas restrains similar impulses on numerous occasions, e.g., *Promises*, 12. In *Brotherhood*, her impulse with regard to serial rapists is "beating them all into bloody pulps," but she recognizes that she cannot. Roarke sees the first as evidence that she is herself and the latter as evidence that "there's my cop" (*Brotherhood*, 329). In other words, her identity as a police officer requires that she not privately mete out violence.

46 *Imitation*, 103. Arriving home, she explains the resulting bruise to Roarke: "Somebody knocked me into this guy's fist when I was trying to stop him from beating this other guy who was whacking off in the subway to a bloody pulp. I couldn't blame the guy, the guy with the fist, because he wasn't aiming at me. But still" (106).

47 *Origin*, 299–300.

48 *Salvation*, 173.

49 *Rapture*, 67.

50 *Ceremony*, 213.

51 *Reunion*, 368; *Conspiracy*, 366.

52 *Devoted*, 346.

53 *Conspiracy*, 78.

54 *Survivor*, 65.

55 *Rapture*, 79. Right before that, a chemi-head, seeing Dallas and Peabody, attempted to escape and "skidded on the wet pavement and banged face first into the lamppost," knocking himself out and bloodying his nose (*Rapture*, 79). Peabody models her approach to street toughs after Dallas (*Divided*, 185–86).

56 *Conspiracy*, 73, 131. Dallas uses violence and threats in the first case, a bribe in the second. In another case, she threatens an informant aroused by pain to keep him from his preferred sex club (*Reunion*, 165, 180).

57 *Reunion*, 157. In a club, again the audience is key (*Conspiracy*, 78). Dallas uses threats of violence in response to an insult from a "grunt loitering in a doorway." She tells his drugged companion that she knows he's carrying illegals because she has "X-ray vision" (*Strangers*, 257). Johnson suggests that whatever progress has been made in combating certain forms of police misconduct, "more common forms of street brutality have proven persistent and intractable" (Johnson, *Street Justice*, 5).

58 *Treachery*, 12.

59 *Treachery,* 124; similarly, *Imitation,* 237: she tells a loitering chemi-head, "If I have to chase you, it's going to piss me off. . . . Then I'll probably slip so that my foot ends up planted in your balls. Just got a question. You got the answer, it's worth ten." She merges threats and the possibility of reward.

60 *Creation,* 311.

61 In *Delusion in Death,* a bystander recording of a crime scene, which he believes shows police officers using excessive force, turns out—as the witness agrees when he watches the footage with Peabody—to only show officers acting in self-defense (*Delusion,* 136–39).

62 *Immortal,* 227–28; *Salvation,* 233–35; *Imitation,* 312. Dallas' detectives do so in *Devoted,* 234–35.

63 *Strangers,* 353. Similarly, *Salvation,* 345–46.

64 *Strangers,* 354.

65 *Rapture,* 203–6.

66 *Rapture,* 204–5, 231. (The encounter is described, in a flashback from a dream, in *Obsession,* 76.) The broader question of parallels between violent, unwanted sex and passionate, desired encounters is raised in *Judgment,* 196; *Innocence,* 116; and *Immortal,* 171. During the mind-controlled encounter Barrow provoked, during which Roarke used Eve sexually while repeating the Gaelic word for "mine," his violent "possession" was linked to his instinctive claiming. In their next encounter, Roarke makes love to her and calls her "my love" in Gaelic, seeking balance here, to replace taking with giving, violence with tenderness. Questions about consent (as "part of the fantasy") arise. Dallas' insistence that he needn't ask does not mean that marriage grants an unconditional right to sexual access, but perhaps that no permission is required to make overtures. It seems significant that consent within a committed long-term relationship requires different strategies and can rely on a personal language of willingness that need not be as explicitly spelled out as is necessary in a single or first encounter. Lennard discusses the episode, especially as it relates to Roarke's control: "He simply comes equipped with a conscience as well as a brain and a penis, and controls all three . . . unfailingly" (*Of Modern Dragons,* 78). Carrington presents an intriguingly parallel account of mind-control in Star Trek: a kiss, and threatened whipping, with Kirk and Uhura (*Speculative Blackness,* 78–80). As with Roarke, Kirk is an unwilling participant in (threatened) violence; for Uhura, like for Dallas, there is a past trauma—interracial violence harking back to slavery in the first case, rape in the other—recalled by the event. Just as Dallas refutes any such connection in later conversations with Roarke, Nichelle Nichols, the actor who plays Uhura, frames the event in terms of kink, not violence. Dallas has implausibly little trauma interfering with her ability to have a sexual relationship with Roarke (or, earlier, others); see Lennard, *Of Modern Dragons,* 78; Goris, "From Romance to Roberts," 405n19.

67 *Rapture*, 217.

68 Body cameras are not worn all the time; even when used, they can be tricked. For instance, in a highly sensitive investigation which must be kept secret, Dallas orders Peabody: “Keep your recorder off me when I remove the eyes Roarke put over the bathroom doorway” (*Treachery*, 77; also 55). On the possibility of tampering with records, see *Betrayal*, 118. Other evidence can be destroyed as well. Dallas allows the destruction of (irrelevant) evidence that shows Nadine having sex with a murder victim, though only after the case is resolved (*Witness*, 309).

69 *Rapture*, 218, 219, 220.

70 *Rapture*, 233, 234.

71 *Obsession*, 65.

72 Dallas takes down a suspect who gets away from his arresting officer in Central (*Imitation*, 158–59); later, she explains that his jaw was dislocated and he has a concussion—and though he claims it’s from her pitching her Pepsi at him, she thinks it’s from when a bunch of officers tackled him in the aftermath of her takedown. In either case, she complains of having to “waste more time on paperwork” (164). She considers such things part of “normal” life in Central (196).

73 *Witness*, 191.

74 *Born*, 305.

75 *Memory*, 58–60. Though he punched Dallas, they come to an amicable agreement; she forgoes the charge of assaulting an officer and tells McNab she’s bleeding because she bit her tongue. On another occasion, a similar takedown of a pickpocket ends with her pressing her boot to his throat, cutting off his air supply for “ten warning seconds” (*Reunion*, 282). Jenkinson also relates a comedy-of-errors apprehension where the suspect makes a baseless complaint of police brutality (*Indulgence*, 44–45).

76 *Born*, 132.

77 *Creation*, 206. Also *Thankless*, 46.

78 *Innocent*, 212. False accusations of sexual assault recur in, for example, *Devoted*, 306–7, and *Reunion*, passim. In *New York to Dallas*, Dallas’ mother uses a false accusation of rape to ensnare a victim who works as a rape counselor. Fake accusations are a problem because rape is so terrible. Gloria DeLauter, a particularly pathological character in Roberts’ Chesapeake Bay series, repeatedly accuses men of sexual assault (e.g., *Inner Harbor*, 137, 180, 300). On frivolous false accusations of sexual harassment, see *Obsession*, 208, 225–27.

79 Peabody intimidates (but does not actually touch) a suspect in interrogation; when the suspect threatens to tell someone, Dallas says, “Who’s going to believe you over cops? And things happen to recordings all the time. Glitchy equipment. How about we unlock her restraints, Peabody? You can do what you did to the last one. I’ve got your back” (*Devoted*, 361). It’s an empty threat, but effective. In “Ritual in Death,” Dallas uses threats to coerce a confession before turning the recorder on (187). At

other times, she keeps her recorder off to give helpful advice to deserving suspects.

80 *Promises,* 294.

81 Peabody suggests that she herself go in with the apprehended killer, since of all the cops "volunteering to handle it . . . [o]ne of them's bound to try to get in some kicks" for the two dead officers (*Survivor,* 356).

82 *Visions,* 325.

83 *Rapture,* 220.

84 *Judgment,* 289.

85 *Conspiracy,* 267.

86 Charles J. Ogletree Jr. and Austin Sarat, "Imaging Punishment: An Introduction," in *Punishment in Popular Culture,* ed. Charles J. Ogletree Jr. and Austin Sarat (New York: New York University Press, 2015), 12.

87 *Loyalty,* 247; *Salvation,* 318–20.

88 In a rare case, the suspect—a writer focused on serial killers—does not believe that Dallas is capable of using the technique she mentions: "I take you into a private room and during our little chat you trip and somehow manage to break your face." He responds with an impassioned defense of her integrity: "You've got attitude for sure, and some innate violent tendencies, but you don't pound on suspects. Too much integrity. You're a good cop." He elaborates on her adherence to "the spirit of the law" if not always "the letter": "Maybe you take shortcuts now and then, stuff that doesn't find its way into your official reports, but you're careful about the lines—the ones you cross, the ones you don't. And beating confessions out of suspects isn't one of your shortcuts" (*Imitation,* 271–72).

89 *Visions,* 333, 337; *Ceremony,* 278–80, 286.

90 *Judgment,* 289, also 290–91.

91 *Seduction,* 311 (and, broadly, 311–14). In a different vein, in a Roberts novel, a foster father tells his young charge that if he continues down his current path, he'll end up back in juvie, then in prison, where rape will be inevitable (*Inner Harbor,* 22).

92 *Brotherhood,* 375.

93 "Ritual," 188.

94 *Devoted,* 358, 363, 365, 370.

95 *Glory,* 30, and, more broadly, 27–30.

96 *Reunion,* 104–6, where the naïve warden at Dockport harbors delusions about rehabilitating its residents.

97 For example, a brutal serial killer and rapist "bled to death" when "an unidentified inmate or guard castrated him and left him lying in his own cage" (*Imitation,* 332). The abusive father of one of Dallas' victims turns out to have met someone meaner in jail: "Picked the wrong con to mess with inside, and ended up bleeding out in the showers thanks to the shiv in his gut" (*Indulgence,* 84). A junkie who stabbed and killed someone for a negligible sum "died in prison when somebody returned the favor"

("Chaos," 22). The implication in such cases is that they got what they deserved.

98 "Midnight," 126.

99 *New York to Dallas*, 5–6.

100 "Taken," 20, 37, 57.

101 Discussing the contemporary United States, prisoner Charlie Morningstar reflects, "Sex is against the law in the prison system. But the fact is that it's still going to go on" (quoted in Robin Levi and Ayelet Waldman, eds., *Inside This Place, Not of It: Narratives from Women's Prisons*, Voice of Witness 8 (San Francisco: McSweeney's Books, 2011), 202). Despite threats of prison rape, the novels describe consensual prison sex: Dallas convinces an inmate to share information on Dunne in exchange for a session with a human LC rather than a droid (*Reunion*, 108); a couple in *Devoted in Death* (308) enjoys regular conjugal visits while one partner is incarcerated.

102 In a real-world comparison, Sarah Chase, currently imprisoned, recounts a relationship with a guard that she at first desired, but then she "began to realize that he was taking advantage of me"; when she attempted to end their relationship, "he got scary," and she was lucky to get help from others. She was harshly penalized, though, for later attempting to cover up their relationship (Levi and Waldman, *Inside This Place, Not of It*, 81–82). Chase's account bears out what another imprisoned woman, Marilyn Sanderson, observes of "sexual assault between staff and inmates": "Sometimes it starts off being consensual, but then later it becomes an abusive situation" (Levi and Waldman, *Inside This Place, Not of It*, 156). The only account relayed by Levi and Waldman that does not seem to have degenerated into abuse is between Victoria Sanchez, currently imprisoned, and a female guard that never progressed beyond kissing and ended, after four years, when the guard quit her job (179–80). Sanchez reflects that when staff suspected the relationship, "they thought it was my fault. If you ever get involved with staff, it's always your fault. You did it, you manipulated" (180).

103 *Reunion*, 111–12, 113, 114.

104 In real-world contexts, a staggeringly high percentage of female prisoners have survived previous sexual or domestic abuse; while incarcerated, "abuse often continues for these women, who face sexual, physical, and mental abuse at the hands of prison staff" (Michelle Alexander, "Foreword: Standing without Sweet Company," in Levi and Waldman, *Inside This Place, Not of It*, 13). Angela Davis remarks on the "pervasive vulnerability of imprisoned women to sexual abuse" in her *Are Prisons Obsolete?* (New York: Seven Stories Press, 2003), 80, or, more broadly, 77–83. The testimonies of currently and formerly imprisoned women compiled by Levi and Waldman illustrate the commonplace and devastating practice of forcible rape as well as coercion and abuse of power by prison staff and guards (Levi and Waldman, *Inside This Place, Not of It*,

18–19, 81, 96–98, 112–13, 115–17, 145, 156–57, 178–79, 196). The book also includes excerpts from a longer report, "Women in Detention in the United States," including reports on sexual abuse (232–34, 262–69). While violence by other prisoners is possible, they found sexual relationships between inmates typically consensual.

105 A newly incarcerated mother bribes a guard to let her son visit her in prison, and the son kills her; Dallas is deeply angry and says, "Asses will be thoroughly kicked" (*Born*, 331).

106 Davis writes, "The prison reveals congealed forms of antiblack racism that operate in clandestine ways" (Davis, *Are Prisons Obsolete?*, 25).

107 *Kindred*, 239; information on her sentence, *Kindred*, 296. The woman in question, importantly, was manipulated by a male partner to take a more extensive sentence rather than a lesser one by implicating him.

108 *Immortal*, 218. Also *Survivor*, 114; *Visions*, 273. Joshua Price discusses the impact of parole supervision and "the experience of being subject to the arbitrary tyrannies and caprices of parole agents unaccountable to the public or the courts" on previously incarcerated people and their families in *Prison and Social Death* (New Brunswick, N.J.: Rutgers University Press, 2015), 107.

109 *Kindred*, 167.

110 *Immortal*, 216.

111 James, *Talking about Detective Fiction*, 153.

112 *Obsession*, 89.

113 Although gender differences are relevant, particularly given that women are the primary victims of sexual violence in the In Death universe, here a thought experiment may prove useful. Imagine the victim as a woman who made a rude overture, then lifted her skirt when prompted by a male cop; that cop then repeatedly and roughly jammed several fingers into her vagina, causing her significant pain. Imagine that the cop and his wife, who had been standing by, then joked about the incident as a refreshing start to their day.

114 Dallas repeatedly speculates, too, that people enjoy murder "as long as it isn't too close." She thinks, "It's reassuring. Somebody's dead, but we're not" (*Imitation*, 126). The role of seeing—visual evidence, affect—is worth further exploration.

115 Davis, *Are Prisons Obsolete?*, 10. Ogletree and Sarat argue for the key role of mass media, especially film and television, "in shaping and transforming political and legal life" (Ogletree and Sarat, "Imaging Punishment," 3). I would argue that novels potentially offer more room for reflection and resistance when readers employ critical reading strategies, though critical viewing strategies are useful as well.

116 *Creation*, 285. Dallas tells a witness who expresses worries about entrapment, "You watch too many cop shows" (*Treachery*, 125); other references include *Thankless*, 355. Robb/Roberts plays with metafiction (e.g.,

Devoted in Death, 79, and *Savor the Moment*, 287; and Vivanco, *For Love and Money*, 112, gives another example).

117 *Calculated*, 7. Similarly, an actress points to parallels between their jobs: seemingly "exciting, glamorous," but really "a job, with its ups and downs like any" (*Betrayal*, 13).

118 Bonilla-Silva, *Racism without Racists*, 2.

119 Alexander, in *The New Jim Crow*, chronicles a shift from slavery to Jim Crow to "law and order" rhetoric.

120 Holland, *Erotic Life of Racism*, 4. Roach points out its "dual senses": "really great" and "unrealistic" (Roach, *Happily Ever After*, 96). Toni Morrison insists that "the world does not become raceless or will not become unracialized by assertion. The act of enforcing racelessness in literary discourse is itself a racial act" (Morrison, *Playing in the Dark*, 46).

121 In Death's universe is saturated by what sociologist Eduardo Bonilla-Silva calls "color-blind racism" (Bonilla-Silva, *Racism without Racists*, 7). The pretense that race plays no role is a central facet of the new, post–Jim Crow racism. On this new racism and state-sponsored violence against black people, consult his *Racism Without Racists*, esp. 43–51. Frankenberg offers a helpful reframing of "color-blindness" as "a double move toward 'color evasiveness' and 'power evasiveness'" (Frankenberg, *White Women, Race Matters*, 14). Toni Morrison observes evasiveness in literature: "In matters of race, silence and evasion have historically ruled literary discourse. Evasion has fostered another, substitute language in which the issues are encoded, foreclosing open debate." She continues, "The habit of ignoring race is understood to be a graceful, even generous, liberal gesture" (Morrison, *Playing in the Dark*, 9, 9–10). Even if race is not formally acknowledged, though, it can be discussed. *Star Trek* combines interracial harmony as a taken-for-granted element of its utopian future with extensive "allegorical treatments of race and racism" (Carrington, *Speculative Blackness*, 160). Octavia Butler's *Kindred* (Boston: Beacon, 2003 [1979]) is an excellent example of speculative fiction's directly addressing race and racism as well as the relationship between past, present, and future.

122 The elimination of the death penalty is mostly implicit, with references to multiple consecutive life sentences for particularly awful crimes. Direct references to its abolition appear rarely after its first mention in *Glory in Death*; for instance, a retired cop and political figure wants to reinstate executions ("Interlude," 43), and Dallas refers to executions once having been acceptable (*Delusion*, 325).

123 *Imitation*, 120.

124 *Naked*, 241; "Interlude," 20. The commonplace nature of same-sex dating and marriage (noted by Goris, "From Romance to Roberts," 410) illuminates a tension: although Dallas encounters quite a few people in the course of her daily life who date, cohabit with, or marry people of the

same sex, and some who are involved with both men and women, none number among her friends.

125 *Judgment,* 49, 56. These and a brief reference to Hitler and "people who think white's right" (*Delusion,* 240) are among the series' few references to "essentialist" (Frankenberg, *White Women, Race Matters*) or "biological" (Bonilla-Silva, *Racism without Racists*) racism.

126 *Judgment,* 107, 57. Latinx characters in the novels include a handful of cops, a prisoner (*Reunion*), a priest and his community (*Salvation*), and several maids ("Eternity," 12, 17; *Big Jack*).

Chapter 5

1 *Festive,* 320. Also *Obsession,* 25; *Devoted,* 273. In *Brotherhood,* Dallas proposes a modification: "Even if you're an asshole" (44). Appropriately, in that installment the victims she stands for *were* awful (174, 382–83).

2 *Rapture,* 49.

3 *Strangers,* 1; similarly, *Delusion,* 30: "Murder could happen . . . to anyone, anywhere, anytime." Robb is partly right and partly wrong. All human beings are vulnerable to murder and violence, but not all are equally exposed to its ravages. Judith Butler puts the sign's sentiment slightly differently: "In a way, we all live with this particular vulnerability, a vulnerability to the other that is part of bodily life, a vulnerability to a sudden address from elsewhere that we cannot preempt." What Butler attends to that Robb does not, at least not in this context, is the way that "this vulnerability . . . becomes highly exacerbated under certain social and political conditions" (Butler, *Precarious Life: The Powers of Mourning and Violence* [London: Verso, 2006], 29). Beyond the "radically inequitable ways that corporeal vulnerability is distributed globally" (30), there is—as Robb writes in some of the novels I explore in this chapter—uneven distribution of violence even within New York.

4 Bonilla-Silva prefers "racial practices" ("behaviors, styles, cultural affectations, traditions, and organizational procedures that help maintain white rule") to "discrimination." The latter is linked to bad acts, actors, and intentions rather than structures and routines (Bonilla-Silva, *Racism without Racists,* 62–63n1). Neither individual discrimination nor large-scale racial inequality receives sustained attention. Karen Fields and Barbara Fields note that "the most consequential of the illusions racecraft underwrites is concealing the affiliation between racism and inequality in general" (Fields and Fields, *Racecraft: The Soul of Inequality in American Life* [London: Verso, 2012], 261).

5 *Naked*; similarly, *Witness,* 50.

6 *Strangers,* 1.

7 *Strangers,* 127. Also *Immortal,* 214; *Treachery,* 6.

8 *Loyalty,* 85; *Portrait,* 9; *Treachery,* 78–79.

9 *Conspiracy,* 3.

10 *Conspiracy,* 74. Similarly, *Imitation,* 8, and *Seduction,* 37: "It was a cycle no one, particularly the city fathers, seemed to be able to break."

11 *Survivor,* 263; *Born,* 219, 283.

12 *Conspiracy,* 4. On the intractability of the human propensity for violence, see *Conspiracy,* 102, and *Fantasy,* 285. Susan Sontag uses photography showing suffering to address human compassion, complicity, and the linked questions of attention and action. She remarks on "how much suffering caused by human wickedness there is in the world we share with others. Someone who is perennially surprised that depravity exists, who continues to feel disillusioned (even incredulous) when confronted with evidence of what humans are capable of inflicting in the way of gruesome, hands-on cruelties upon other humans, has not reached moral or psychological adulthood" (Sontag, *Regarding the Pain of Others* [New York: Picador, 2003], 114).

13 *Conspiracy,* 3. On another occasion, a novel refers to the "human garbage" in an alley—though it turns out to be a VR program (*Rapture,* 1).

14 *Conspiracy,* 3. One cynical campaign "promises to fight the good fight against neglect, crime, and the general decay of that ailing sector of the city" (*Witness,* 50). Lauren Berlant refers to "the structural intractability of a problem the world can live with" in her article "Slow Death (Sovereignty, Obesity, Lateral Agency)," *Critical Inquiry* 33 (2007): 762.

15 *Strangers,* 165.

16 *Conspiracy,* 6; similarly, *Imitation,* 42. "Though she'd been brought up in wealth and privilege," Louise shares this awareness (*Portrait,* 101). The clinic she runs in a poor neighborhood "was a steady beam of light in a very dark world."

17 *Conspiracy,* 5.

18 *Conspiracy,* 4.

19 Death, especially slow death, stands distinct from murder. As Berlant writes, "Slow death, or the structurally motivated attrition of persons notably because of their membership in certain populations is neither a state of exception nor the opposite, mere banality, but a domain of revelation where an upsetting scene of living that has been muffled in ordinary consciousness is revealed to be interwoven with ordinary life after all" (Berlant, "Slow Death," 761). On ordinary deaths and slow deaths, consult also Elizabeth A. Povinelli, *Economies of Abandonment: Social Belonging and Endurance in Late Liberalism* (Durham, N.C.: Duke University Press, 2011). Dallas speculates that the murderer counts on no one investigating these deaths too closely. She finds a way to spin it to interest the media despite the fact it would usually not make good copy (*Conspiracy,* 133–34).

20 *Conspiracy,* 10, 27.

21 *Rapture,* 69.

22 Also consult *Portrait,* 242. For a similar discussion about expensive virility and fertility drugs, see *Seduction,* 125, 180. Berlant observes,

"Biopower operates when a hegemonic bloc organizes the reproduction of life in ways that allow political crises to be cast as conditions of specific bodies and their competence at maintaining health or other conditions of social belonging; thus this bloc gets to judge the problematic body's subjects"—or, I might suggest, the problematic subjects' bodies—"whose agency is deemed to be fundamentally destructive" (Berlant, "Slow Death," 765 and passim).

23 *Glory*, 2.

24 *Glory*, 2; *Conspiracy*, 108.

25 *Conspiracy*, 174.

26 *Conspiracy*, 350. Artificial organs raise questions about the boundaries between human and droid (*Origin*, 68–69).

27 *Portrait*, 304.

28 *Divided*, 156. Similarly, see *Calculated*, 92; *Holiday*, 180 ("Nothing's better than genuine").

29 On the last of these points, see *Immortal*, 127.

30 *Conspiracy*, 363. Similarly, the murderers in *Indulgence in Death* chose victims who lacked "their pedigree, their privilege to be important by birth" (315).

31 *Conspiracy*, 365.

32 *Conspiracy*, 107, 67.

33 In *Origin in Death*, "the science fiction generic identity" that had been "simply part of the setting" of Robb's universe (Goris, "From Romance to Roberts," 411) moves to the fore, invoking "much sharper senses of futurity and alienation" and "mak[ing] horribly real a dystopic warning of evil growth and unending revenance" (Lennard, *Of Modern Dragons*, 80, 82).

34 Dallas is skeptical in general about scientific research. In *Seduction in Death*, banned medical experimentation is implicated in the birth of one of the villains. But Dallas also worries about cloned cows and pigs getting intelligence and coming for human beings in a revenge fantasy (*Survivor*, 205–6). She is leery of commonplace technology as well, including networked vending machines (*Origin*, 26–27). On the one hand, such worries seem ridiculous and humorous. On the other hand, they weave a thread of unease about the reach of technology through the novels despite their general acquiescence to invasive government surveillance.

35 Similarly, the DA wants a stronger case before pursuing warrants because the suspects are "wealthy men, who can afford an army of very slick attorneys" (*Indulgence*, 314).

36 *Origin*, 216.

37 *Origin*, 6.

38 *Origin*, 30, 30–31.

39 *Origin*, 39, 105.

40 *Origin*, 262, 263.

41 Nadine Furst's working title for *The Icove Agenda* was *Deadly Perfection: The Icove Agenda* (*Salvation*, 80). Of the doctor, Dallas sums up, "He was a perfectionist" (*Origin*, 106; similarly, 170).

42 *Origin*, 333, 264.

43 *Origin*, 264, 267.

44 *Origin*, 267, 292, 293.

45 *Origin*, 201.

46 *Rapture*, 239.

47 *Origin*, 182.

48 *Immortal*, 1.

49 *Origin*, 182, 211, 91, 101.

50 *Origin*, 169.

51 *Origin*, 174, 176. Louise raises similar questions about "selecting traits, eliminating others," which come down to the question of "who decides" on the "parameters" (212).

52 *Immortal*, 40.

53 For instance, Zoner (analogous to marijuana) is mostly harmless; plenty of people, when investigated, turn out to have a bust for Zoner in their youth. At the other end of the spectrum, Zeus (like PCP) makes users extra strong and gives them a feeling of invincibility—and often leads to violence. Funk, not entirely dissimilar to methamphetamines, is especially addictive. Funky junkies become increasingly jittery and unable to focus the longer they use.

54 An exception would be *Survivor*, 117–18.

55 Robb often plays with literary analogues and antecedents (e.g., *Witness in Death* pays homage to Agatha Christie), especially in the novellas. "Chaos in Death" engages *The Strange Case of Dr. Jekyll and Mr. Hyde*; "Taken in Death" plays off Hansel and Gretel; the villain in "Wonderment in Death" (in an anthology entitled *Down the Rabbit Hole*) is obsessed with *Alice in Wonderland*. As to whether Dallas has "a touch of sight" or merely well-honed instincts, see *Indulgence*, 24.

56 For example, *Fantasy*, 137.

57 The killer in *Portrait in Death* murders and photographs young people to capture their light, believing he can take it inside himself and gain immortality: "*They will say I am mad, but I have found sanity. I have found Truth and Salvation*" (*Portrait*, 2, emphasis in original). He declares, "What I do is not simply for myself, but for all mankind" (*Portrait*, 285). He is not, he insists, "some kind of monster" but "a savior" (*Portrait*, 343). The killer in "Haunted in Death" has a long family history of mental illness (314). In two exceptions, Allika Straffo suffers depression after her young son dies (*Innocent*, 131); Peabody, feeling down, insists that "depression did *not* run in her family, and she wasn't going to be the first to spiral down into it" (*Seduction*, 117, emphasis in original).

58 “Chaos,” 10; also “Taken,” 61. Drugs and mind control can induce “fatal delusions” (“Wonderment,” 46) in otherwise previously healthy people (e.g., *Delusion, Rapture,* “Chaos”).

59 The murderer in *Concealed in Death* was not quite normal, suffering from depression after his mother’s suicide; it was committing the first murder of a dozen that led to his break with reality and his ongoing institutionalization. In “Possession in Death,” the grief accompanying the loss of a man’s beloved and his career turns him into a criminal, setting him on the path of murdering young women. When a woman with whom one man was intimately, though not sexually, involved is killed, it “derailed his train” (*Creation,* 260).

60 “Midnight,” 133, 201. Other examples include the killers in *Thankless in Death* and *Delusion in Death* (e.g., 237, 267). Dallas reflects, “Sometimes the unspeakable can come from the decent. And sometimes, it’s possible to make yourself decent out of the unspeakable. I know about this” (*Innocent,* 367). On the overlap and distinctions between killers and monsters, see *Indulgence,* 232–34. Other characters raise similar questions (*Imitation,* 122). A related question concerns luck rather than morality: Roarke wonders why, when he had every disadvantage and the children killed in a home invasion every advantage, “I come to this and those children are dead?” (*Survivor,* 258).

61 *Conspiracy,* 145.

62 *Rapture,* 253 (though the killer takes a different stance, 282). Dallas makes a similar observation in other cases (e.g., *Creation,* 126); Mira expresses a slightly different opinion elsewhere: “Sometimes a killer is born, sometimes he is made” (*Imitation,* 200). More reflection can be found in *Visions,* 338, regarding the abused serial killer, and in *Innocent,* 319, regarding a ten-year-old “sociopath with homicidal tendencies”; Roarke speculates that Rayleen Straffo “must be very, very sick” (*Innocent,* 289). The why is unclear. “There are some questions that don’t have answers. You’ve got to let them be” (*Innocent,* 309, 370).

63 Mental defect is often connected to criminality (e.g., “Midnight,” 125; “Eternity,” 108; *Conspiracy,* 307; *Judgment,* 46; *Betrayal,* 37).

64 *Ceremony,* 68; *Seduction,* 37, 290; *Imitation,* 103; *Delusion,* 256. On beggars’ licenses, see Ruthann Robson, *Dressing Constitutionally: Hierarchy, Sexuality, and Democracy from Our Hairstyles to Our Shoes* (New York: Cambridge Unversity Press, 2013), 11–12.

65 *Conspiracy,* 3. It connects them to the “poor and displaced” who suffer.

66 Although sexual brutality is more common as a pathology (e.g., *Imitation,* 150), in other cases purportedly abnormal sexuality involves impotence (*Creation,* 103) or asexuality (“Midnight,” where Dallas notes the killer had “never had a healthy sexual relationship” [160], then describes him as “highly asexual” [175]). Another detective describes a perpetrator who seems to have no interest in sex as “a sick fuck” (*Delusion,* 291), a

term also used for a handyman who preyed on a thirteen-year-old girl (*Concealed*, 97). On asexuality, consult Julia Sondra Decker, *The Invisible Orientation: An Introduction to Asexuality* (New York: Carrel Books, 2014).

67 Cara Leibowitz calls words like "idiot" and "moron" "highly ableist terms with a sordid history" (Leibowitz, "Everyday Ableism and How We Can Avoid It," March 3, 2015, http://thebodyisnotanapology.com/magazine/everyday-ableism-and-how-we-can-avoid-it/). On ableism, see Fiona Kumari Campbell's "Refusing Able(ness): A Preliminary Conversation about Ableism," *M/C Journal: A Journal of Media and Culture* 11, no. 3 (2008), http://journal.media-culture.org.au/index.php/mcjournal/article/viewArticle/46/0, in which Campbell notes that "a chief feature of an ableist viewpoint is a belief that impairment or disability (irrespective of 'type') is inherently negative and should the opportunity present itself, be ameliorated, cured or indeed eliminated." Campbell defines ableism as "a network of beliefs, processes and practices that produces a particular kind of self and body (the corporeal standard) that is projected as the perfect, species-typical and therefore essential and fully human. Disability then, is cast as a diminished state of being human" (Campbell, "Inciting Legal Fictions: Disability's Date with Ontology and the Ableist Body of Law," *Griffith Law Review* 10, no. 1 [2001]: 44n5). On why slurs matter and how they operate, consult *Redksins*, King's exploration of the Washington, D.C. NFL franchise's team name. Although King focuses on racial slurs, much of what he writes about the term (which he renders "r*dskins") applies to ableist epithets. Indeed, there are crucial parallels between ableism and "anti-Indian racism [that] persists in part because it is normalized, taken for granted, and familiar" (58).

68 *Loyalty*, 58. Similarly, a slow vehicle "limped along like a blind, three-legged dog" (*Visions*, 2).

69 Louise DiMatto asks, "What, do I look simple?" when Dallas asks her if she's cooking for a dinner party (*Visions*, 219).

70 *Creation*, 204–7, quote from 206. Roarke remarks on Dallas' "compassion for the distress and confusion of a scared little boy inside a man's body" (*Creation*, 208; similarly, *Concealed*, 347).

71 In contrast, some books rely on disability of a protagonist as a plot device or as a metaphor for character. Take Teresa Medeiros, *Yours until Dawn* (New York: Avon Books, 2004). Its hero, Gabriel Fairchild, once angelic looking, had been blinded and scarred aboard the Trafalgar when he tried but failed to save Admiral Nelson's life. Believing himself rejected by the young woman he wished to marry, Fairchild becomes reclusive and surly. He eventually recovers his sight, falls into real love with the young woman, and takes his rightful place as earl. Consult also Ridley, "Some Thoughts on 'Physically Disabled Protagonists,'" *Love in the*

Margins, October 27, 2013, http://loveinthemargins.com/2013/10/27/some-thoughts-on-physically-disabled-protagonists/.

72 Trey Ziegler, who drugged, raped, and blackmailed several women, was murdered in *Festive in Death.*

73 To take only one example, see *Imitation,* 58. Countervoices arise: not only does McNab like Peabody and appreciate her ass (e.g., *Survivor,* 191), so too no women denigrate it.

74 *Brotherhood,* 71.

75 "Eternity," 34.

76 *Survivor,* 37.

77 "Eternity," 33.

78 *Big Jack,* 237, emphasis in original. He elaborates, "Most physical ailments were temporary and easily rectified," but "mental illness was nothing but an embarrassment to anyone associated with the patient."

79 *Purity,* 92. "If disability is conceptualized as a terrible unending tragedy, then any future that includes disability can only be a future to avoid. A better future, in other words, is one that excludes disability and disabled bodies; indeed it is the very *absence* of disability that signals this better future. The *presence* of disability, then, signals something else, a future that bears too many traces of the ills of the present to be desirable" (Alison Kafer, *Feminist, Queer, Crip* [Bloomington: Indiana University Press, 2013], 2, emphasis in original).

80 *Purity,* 116.

81 *Purity,* 116. McNab jokes about it to put others at ease (*Purity,* 148). Overall, there is great attention to his affect (e.g., 97, 113) and the need for others to manage their affect around him (114). In a slightly different register, teenager Jamie Lingstrom views McNab in motivational terms: "Jamie thought he was pure hero stuff now that he'd been wounded in the line. Here he was half-frozen and pushing on with the job." Persisting despite all obstacles was "what cops did" (133). On narratives of overcoming, consult ch. 4 of Kafer, *Feminist, Queer, Crip.*

82 *Rapture,* 185–86.

83 *Purity,* 315; *Visions,* 280–86.

84 *Witness,* 252.

85 *Origin,* 32, mentions Peabody's "complete recovery from being injured in the line." Psychological traumas, sometimes stemming from physical injury, may have longer-term consequences. One detective badly injured in the line "lost her belly" for street policing (*Treachery,* 217).

86 A character "paralyzed from the waist down for six weeks," and laid up for twice that after "she'd taken a hit for the President" while serving as a Secret Service agent, recovered fully and went to work for Roarke in security (*Divided,* 91).

87 The doctors at the time summed up her condition: "*Beaten, raped. Long-term sexual and physical abuse. Suffering from malnutrition,*

dehydration, severe physical and emotional trauma." One concludes, "*She's lucky to have survived*" (*Seduction*, 166, emphasis in original).

88 In contrast, in *Concealed in Death*, the bones of a dozen girls reveal the neglect some suffered in life (e.g., 284). As for trauma's invisible traces, these recur throughout.

89 One might consider Dallas' management of her trauma and associated reactions part of a chronic illness, but PTSD here is an invisible disability. Mental illness in general typically remains latent or undiagnosed until it causes illness or reactions.

90 *Purity*, 163–64. When a cop retires very early, with "no disability, no mental fatigue," it hints that some corruption was involved (*Conspiracy*, 130). The possibility of pensioning off cops with disability contrasts with actual practice, where no cops seem to be permanently disabled in the line of duty. When Trueheart is injured and (temporarily) paralyzed, Dallas worries because "he needs to be a cop" (*Witness*, 252). When he regains consciousness, Peabody tells Dallas and signals as "the best part: he's responding to stimuli. There's no paralysis" (258). It is not just disability as the inability to do productive work, but the inability to work in a chosen vocation that is at stake here.

91 Indeed, an unnamed e-detective does his work competently while seated: he "rode a wheeled stool up and down a counter, his baggies and skin tank red and orange blurs, his ring-studded fingers flying over keys and controls" (*Fantasy*, 160).

92 "Possession," 62, 61.

93 Whether inability to hear counts as a medical condition for which one ought to seek cure or remediation remains an active debate. Deaf people often characterize their community as a linguistic and cultural minority rather than a population of disabled individuals. On the conceptual transition from "hearing loss" to "Deaf gain," consult H-Dirksen L. Bauman and Joseph M. Murray, "Reframing: From Hearing Loss to Deaf Gain," trans. from ASL by Fallon Brizendine and Emily Schenker, *Deaf Studies Digital Journal* 1 (2009), accessed March 10, 2016, http://dsdj.gallaudet.edu/assets/section/section2/entry19/DSDJ_entry19.pdf; and on the notion of "Deafhood" as an aspect of the self that is not purely biological but also socially constituted, consult Paddy Ladd, *Understanding Deaf Culture: In Search of Deafhood* (Clevedon, UK: Multilingual Matters, 2003). I am grateful to Kirk VanGilder for these references.

94 One rare mention of a mobility aid appears in a paean to New York's diverse populace, accomplished via a juxtaposition meant to amuse: "A transvestite, who easily topped six and a half feet, toddled along on skinny blue heels. She shook back her golden waterfall of hair as she delicately tested a melon for ripeness. . . . Eve watched a tiny woman, well past her century mark, bump up in her seated scooter. The tranny and the centenarian seemed to chat amiably while they selected fruit" (*Strangers*, 365). This mobility aid fits smoothly into the narrative flow

and is not singled out as a sign of debility, though it is associated with age. Peabody briefly mentions appreciating the city's "diversity and all" (*Reunion,* 281). A few other mentions of trans people as spectacle include, on Halloween, "a ghoul, a six-foot pink rabbit, and a mutant transsexual crossed the street" (*Ceremony,* 294).

95 *Portrait,* 76.

96 *Imitation,* 161.

97 *Holiday,* 8.

98 *Portrait,* 87. Indicating the depth of this sentiment, pity is also used with regard to a tortured murder victim (*Creation,* 34).

99 *Portrait,* 87.

100 Vivanco explores a novel with an intellectually disabled hero in *Pursuing Happiness,* 45–61. She notes the link between ability and the ability to work and signals the crucial role of the work ethic in American mythologies.

101 Kafer, *Feminist, Queer, Crip,* 21 and for more on the novel, see 70–74.

102 Kafer, *Feminist, Queer, Crip,* 83, emphasis in original.

103 Kafer, *Feminist, Queer, Crip,* 10. "Disability in the United States is often viewed as an unredeemable difference. Disability and the disabled body are problems that must be solved technologically, and there is allegedly so much cultural agreement on this point that it need not be discussed or debated. Disability, then, plays a huge, but seemingly uncontested, role in how contemporary Americans envision the future" (74).

104 On J. Halberstam's treatment of "longevity," consult Kafer, *Feminist, Queer, Crip,* 40–41.

105 *New York to Dallas,* 10, 243; *Survivor,* 358.

106 There is no mention of pain, mobility limitations, or inability to continue her work. Of course, this is not to suggest that any of these things would justify self-termination either. The link between disability and death emerges elsewhere too. Roarke watches an old Bette Davis video in which "she goes blind and dies in the end" (*Loyalty,* 17). Disability leads, if not causally then conceptually, to death.

107 *Origin,* 47, 49.

108 *Survivor,* 246. The parents lost their daughter to murder in *Naked in Death,* then later adopted Kevin, "whose junkie mother had deserted him" (*Thankless,* 302). Also *Thankless,* 369–70.

109 *Loyalty,* 13. Another primary doesn't bother to identify a Jane Doe; Dallas says "she's in the wrong business" (*Immortal,* 144). These attitudes are not limited to police; a killer steals a dead woman's ID and isn't worried that her family might have been looking for her: "She was a street LC with a funk habit" (*Memory,* 363). Deaths of cops and cops' families get more attention—in part because cops have to be able to do their job (*Kindred,* 97–98).

110 *Strangers*, 245–48. Dallas had arranged for the investigation before the woman agreed to cooperate, but uses the promise of a renewed investigation to induce cooperation.

111 Notable jerk victims include the serial gang-rapists in *Brotherhood in Death* (383); the Icoves (*Origin*, 136); and the impostor-priest in *Salvation in Death* (286). One murderer says to Dallas, "I didn't think any investigator looking into Richard's life to solve his death would work overly hard on the case once they discovered the kind of man he was" (*Witness*, 330, and also 261, 337). Similarly, see "Missing," 257; *Treachery*, 58.

112 *Loyalty*, 188.

113 Moreover, Dallas also imagines the deaths—almost as if a recreation of the events—through both the victim's mind and the killer's mind. As Roarke describes it, "It's more than standing for the dead, which is vicious enough to bear. But you walk with them through it" (*Kindred*, 85). She also has an ability to imagine the perspectives of "the mad and the vicious" (*Seduction*, 102).

114 Examples include Commander Whitney (*Glory*, 10); Roarke (*Immortal*, 212; *Fantasy*, 272–73); Summerset (*Survivor*, 236); Feeney (*Ceremony*, 50); Peabody (*Ceremony*, 54–55); and Amaryllis Coltraine (*Promises*, 221). With the exception of Coltraine, who had complained posthumously via dream, sooner or later all apologize for having misjudged her.

115 *Judgment*, 263.

116 *Immortal*, 111; "Haunted," 288–89.

117 *Origin*, 290.

118 Martha Nussbaum argues that "an ethics of impartial respect for human dignity will fail to engage real human beings unless they are made capable of entering imaginatively into the lives of distant others and to have emotions related to that participation" (Nussbaum, *Poetic Justice: The Literary Imagination and Public Life* [Boston: Beacon Press, 1995], xvii). Nussbaum is not suggesting "substituting empathetic imagining for rule-governed moral reasoning" but rather the utility of "literary imagination [as] a part of public rationality" (xvi).

119 Everyone seems to agree that imagination is vital for transformation. bell hooks has pointed out, "To be truly visionary we have to root our imagination in our concrete reality while simultaneously imagining possibilities beyond that reality" (hooks, *Feminism Is For Everybody: Passionate Politics* [Cambridge, Mass.: South End Press, 2000], 110). See also Ytasha L. Womack, *Afrofuturism: The World of Black Sci-Fi and Fantasy Culture* (Chicago: Lawrence Hill Books, 2009), 24, 44; and Kafer, *Feminist, Queer, Crip*, 46. Roach's proposed reparative reading of romance foregrounds the role of imagination (Roach, *Happily Ever After*, 184).

Conclusion

1 *Delusion*, 220. "If knowledge of social injustice, such as slavery, makes it difficult to maintain the fantasy pleasure of the romance novel, may the reverse also be true, that the fantasy pleasure of romance makes it difficult to maintain knowledge of social injustice?" (Roach, *Happily Ever After*, 140). Love sustains in good times and bad ("Wonderment," 38).

2 "Wonderment," 13. One might consider that for all their verisimilitude, billionaire romances are basically paranormal fiction. Regular rules of the universe are suspended. Unlimited wealth is another kind of magic. A poor or middle-class woman who finds herself involved with a billionaire has entered an alternate universe just as surely as if she accidentally stepped through a portal to another world. Courtney Milan's *Trade Me* (Published by author, 2015) appropriates and subverts common tropes in the billionaire subgenre represented by, inter alia, the Harlequin Presents line.

3 Tensions exist among overlapping narratives and competing registers. Dallas' work precludes happiness predicated on the eradication of negative affect, which Jonathan Allan suggests is "the lesson of romance" (Allan, "Reading the Regis Roundtable," 4). In Death's open-ended seriality thwarts any once-and-for-all answers except the unwavering commitment between Dallas and Roarke.

4 When a homeless man with an addiction to funk witnesses a crime, Dallas trades him a pair of her good quality sunglasses for information and tells the uniforms on duty that no, they shouldn't transport him to a shelter for rehabilitation. She thinks, "It's what—technically—should be done, and maybe, she thought, morally. But realistically? He'd be out within a week, have lost his turf, and very likely be worse off than now" (*Calculated*, 215).

5 A burgeoning literature on charity and philanthropy asks whether and how they should be guided by market imperatives and mechanisms, both as to how they help and whom they help; another significant consideration is whether distance makes a difference. Appealing to measurable outcomes, utilitarian philosopher Peter Singer argues that, assuming the equal worth of all human lives, money spent saving the lives of the extremely poor in the developing world is more effective (Singer, *The Most Good You Can Do: How Effective Altruism Is Changing Ideas about Living Ethically* [New Haven, Conn.: Yale University Press, 2015], 111–15) and that distance makes no difference to the obligation to assist (Singer, *Famine, Affluence, and Morality* [Oxford: Oxford University Press, 2016], 7–9, 54). Jeremy Beer instead advocates "philanthropolocalism," which "posits that the primary purpose of philanthropy ought to be *to increase opportunities for and strengthen the possibilities of authentic human communion*" (Beer, *The Philanthropic Revolution: An Alternative History of American Charity* [Philadelphia: University of Pennsylvania Press, 2015], 99, emphasis in original). Eschewing any attempt to save "humanity, the nation, the global community, or any

other agglomeration of humans in the abstract . . . the philanthropolocalist concern is to promote human flourishing within the local community, not to 'change the world' through the technologies of social entrepreneurship." Beer's history of charity, his distinctions between charity and philanthropy, and the connections he draws between philanthropic hubris and eugenic ideals of social improvement are insightful and useful. I am less convinced by his focus on personal and local giving to those with whom one is already connected. This model takes no account of barriers to entry for those excluded from existing networks of patronage and charity.

6 *Immortal,* 19.

7 On the paradoxical history of prisons, consult Caleb Smith, *The Prison and the American Imagination* (New Haven, Conn.: Yale University Press, 2009), and Naomi Murakawa, *The First Civil Right: How Liberals Built Prison America* (New York: Oxford University Press, 2014).

8 Johnson, *Street Justice,* 280.

9 Amira Jarmakani makes a similar point in her study of "desert romances" and American representations of Arabs and Muslims after 9/11: instead of aiming simply for more inclusive representations as a solution, one should read existing stories in new ways. See Jarmakani, *An Imperialist Love Story: Desert Romances and the War on Terror* (New York: New York University Press, 2015), 191–92.

10 I neither wish to chastise Robb for occasional lapses into stereotype nor to offer absolution; I have no standing to do so. Those interested in theoretical exploration of, or practical advice for, writing characters outside one's experience will find myriad resources online. Mikki Kendall's blog provides an excellent starting point. See Kendall, "Diversity, Political Correctness and the Power of Language," April 30, 2016, https://mikkikendall.com/2016/04/30/diversity-political-correctness-and-the-power-of-language/. On her blog, The Rejectionist, white novelist Sarah McCarry's September 8, 2015 post "On Totems," in dialogue with Nambe Pueblo Indian literary scholar and blogger Debbie Reese (http://americanindiansinchildrensliterature.blogspot.com), gives a useful reflection: see http://www.therejectionist.com/2015/09/on-totems.html.

11 Nussbaum, *Poetic Justice,* xvii.

12 In his account of how anti-Indian racism makes possible the use of "Redskins" as the official name for the NFL franchise in Washington, D.C., King argues for the central role of thoughtlessness in making possible attachment to the name. By thoughtlessness, he means that people "act without thinking, without considering their social location, without incorporating alternative interpretations, without listening to others, and often without question. Such thoughtlessness demonstrates the power of privilege and socialization as well as an associated underdevelopment of critical literacies" (King, *Redskins,* 47).

13 Dillard, *Living by Fiction,* 152.

Works Cited

Works by J. D. Robb

In Death novels and novellas appear here in their order within the series chronology. I cite the editions used in preparing this volume. Novels 1–40 are mass market paperback editions, while novels 41–42 are hardcover editions.

Naked in Death. In Death 1. New York: Berkley, 1995.

Glory in Death. In Death 2. New York: Berkley, 1995.

Immortal in Death. In Death 3. New York: Berkley, 1996.

Rapture in Death. In Death 4. New York: Berkley, 1996.

Ceremony in Death. In Death 5. New York: Berkley, 1997.

Vengeance in Death. In Death 6. New York: Berkley, 1997.

Holiday in Death. In Death 7. New York: Berkley, 1998.

"Midnight in Death." In J. D. Robb, *Three in Death*, 119–226. New York: Berkley, 2008.

Conspiracy in Death. In Death 8. New York: Berkley, 1999.

Loyalty in Death. In Death 9. New York: Berkley, 1999.

Witness in Death. In Death 10. New York: Berkley, 2000.

Judgment in Death. In Death 11. New York: Berkley, 2000.

Betrayal in Death. In Death 12. New York: Berkley, 2001.

"Interlude in Death." In J. D. Robb, *Three in Death*, 1–118. New York: Berkley, 2008.

Seduction in Death. In Death 13. New York: Berkley, 2001.

Reunion in Death. In Death 14. New York: Berkley, 2002.

Purity in Death. In Death 15. New York: Berkley, 2002.

Portrait in Death. In Death 16. New York: Berkley, 2003.

Imitation in Death. In Death 17. New York: Berkley, 2003.

Big Jack. New York: Berkley, 2010.

Divided in Death. In Death 18. New York: Berkley, 2004.

Visions in Death. In Death 19. New York: Berkley, 2005.

Survivor in Death. In Death 20. New York: Berkley, 2005.

Origin in Death. In Death 21. New York: Berkley, 2005.

Memory in Death. In Death 22. New York: Berkley, 2006.

"Haunted in Death." In J. D. Robb, *Three in Death*, 227–355. New York: Berkley, 2008.

Born in Death. In Death 23. New York: Berkley, 2007.

Innocent in Death. In Death 24. New York: Berkley, 2007.

Creation in Death. In Death 25. New York: Berkley, 2008.

"Eternity in Death." In J. D. Robb, *Time of Death*, 1–108. New York: Jove, 2012.

Strangers in Death. In Death 26. New York: Berkley, 2008.

Salvation in Death. In Death 27. New York: Berkley, 2009.

"Ritual in Death." In J. D. Robb, *Time of Death*, 109–98. New York: Jove, 2012.

Promises in Death. In Death 28. New York: Berkley, 2009.

Kindred in Death. In Death 29. New York: Berkley, 2010.

"Missing in Death." In J. D. Robb, *Time of Death*, 199–294. New York: Jove, 2012.

Fantasy in Death. In Death 30. New York: Berkley, 2010.

Indulgence in Death. In Death 31. New York: Berkley, 2011.

"Possession in Death." In J. D. Robb et al., *The Other Side*, 1–80. New York: Jove, 2010.

Treachery in Death. In Death 32. New York: Berkley, 2011.

New York to Dallas. In Death 33. New York: Berkley, 2012.

"Chaos in Death." In J. D. Robb et al., *The Unquiet*, 1–95. New York: Jove, 2011.

Celebrity in Death. In Death 34. New York: Berkley, 2012.

Delusion in Death. In Death 35. New York: Berkley, 2012.

Calculated in Death. In Death 36. New York: Berkley, 2013.

Thankless in Death. In Death 37. New York: Berkley, 2013.

"Taken in Death." In J. D. Robb et al., *Mirror, Mirror*, 1–92. New York: Jove, 2013.

Concealed in Death. In Death 38. New York: Berkley, 2014.

Festive in Death. In Death 39. New York: Berkley, 2014.

Obsession in Death. In Death 40. New York: Berkley, 2015.

Devoted in Death. In Death 41. New York: Berkley, 2015.

"Wonderment in Death." In J. D. Robb et al., *Down the Rabbit Hole*, 1–99. New York: Jove, 2016.

Brotherhood in Death. In Death 42. New York: Berkley, 2016.

Works by J. D. Robb and Nora Roberts

Remember When. New York: Berkley Books, 2004.

Works by Nora Roberts

Engaging the Enemy. New York: Silhouette Books, 2003 [1985].

Sea Swept. Chesapeake Bay Saga 1. Jove Books: New York, 1998.

Rising Tides. Chesapeake Bay Saga 2. Jove Books: New York, 1998.

Inner Harbor. Chesapeake Bay Saga 3. Jove Books: New York, 1999.

Chesapeake Blue. Chesapeake Bay Saga 4. Jove Books: New York, 2002.

Vision in White. Bride Quartet 1. New York: Berkley, 2009.

Bed of Roses. Bride Quartet 2. New York: Berkley, 2009.

Savor the Moment. Bride Quartet 3. New York: Berkley, 2010.

Happy Ever After. Bride Quartet 4. New York: Berkley, 2010.

Other fiction

Butler, Octavia E. *Kindred*. Boston: Beacon, 2003 [1979].

James, E. L. *Fifty Shades of Grey*. New York: Vintage Books, 2011.

Medeiros, Teresa. *Yours until Dawn*. New York: Avon Books, 2004.

Meyer, Stephenie. *Twilight*. New York: Little, Brown, 2005.

Milan, Courtney. *Trade Me*. Published by author, 2015.

Non-fiction

Alexander, Michelle. "Foreword: Standing Without Sweet Company." In Levi and Waldman, *Inside This Place, Not of It*, 11–14.

———. *The New Jim Crow: Mass Incarceration in the Age of Colorblindness*. Rev. ed. New York: The New Press, 2011.

Allan, Jonathan A. "Reading the Regis Roundtable: An Outsider's Perspective." *Journal of Popular Romance Studies* 3, no. 2 (2013): 1–6.

Barrett-Fox, Rebecca. "Christian Romance Novels: Inspiring Convention and Challenge." In Gleason and Selinger, *Romance Fiction and American Culture*, 347–68.

Bauman, H-Dirksen L., and Joseph M. Murray. "Reframing: From Hearing Loss to Deaf Gain." *Deaf Studies Digital Journal* 1 (2009). Accessed March 10, 2016. http://dsdj.gallaudet.edu/assets/section/section2/entry19/DSDJ_entry19.pdf.

Beer, Jeremy. *The Philanthropic Revolution: An Alternative History of American Charity*. Philadelphia: University of Pennsylvania Press, 2015.

Berlant, Lauren. "Slow Death (Sovereignty, Obesity, Lateral Agency)." *Critical Inquiry* 33 (2007): 754–80.

Bonilla-Silva, Eduardo. *Racism without Racists: Color-Blind Racism and the Persistence of Racial Inequality in America*. 4th ed. Lanham, Md.: Rowman & Littlefield, 2014.

Butler, Judith. *Precarious Life: The Powers of Mourning and Violence*. London: Verso, 2006.

Campbell, Fiona Kumari. "Inciting Legal Fictions: Disability's Date with Ontology and the Ableist Body of Law." *Griffith Law Review* 10, no. 1 (2001): 42–62.

———. "Refusing Able(ness): A Preliminary Conversation about Ableism." *M/C Journal: A Journal of Media and Culture* 11, no. 3 (2008). Accessed March 10, 2016. http://journal.media-culture.org.au/index.php/mcjournal/article/viewArticle/46/0.

Carrington, André M. *Speculative Blackness: The Future of Race in Science Fiction*. Minneapolis: University of Minnesota Press, 2016.

Celello, Kristin. *Making Marriage Work: A History of Marriage and Divorce in the Twentieth-Century United States*. Chapel Hill: University of North Carolina Press, 2009.

Cohn, Jan. *Romance and the Erotics of Property: Mass-Market Fiction for Women*. Durham, N.C.: Duke University Press, 1988.

Collins, Lauren. "Real Romance: How Nora Roberts Became America's Most Popular Novelist." *The New Yorker*, June 22, 2009.

Crary, Jonathan. *24/7: Late Capitalism and the Ends of Sleep*. New York: Verso, 2013.

Davis, Angela Y. *Are Prisons Obsolete?* New York: Seven Stories Press, 2003.

Decker, Julie Sondra. *The Invisible Orientation: An Introduction to Asexuality*. New York: Carrel Books, 2014.

Derickson, Alan. *Dangerously Sleepy: Overworked Americans and the Cult of Manly Wakefulness*. Philadelphia: University of Pennsylvania Press, 2014.

Dillard, Annie. *Living by Fiction*. New York: Harper & Row, 1983.

Fusco, Coco. "Fantasies of Oppositionality: Reflections on Recent Conferences in Boston and New York." *Screen* 29, no. 4 (1988): 80–93.

Gabaldon, Diana. *The Outlandish Companion*. Vol. 2. New York: Delacorte, 2015.

Gallagher, Winifred. *In the Bag: What Purses Reveal and Conceal*. New York: HarperCollins, 2006.

Gira Grant, Melissa. *Playing the Whore: The Work of Sex Work*. New York: Verso, 2014.

Gleason, William A., and Eric Murphy Selinger, eds. *Romance Fiction and American Culture: Love as the Practice of Freedom?* Burlington, Vt.: Ashgate, 2016.

Glenn, Evelyn Nakano. *Forced to Care: Coercion and Caregiving in America*. Cambridge, Mass.: Harvard University Press, 2012.

Goris, An. "From Romance to Roberts and Back Again: Genre, Authorship and the Construction of Textual Identity in Contemporary Popular Romance Novels." PhD diss., University of Leuven, 2011.

———. "Happily Ever After . . . and After: Serialization and the Popular Romance Novel." *Americana: The Journal of American Popular Culture (1900 to Present)* 12, no. 1 (2013).

———. "Mind, Body, Love: Nora Roberts and the Evolution of Popular Romance Studies." *Journal of Popular Romance Studies* 3, no. 1 (2012): 1–21.

Fields, Karen E., and Barbara J. Fields. *Racecraft: The Soul of Inequality in American Life*. London: Verso, 2012.

Frankenberg, Ruth. *White Women, Race Matters: The Social Construction of Whiteness*. Minneapolis: University of Minnesota Press, 1993.

Frantz, Sarah S. G., and Eric Murphy Selinger, eds. *New Approaches to Popular Romance Fiction: Critical Essays*. Jefferson, N.C.: McFarland, 2012.

Holland, Sharon Patricia. *The Erotic Life of Racism*. Durham, N.C.: Duke University Press, 2012.

hooks, bell. *All About Love: New Visions*. New York: William Morrow, 2000.

———. *Art on My Mind: Visual Politics*. New York: The New Press, 1995.

———. *Feminism Is for Everybody: Passionate Politics*. Cambridge, Mass.: South End Press, 2000.

———. *Remembered Rapture: The Writer at Work*. New York: Henry Holt, 1999.

———. *Writing Beyond Race: Living Theory and Practice*. New York: Routledge, 2013.

———. *Yearning: Race, Gender, and Cultural Politics*. Boston: South End Press, 1990.

Jagose, Annamarie. *Orgasmology*. Durham, N.C.: Duke University Press, 2013.

James, P. D. *Talking about Detective Fiction*. New York: Knopf, 2009.

Jarmakani, Amira. *An Imperialist Love Story: Desert Romances and the War on Terror*. New York: New York University Press, 2015.

Johnson, Marilynn S. *Street Justice: A History of Police Violence in New York City*. Boston: Beacon, 2003.

Kafer, Alison. *Feminist, Queer, Crip*. Bloomington: Indiana University Press, 2013.

Kamblé, Jayashree. *Making Meaning in Popular Romance Fiction: An Epistemology*. New York: Palgrave, 2014.

Kendall, Mikki. "Diversity, Political Correctness and the Power of Language." April 30, 2016. https://mikkikendall.com/2016/04/30/diversity-political-correctness-and-the-power-of-language/.

King, C. Richard. *Redskins: Insult and Brand*. Lincoln: University of Nebraska Press, 2016.

Ladd, Paddy. *Understanding Deaf Culture: In Search of Deafhood*. Clevedon, UK: Multilingual Matters, 2003.

Leibowitz, Cara. "Everyday Ableism and How We Can Avoid It." March 3, 2015. http://thebodyisnotanapology.com/magazine/everyday-ableism-and-how-we-can-avoid-it/.

Lennard, John. *Of Modern Dragons and Other Essays on Genre Fiction*. Penrith, UK: Humanities-Ebooks, 2007.

Levi, Robin, and Ayelet Waldman, eds. *Inside This Place, Not of It: Narratives from Women's Prisons*. Voice of Witness 8. San Francisco: McSweeney's Books, 2011.

Little, Denise, and Laura Hayden, eds. *The Official Nora Roberts Companion*. New York: Berkley, 2003.

Morrison, Toni. *Playing in the Dark: Whiteness and the Literary Imagination*. Cambridge, Mass.: Harvard University Press, 1992.

Mukherjea, Ananya. "My Vampire Boyfriend: Postfeminism, 'Perfect' Masculinity, and the Contemporary Appeal of Paranormal Romance." *Studies in Popular Culture* 33, no. 2 (2011): 1–20.

Murakawa, Naomi. *The First Civil Right: How Liberals Built Prison America*. New York: Oxford University Press, 2014.

Nussbaum, Martha C. *Poetic Justice: The Literary Imagination and Public Life*. Boston: Beacon Press, 1995.

Ogletree Jr., Charles J., and Austin Sarat. "Imaging Punishment: An Introduction." In *Punishment in Popular Culture*, edited by Charles J. Ogletree and Austin Sarat, 1–20. New York: New York University Press, 2015.

Paoletti, Jo B. *Sex and Unisex: Fashion, Feminism, and the Sexual Revolution*. Indianapolis: Indiana University Press, 2015.

Povinelli, Elizabeth A. *Economies of Abandonment: Social Belonging and Endurance in Late Liberalism*. Durham, N.C.: Duke University Press, 2011.

Price, Joshua M. *Prison and Social Death*. New Brunswick, N.J.: Rutgers University Press, 2015.

Rankine, Claudia. *Citizen: An American Lyric*. Minneapolis: Graywolf, 2014.

Regis, Pamela. *A Natural History of the Romance Novel*. Philadelphia: University of Pennsylvania Press, 2003.

Ridley. "Some Thoughts on 'Physically Disabled Protagonists.'" *Love in the Margins*. October 27, 2013. http://loveinthemargins.com/2013/10/27/some-thoughts-on-physically-disabled-protagonists/.

Roach, Catherine M. *Happily Ever After: The Romance Story in Popular Culture*. Bloomington: Indiana University Press, 2016.

Roberts, Thomas J. *An Aesthetics of Junk Fiction*. Athens: University of Georgia Press, 1990.

Robson, Ruthann. *Dressing Constitutionally: Hierarchy, Sexuality, and Democracy from Our Hairstyles to Our Shoes*. New York: Cambridge University Press, 2013.

Rodale, Maya. *Dangerous Books for Girls: The Bad Reputation of Romance Novels Explained*. Middletown, Del.: n.p., 2015.

Selinger, Eric Murphy. "Editor's Introduction: Nothing But Good Times Ahead: A Special Forum on Jennifer Crusie." *Journal of Popular Romance Studies* 2, no. 2 (2012).

———. "How to Read a Romance Novel (and Fall in Love with Popular Romance)." In Frantz and Selinger, *New Approaches*, 33–46.

———. "Review: Rereading the Romance." *Contemporary Literature* 48, no. 2 (2007): 307–24.

Selinger, Eric Murphy, and Sarah S. G. Frantz. "Introduction." In Frantz and Selinger, *New Approaches*, 1–20.

Selinger, Eric Murphy, and William A. Gleason. "Introduction: Love as the Practice of Freedom?" In Gleason and Selinger, *Romance Fiction and American Culture*, 1–21.

Singer, Peter. *Famine, Affluence, and Morality*. Oxford: Oxford University Press, 2016.

———. *The Most Good You Can Do: How Effective Altruism Is Changing Ideas about Living Ethically*. New Haven, Conn.: Yale University Press, 2015.

Smith, Caleb. *The Prison and the American Imagination*. New Haven, Conn.: Yale University Press, 2009.

Snodgrass, Mary Ellen. *Reading Nora Roberts*. Santa Barbara, Calif.: Greenwood, 2010.

Sontag, Susan. *Regarding the Pain of Others*. New York: Picador, 2003.

Teo, Hsu-Ming. *Desert Passions: Orientalism and Romance Novels*. Austin: University of Texas Press, 2012.

Turnaturi, Gabriella. *Betrayals: The Unpredictability of Human Relations*. Translated by Lydia G. Cochrane. Chicago: University of Chicago Press, 2007.

Valeo, Christina A. "The Power of Three: Nora Roberts and Serial Magic." In Frantz and Selinger, *New Approaches*, 229–40.

Vivanco, Laura. *For Love and Money: The Literary Art of the Harlequin Mills & Boon Romance*. Penrith, UK: Humanities-Ebooks, 2011.

———. *Pursuing Happiness: Reading American Romance as Political Fiction*. Penrith, UK: Humanities-Ebooks, 2016.

———. "Sleepless Masculinity." December 23, 2014. http://www.vivanco.me.uk/blog/post/sleepless-masculinity.

Wajcman, Judy. *Pressed for Time: The Acceleration of Life in Digital Capitalism*. Chicago: University of Chicago Press, 2015.

Weeks, Kathi. *The Problem with Work: Feminism, Marxism, Antiwork Politics, and Postwork Imaginaries*. Durham, N.C.: Duke University Press, 2011.

Wendell, Sarah. *Everything I Know about Love I Learned from Romance Novels*. Naperville, Ill.: Sourcebooks Casablanca, 2011.

Wendell, Sarah, and Candy Tan. *Beyond Heaving Bosoms: The Smart Bitches' Guide to Romance Novels*. New York: Fireside, 2009.

Womack, Ytasha L. *Afrofuturism: The World of Black Sci-Fi and Fantasy Culture*. Chicago: Lawrence Hill Books, 2013.

Zelizer, Viviana A. *The Purchase of Intimacy*. Princeton, N.J.: Princeton University Press, 2005.

Index

The index lists characters by the name typically used in the series; for example, both Mavis Freestone and Charlotte Mira appear under M.